TRANSFORMATION NOW!

TRANSFORMATION NOW!

Toward a Post-Oppositional Politics of Change

AnaLouise Keating

UNIVERSITY OF ILLINOIS PRESS
Urbana, Chicago, and Springfield

Library of Congress Control Number: 2013950024

I dedicate this book to Paula Gunn Allen,
Gloria Anzaldúa, and other threshold theorists,
nepantleras, almas afines, El Mundo Zurdist@s

Fuego, inspire and energize us to do the necessary work,
and to honor it
 as we walk through the flames of transformation.
 May we seize the arrogance to create outrageously
 soñar wildly—for the world becomes as we dream it.

Gloria Anzaldúa

Contents

Giving Thanks

Stand on the shoulders of giants.

Google Scholar

We must be motivated by love in order
to undertake change—love of self, love
of people, love of life. Loving gives us the
energy and compassion to act in the face
of hardship; loving gives us the motivation
to dream the life and work we want.

Gloria Anzaldúa, "Foreword, 2001"

Where do I even begin, to name the intellectual and spiritual giants whose lives and works have supported me, opened new vistas, encouraged me in my work, energized and inspired me with love? (*If only I could thank everyone, simultaneously; I don't want to leave anyone out or diminish the contributions of anyone.*) This book represents the culmination of another piece of my life's journey, and everyone I've interacted with over the past decade has left their mark on the ideas and words in this book. Every author whose work I cite in *Transformation Now!* has been instrumental to my development. I thank them all.

I'm grateful to my graduate students at Texas Woman's University. Our discussions and explorations of contemporary theories and (trans)disciplinary knowledge formations have been invaluable to me, as I've tried to think through and—whenever possible—*beyond* oppositional thought. I'm especially grateful to Reanae McNeal and Erica Granados De La Rosa, who offered to allow me to include their womanist invitational syllabi in this book. Thanks to Jacqui Alexander, Michele Tracy Berger, Reanae Bredin, Jessica

Camp, Angela Cotten, Betsy Dahms, Victoria Genetin, Kathleen Guidroz, Robyn Henderson-Espinoza, Marilyn Frye, Sarah Hoagland, Irene Lara, Layli Maparyan, Carrie McMaster, Reanae McNeal, Kimberly Merenda, Deborah A. Miranda, Sonia Saldívar-Hull, and Ann Waters for their assistance with various writerly-readerly activities, ranging from feedback on earlier chapter drafts to encouragement and reality checks along the way.

The external reviewers' generous feedback and terrific suggestions have been instrumental in assisting me as I take my thinking further, and I am tremendously grateful for their thoughtful attention to this project. Irene Lara: thank you for your excitement about the initial proposal. Suzanne Bost and Aimee Carrillo Rowe: you gave me new lens with which to view my project. Your encouragement emboldened me, and I cannot fully articulate my gratitude. This book is so much stronger, thanks to your insightful suggestions. But, of course, all errors, limitations, and excessive provocations are my own.

I explored many of these ideas in conversation with Gloria Anzaldúa—conversations that are ongoing but that originated back in the mid 1990s. Her generosity, intellectual humility, and confidence in my work have been sustaining and life-altering. I am especially grateful for her encouragement that I "rock the boat" and question the shibboleths of our various movements. (*You left us too early, comadre.*) I'd also like to thank the North Texas weather, February 2011 (the "snowpocalypse": rain-followed-by-freezing temperatures-and-then-snow) and the city of Denton's limited street apparatus (the lack of salting or sanding or plowing), which kept our schools closed and encouraged (*forced?*) us to stay home, unable/unwilling to venture out. You gave me unexpected, unbroken, unbidden time to think, to develop this book project.

Thanks to Jimmie Lyn Harris and the other F.I.R.S.T. librarians (the Faculty, Information and Research Support Team) at Texas Woman's University, for tracking down so many sources for me. Thanks to Claire L. Sahlin, supportive colleague and department chair. I am very grateful for your support over the years and for your timely suggestion for how I might address the publisher's request to remove section epigraphs. I'm also very grateful to Gail Orlando, whose time-saving office assistance, thoughtful pro-active recommendations, and serendipitous conversations are irreplaceable.

I'm extremely grateful to my editor, Larin McLaughlin, for her initial interest in my (some might say provocative) idea for this project. Without her interest, would I have continued? I don't know. Thank you, Larin! Thanks for your confidence in this project, your appreciation for what I'm trying to do, and your acceptance of my quirky stylistic choices and concepts (like the exclamation point in my title and the italicized parenthetical comments). Thanks to Jennifer Comeau Reichlin, Dawn M. Durante, Roberta J. Sparenberg, and the other folks at the University of Illinois Press. Thanks very much to Deborah Oliver for doing such superb copyediting on this manuscript. *Transformation Now!* is my ninth book, which means that I've worked with a lot of copyeditors. You are the best. I appreciate your thoughtful questions, careful explanations, and great suggestions, as well as your leniency with my nontraditionalist approach to many writing-related items in this book.

I've been wrestling with and revising some of the concepts in *Transformation Now!* for years, and portions of several chapters were previously published in earlier versions. An earlier version of part of chapter 1 was published as "From Intersections to Interconnections: Lessons for Transformation from *This Bridge Called My Back: Radical Writings by Women of Color*" in *The Intersectional Approach: Transforming the Academy through Race, Class, and Gender*, ed. Michele Tracy Berger and Kathleen Guidroz (Durham: University of North Carolina Press, 2009); an earlier version of part of chapter 3 was published as "(De)Centering the Margins? Identity Politics and Tactical (Re)Naming" in *Other Sisterhoods: Literary Theory and U.S. Women of Color*, ed. Sandra Kumamoto Stanley (Urbana: University of Illinois Press, 1998); and an earlier version of part of chapter 5 was published as "Back to the Mother? Feminist Mythmaking with a Difference" in *Feminist Interpretations of Mary Daly*, ed. Sarah Lucia Hoagland and Marilyn Frye (University Park: Pennsylvania State University Press, 2000), 294–331. Although they probably wouldn't recognize parts of my arguments, given how much my ideas have shifted over the years, I'm extremely grateful to these editors both for the opportunity to think about these topics and for their comments on the early drafts.

The longer I live, the more enormously grateful I am for my parents, Tom and Joann Keating, for giving me such a solid foundation and so many lessons in how to forge commonalities without ignoring differences, how to define equality and fairness in nuanced, context-specific ways. Thanks to my sister, Jane Keating Vraspier, and my nephew, Quinn Vraspier, for assisting me as I tried to figure out the cover art. And, of course, I thank my family, Eddy Lynton and Jamitrice Keating-Lynton, for building their lives with mine, for the many daily lessons our lives together make possible, for the humor we share, for the insights we create. You have been generous, supportive, and wise; I am very blessed to have you in my life. (I expect to be seeing you both publish your own books pretty soon!) As always, I am so grateful to the orishas, espíritus, and ancestors for guiding me, whispering words of encouragement that nourish my body-heart-mind-spirit and inspire my vision.

Post-Oppositional Resistance?

Threshold Theories Defined and Enacted

> Wars. So many wars. Wars outside and wars inside. Cultural wars, science wars, and wars against terrorism. Wars against poverty and wars against the poor. Wars against ignorance and wars out of ignorance. My question is simple: Should we be at war, too, we, the scholars, the intellectuals? Is it really our duty to add fresh ruins to fields of ruins? Is it really the task of the humanities to add deconstruction to destruction? More iconoclasm to iconoclasm? What has become of the critical spirit? Has it run out of steam?
>
> Bruno Latour, "Why Has Critique Run Out of Steam?"

> Some forty-odd years after the Civil Rights movement, we are still seeking solutions to racism. The question is how shall we dismantle or redeem the systems that have been put in place to perpetuate racism? To date there have been few answers to this question. There are even fewer options for defining self and society as constructs that do not emerge out of conflict, but out of a full awareness of the realities of the universe and our connections in it.
>
> Barbara A. Holmes, *Race and the Cosmos*

A typical response when I witness, experience, or in other ways am confronted with racism, sexism, homophobia, imperialism, colonialism, or other forms of social injustice—whether this injustice is reported in the news, experienced by my family/friends/self, or expressed in my classrooms, at conferences, or in the books, articles, and websites I read—is to react oppositionally. My blood pressure rises, my muscles tense. I condemn and reject the ignorant views, the stereotypes, the oppressive treatment. I fight back. Indeed, such reactions have become so automatic that they seem like human nature (*you push me and/or my people, and I'll push back*)[1] or like common sense (*I mean— what's the alternative to fighting back? Should I become a doormat, a pushover? Should I silence myself and just allow the violence—the unfair situation—to continue? Should I ignore the injustice, avert my gaze, remain oblivious?*). My commitment to challenging social injustice has defined me and shaped my career so extensively that at times I've described myself by what I oppose: my work is anti-racist, anti-sexist, anti-homophobic, anti-white-supremacist, and so on. (*Look at me: The crusading scholar!*)

My undergraduate and graduate work trained me to think oppositionally, to structure my articles and book chapters as a series of binary discussions that proceed through nuanced contrasts: first, describe other scholars' theories and perspectives; second, demonstrate the limitations in their views; third, explain why my views are superior to those of other scholars; fourth, persuade readers to reject the other scholars' views and embrace mine. I've developed an oppositional toolkit—an arsenal, as it were—filled with all sorts of strategies, methods, and approaches that enable me to poke holes in other people's arguments, demonstrate the flaws in their thinking, and persuade readers that my theories are better—more all-encompassing, more insightful, more effective, more worthy of respect. In short, I've been trained to demonstrate that my perspectives are right and those of others are wrong. I've honed my debate skills and sharpened my oppositional consciousness so thoroughly that they've become second nature. As I define the term, *oppositional conscious- ness* represents a binary either/or epistemology and praxis that structures our perceptions, politics, and actions through a resistant energy—a reaction against that which we seek to transform. Oppositional consciousness can take a variety of modes and occurs both inside and outside academic settings (classrooms, journals, etc.).[2]

I've lost count of the number of times that I've waded into an argument, jumped into the fray. And I confess, at this point in my career, these intellectual oppositional battles have become kind of fun. I enjoy the scholarly skirmishes, the critical banter, the opportunities to think on my feet, to use my words, my research, and my ideas in a righteous crusade for a better future. I relish the battle, and I love winning; I want to be right! (*Just ask my family.*) I'm not alone in my oppositional approach; I've learned from the best, modeling myself on the leading scholars in my academic fields, adopting their "murderous maneuvers of dialectical reasoning that negate another's position as wrong in order to affirm our own position as right—as *the* one (and only) position" (Kirby, 228, original emphasis).

But like Bruno Latour, I wonder: Given the many forms of violence we experience today—environmental violence, military violence, ethnocentric violence, gender-based violence, and the list goes on and on and on—"Should we be at war, too, we, the scholars, the intellectuals? Is it really our duty to add fresh ruins to fields of ruins?" While Latour refers specifically to the "science wars" between career scientists and sociologists of science, his questions can be applied more generally both to contemporary academic life and to those of us involved in progressive social-justice work.[3] (I define "us" broadly, to include people inside, outside, or straddling the academy; people who are students, professors, student-professors, lifelong learners, voracious readers, mindful activists, and more.) To be sure, oppositional politics and other forms of oppositional consciousness have been vital, enabling us to survive under hostile conditions and make important social change. However, I question the long-term effectiveness of our oppositional politics and thinking. As I explain in the following pages, these oppositional approaches—wherever they occur . . . in the academy, on the street, in daily life, or in the words we speak, read, and think—are too limited to bring about the long-term transformation we need. Oppositional politics and oppositional thinking have not enabled us to radically transform society. As Barbara Holmes suggests in the second epigraph to this introduction, our struggles against racism—and, I would add, against classism, sexism, homophobia, and other forms of discrimination and oppression—have not enabled us to "dismantle or redeem the systems" that created and reinforce these unjust structures. We remain immersed in conflict—conflicts that often subtly reinforce the very systems against which we struggle.[4] This oppositionality saturates us and limits our imaginations; we define "self and society" in antagonistic, conflict-driven terms that prevent us from obtaining a more ample "awareness of the realities of the universe and our connections in it." Without this larger vision, we remain locked in an embattled, us-against-them status quo.

Transformation Now! grew from my belief that these oppositional energies, politics, epistemologies, and battles are inadequate. We must use them less frequently and, perhaps, move beyond them. We must take new risks and create additional tools and strategies. Like M. Jacqui Alexander, I believe that "[o]ur oppositional politic has been necessary, but it will never sustain us; while it may give us some temporary gains. . . . it can never ultimately feed that deep place within us: that space of the erotic, that space of the soul, that space of the Divine" (99). Hence this book's title, with its demand for immediate change—the immediacy underscored, the demand heightened by the exclamation point. The transformations I call for and attempt to enact are theoretical, thematic, and methodological. I am interested in transforming several recurring strands that occur across a broad range of disciplines. These strands hinge on dichotomous epistemological and ontological frameworks and include the following: (1) an overemphasis on narrow definitions of difference and identity, defined in exclusionary, either/or terms; (2) a subsequent underemphasis on commonalities, defined *not* as sameness but as points of complex connections; (3) the limited knowledge and use of women-of-colors theorizing in a variety of academic fields, ranging from literary studies of the Americas to women's studies;[5] and (4) the oppositional consciousness and energies generally found in social-justice work and in academic critique. But here's the really tricky thing: I can't simply reject these four strands because to do so would inadvertently yet automatically enact the dichotomous thinking I want to transform! And so, rather than entirely dismiss these four strands, I engage them, gently pushing, prodding, and pulling them in new directions.

Each chapter has at least one additional, more specific transformational focus: the dominance of intersectionality and intersectional theory as a framework to understand difference in feminist scholarship, women's and gender studies (WGS), and queer theory (chapter 1); canonical definitions of "American" selfhood and mainstream understandings of individualism (chapter 2); conventional identity politics (chapter 3); critiques of universalism and feminist revisionist mythmaking (chapter 4); self-help literature and the New Age movement (chapter 5); and critical pedagogy (chapter 6). I use these chapter-specific topics to illustrate a key aspect of my call for transformation: the centering of woman-of-colors texts. Each chapter proceeds by foregrounding theories by women of colors, putting these theories in dialogue with additional theoretical and disciplinary perspectives.

I focus on twentieth- and twenty-first-century women-of-colors theorizing because these theories are the most potentially transformational theories that I've ever encountered (*and I have studied many theories*). They give me the intellectual grounding and tools to understand, challenge, and alter the existing frameworks and paradigms. They are riskier, more innovative and imaginative . . . rich with the potential to transform. The theories I explore in the following chapters have called out to me, inviting me to use them in new ways. They embolden and encourage me. (*"Ándale! Ándale!" They urge. "Take your ideas further—go ahead, . . . challenge that shibboleth, poke a few holes in the status quo."*) To be sure, women-of-colors theorists and authors have not received the attention they deserve; this work is underrepresented in academic thought. But my motivation here is not, primarily, representational. In other words, I do not underscore the value of women-of-colors theories *because* I want women of colors to be more fully represented in the scholarship (*although I do very much desire this increased representation*). Nor does my emphasis on women-of-colors work grow from my own women-of-colors status. I showcase these theories and theorists because of their intellectual power to provoke and transform.

Throughout *Transformation Now!* I enact the post-oppositional theorizing that I call for. I interrogate some of the diverse forms that binary-oppositional thought can take while resisting the (*very strong*) temptation to react oppositionally. I aspire to offer viable additions and alternatives to the oppositional forms of consciousness and politics that currently drive social-justice theorizing, activism, and academic disciplines. I develop nonoppositional theories and relational methods that insist on a realistic politics of hope and the possibility of planetary citizenship. Through unlikely dialogues and startling juxtapositions, *Transformation Now!* builds on women-of-colors theories, texts, and perspectives—offering alternatives to difference-based scholarship. The book enacts a variety of multidirectional, multidisciplinary, multivoiced conversations, provocative dialogues in which all parties are transformed.

But what's so bad about oppositional consciousness?

Although oppositional consciousness, politics, and thinking have been necessary to our survival, enabling us to resist and sometimes partially reform oppressive social practices and structures, oppositionality is not as useful today as it was in the past century. I attribute these limitations to the underlying binary systems on which our oppositional epistemologies and practices are generally based. This dichotomous framework defines reality—and, by extension, knowledge, ethics, and truth—in limited, mutually exclusive terms. In this either/or system, we have only two options: Either *I'm* right and I win, or *you're* right and you win. This binary structure flattens out commonalities, reducing them to sameness: Our views are either entirely the same or they're entirely different. And, if our views are *not* the same—if they're different—then one of us (*me, I hope!*) is right and the other one (*you, I will argue!*) is wrong. There's no room for contradiction (*we're both right, even though our views seem strikingly different*); for overlapping perspectives and friendly disagreements (*we're both partially right and partially wrong*); for the building of new truths (*let's take your perspective, my perspective, and at least one more perspective and develop several synergistic alternatives—new perspectives!*); or for whatever other complex commonalities our imaginations might cook up. We remain locked into our already-existing opinions, which we cling to with desperation and fierce determination. As Flora Bridges notes, in oppositional discourse

> what becomes normative, "right," and regulatory within the culture is determined by beating down or stamping out various other alternatives. Norms and values are established by way of domination. In this mental framework the possibility for both/and is destroyed. Both/and thinking is basically determined as irrational, primitive, or illogical. What results is a ravaging, hate-filled dogmatic form of establishing cultural values. (71)

Embattled and besieged, we harden ourselves to protect our current beliefs, values, theories, and worldviews. Because any slippage—any willingness to consider alternative perspectives—seems to weaken our position and expose us to attack, we refuse to seriously consider the limitations in our current perspectives. (*It's us against them. Me against you.*) Differences are drained of complexity and defined in narrow, either/or terms that limit our options and strangle our imaginations. Mark Lawrence McPhail makes a similar point, noting that "argumentative language perpetuates division and fragmentation because it assumes *that competing positions are in fact mutually exclusive*" (*Zen* 99, original emphasis).

These violent oppositional perspectives—in which only one of us can be right and the other must be wrong—have their source at least partially in an inflexible ontological framework that posits a distinct separation between human beings and reality, divides this reality into discrete parts, and defines truth in narrow, rigid terms. Mutual exclusivity and either/or thinking is built into this framework. As McPhail explains, critical discourse relies on an antagonistic, dichotomous worldview and an essentialist epistemological structure, or what he calls negative difference. According to McPhail, "the problem of language in Western culture in its most extreme form . . . reifies the existence of an essential reality, a reality 'out there,' separate and distinct from the human agents that interact within it. This belief in separateness has, indeed, made us strangers, and has created a language of negative difference that manifests itself in the social and symbolic realities of race, gender, and rhetoric" ("Complicity" 1–2).

This principle of negative difference, with its dichotomous epistemology and ontology, shapes academic scholarship. Most (if not all) of us educated in western school systems have been trained to think in disconnectionist terms, to look for the differences (defined narrowly) between our views and those of others, and to heighten these differences while ignoring possible points of connection.[6] By challenging other people's theories, we affirm, support, and develop our own. While difference-inflected dialogue can offer valuable opportunities for intellectual development and creative explorations, we greatly diminish our possibilities for growth by assuming that these differences between our views and others' are permanent and cannot be bridged, transformed, or in other ways resolved. As McPhail notes, critical academic discourse is based on and grounded in disagreement: "all polemic is presupposed by an agreement to disagree, to take positions that are assumed to be mutually exclusive and *essentially* at odds with one another" (*Zen* 59, original emphasis). This antagonistic foundation, with its mutually exclusive options, transforms conversations into battles, making it almost impossible to develop creative compromise or generate innovative hybrid perspectives that draw from strikingly different views.

Our overreliance on these binary forms of oppositional consciousness limits activist-scholars in at least three interrelated ways: as I've just discussed, we're locked into the existing system (which shapes and reinforces the social problems we aspire to change); we can't imagine alternatives to this status quo, with its essentializing dichotomous definition of reality; and we internalize our oppositional approach so thoroughly that we use it against each other. In short, these oppositional energies limit our vision for change, restrict our options, and inhibit our ability to create transformational alliances. Oppositional consciousness usually prevents scholars from seeing alternatives because the arguments are grounded in the systems, framework, and worldview that we're trying to transcend. We've become trapped. Our overreliance on this binary framework imprisons us within the very system that we're trying to transform. Rather than think for ourselves and reflect thoughtfully on the most effective ways to address the specific situations at hand, we automatically fight back, trying to dish out even more than we or our allies have received. Locking us into a reactionary stance, these oppositional energies harm us as students, teachers, scholars, and colleagues.

In addition to inhibiting our ability to develop and implement innovative strategies for progressive social change, oppositional thinking erodes our alliances and communities. As the histories of numerous social movements have demonstrated, all too often oppositional politics fragment from within, damaging the individual and the group.[7] These hostile, oppositional energies become poisonous when we direct them at one another, as we too often do. Because oppositional thinking is premised on a series of winners and losers, we struggle fiercely to come out on top—as one of the winners (or, better yet, as The Ultimate Winner). We engage in all sorts of battles. All too often, and despite our best intentions, we enact what Timothy Powell describes as "corrosive exchanges" ("All Colors" 168) and embark on "[a] downward spiral of ever more hostile counter-accusations that tend to irrupt when a multiplicity of contentious and contrasting cultural points of view come into contact" (175). This fractured approach leads to divisive politics anchored in what Jacqui Alexander describes in "Remembering *This Bridge*, Remembering Ourselves" as "mono-thinking: the mistaken notion that only one kind of justice work leads to freedom" (98). As Alexander notes, reflecting on her own experiences in social-justice movements, oppositional politics' limited approach relies on reductive thinking that prevents social-justice actors from creating broad-based movements for social change:

> We named this process of fragmentation colonization, usually understood as a set of exploitative practices in political, ideological, and aesthetic terms, but also linked in minute ways to dualistic-hierarchical thinking: divisions among mind, body, spirit; between sacred and secular; male and female; heterosexual and homosexual; in class divisions; in divisions between the Erotic and the Divine. We saw its operation creating mono-thinking: *the mistaken notion that only one kind of justice work leads to freedom.* Presumably, organizing for a decent, just, living wage is not connected to anti-racist work, to anti-homophobia work, to organizing against the U.S state in Vieques. Such thinking is always premised in negation, often translated into singular explanations for oppression. (98–99, emphasis added)

Like McPhail's principle of negative difference, the "mono-thinking" that Alexander describes relies on (and reinforces) an essentializing, binary framework that defines reality too narrowly, in inflexible unchanging terms. When our politics are driven by mono-thinking, we assume that there is an absolute "best practice" and "best theory" to effect change. This assumption compels us to focus too narrowly on this single approach (*say, for instance, anti-racism*). Rather than work with those who use other approaches and draw on different theories, we judge them as somehow inferior—as lacking. (*Too often, of course, this judgment seems logical because our potential colleagues have defined their own approach as "the best."*)

Our internal fragmentations—our intra-divisions, as it were—have their source at least partially in the oppositional energies (and the dichotomous thinking behind them) that the groups used to combat social oppression. We can't turn off the negative energies once we remove ourselves from the battlefield. We take these energies with us, into our work, our homes, our minds, our bodies, our souls. They eat away at us, devouring us as we direct this oppositional thinking at one another and at ourselves. We fragment. We crumble. We deteriorate from within. And then we regroup. We begin again. And on to the next corrosive battle.

Too often, we've so closely associated our theories and scholarly/activist/political perspectives with our personal identities and our self-esteem that we become even more adamant about our views, even more reluctant to change. Even a slight shift in opinion can be viewed as defeat—a wound to one's selfhood. In such instances, we're no longer arguing in order to communicate our perspective, protect our values, and/or defend our theories. We're struggling for our psychic lives—fighting to defend our Selves—our self-definitions and self-worth. In such instances, if you attack my theory, you're attacking me. The friendly banter dissolves into acrimonious debate.

How could we even assume that these oppositional politics could effect the permanent, progressive change we so desperately need? After all, the oppositional thinking we employ relies on (and therefore unintentionally reinforces) the existing (unjust, oppressive) frameworks that we're trying to transform! Even if oppositionality's dichotomous approach to reality seems "hardwired" into our brains, as some scientists suggest, I'm tired of the knee-jerk reactions and the recycled theories and practices.[8] I'm exhausted with this divisive mono-thinking and the negative difference on which it relies. It's time to break out of our oppositional frameworks—at least occasionally. We need additional tools and tactics, nonbinary forms of oppositional consciousness that enable us to explore, discover, and create commonalities. Fortunately, we don't need to start from scratch: Women-of-colors scholarship and other threshold theories have opened the way.

Threshold theorizing . . . defined and enacted

Transformation Now! has its source in my belief that radical progressive change—on individual, collective, and planetary levels—is urgently needed and in fact possible, although not necessarily easy to achieve.[9] In this book, I call for, explore, and attempt to enact alternatives to conventional opposi-tional thinking and scholarship. I describe these alternatives as "threshold theories" to underscore their nonbinary, liminal, potentially transformative status. As I use the term, *thresholds* represent complex interconnections among a variety of sometimes contradictory worlds—points crossed by multiple in-tersecting possibilities, opportunities, and challenges. Like thresholds—that mark transitional, in-between spaces where new beginnings, and unexpected combinations can occur—threshold theories facilitate and enact movements "betwixt and between" divergent worlds, enabling us to establish fresh con-nections among distinct (and sometimes contradictory) perspectives, reali-ties, peoples, theories, texts, and/or worldviews. I borrow the phrase "betwixt and between" from Victor Turner. Building on the work of anthropologist Arnold van Gennep, Victor Turner uses this phrase to describe the middle, liminal stage he finds in human rituals—a fluid, nonhierarchical, paradoxi-cal stage in which participants "are neither living nor dead from one aspect, and both living and dead from another. Their condition is one of ambigu-ity and paradox, a confusion of all the customary categories" (96–97). As I demonstrate throughout *Transformation Now!*, this category confusion is a crucial component in threshold theories. When we enact threshold theoriz-ing, we shift "betwixt and between" established categories, enacting what I've elsewhere described as both/and/neither/nor thinking—negotiations between (and within) affirmation and negation—that facilitate the invention of additional possibilities.[10]

Threshold theories inspire us to be bold, to dream big, to affirm the pos-sibility of transformation, to envision radical change. Thresholds mark crisis points, spaces where conflicting values, ideas, and beliefs converge, unsettling fixed categories of meaning. These theoretical thresholds open up dangerous, uncomfortable locations—for both readers and writers. Threshold theories are frictional, containing partial assertions and not-quite-this-but-not-quite-that perspectives. This oscillating ambivalence makes threshold theories complex, contradictory, and multiplicitous. Threshold theories draw from numerous perspectives and offer no final destination, no permanent fixed truths.

Threshold theories demand that we stretch! They challenge us to re-examine and perhaps change our thinking, our worldviews, our actions. Neither entirely inside nor fully outside any single theoretical perspective, threshold theories invite us to consider and perhaps occupy ambivalent insider/outsider positions in relation to a variety of more established theoretical views. In many ways, threshold theories' ambivalent insider-outsider oscillations resemble what Walter Mignolo describes as "border thinking." But I describe these theories as "thresholds" rather than "borders" to underscore both their ability to contain and transform multiple opposing perspectives and their promise of transformation.

Grounded in a framework of interconnectivity—a metaphysics of interconnectedness, as it were—threshold theories are relational. Whereas border thinking generally begins from a point of breakage—from the "subaltern perspective[,] emerging from the cracks between civilization and culture" (Mignolo 44), threshold theories start elsewhere—with the presupposition that we are intimately, inextricably linked with all human and nonhuman existence. Each individual being is interrelated with all that exists—on multiple levels and in multiple ways, ranging from economics and ecology to language, social systems, and energy.[11] By thus positing our radical interconnectedness, threshold theories contain but exceed the exclusionary ontological frameworks, the principle of negative difference, and the either/or thinking found in oppositional consciousness and other Enlightenment-based worldviews. As I indicate in more detail later in this introduction, my use of the word *radical* (with its Latin origin in *roots*) is quite intentional: Threshold theories are premised on a shared commonality (not sameness)—a complex commonality so spacious that it embraces difference—even apparently mutually exclusive differences. By positing complex, contradictory commonalities, threshold theories—and the relational thinking that they produce and on which they rely—enable us to redefine and reconceive conflicts and fragmentation. When we view conflicts from these relational perspectives, we simultaneously acknowledge and look beneath surface judgments, rigid labels, and other divisive ways of thinking. We don't reject these divisions, but we don't become trapped in them, either. We seek commonalities and move toward healing. As I intend to demonstrate in *Transformation Now!*, this radically relational approach can facilitate the development of post-oppositional resistance and nonbinary forms of oppositional consciousness.[12]

But enough abstract talk! Let's look at Gloria Anzaldúa's theories and practice of *nepantleras* and *nepantla* to consider some of the forms that these nonoppositional threshold theories can take. Drawing on her own experiences with a variety of social-justice movements and academic organizations, as well as her innovative understanding of the Náhuatl term *nepantla*, Anzaldúa coined the term *nepantlera* in her post-*Borderlands* work as she developed an expansive alternative to Chicana lesbian identity politics. For Anzaldúa, the nepantlera represents a type of threshold person or world traveler: someone who enters into and interacts with multiple, often conflicting, political/cultural/ideological/ethnic/etc. worlds and yet refuses to entirely adopt, belong to, or identify with any single belief, group, or location.[13]

Anzaldúa invents the word *nepantlera* by taking the common Náhuatl word for "in-between space," *nepantla*, and expanding its meaning to include ontological, epistemological, and ethical dimensions. In Anzaldúa's philosophy, *nepantla* represents temporal, spatial, psychic, intellectual forms of liminality and potential transformation. As she explains in her preface to *this bridge we call home*, "I use the word nepantla to theorize liminality . . . and to talk about those who facilitate passages between worlds, whom I've named nepantleras. I associate nepantla with states of mind that question old ideas and beliefs, acquire new perspectives, change worldviews, and shift from one world to another" ("Preface" 1). In Anzaldúa's work, *nepantla* signals crisis points, potential shifts in meaning, and a resistance to facile either/or frameworks. As Sarah Ohmer suggests, Anzaldúa's nepantla is charged with multiple oppositional energies, for it includes "a clash of opposites, un enfrentamiento with oppositional movements of identities and ideologies in which the self sways, but is not fixed, and remains ambivalent" (153). This mobile, ambivalent multiplicity triggers a shift from binary-oppositional consciousness and mono-thinking. Perhaps nepantla can best be described as particularly chaotic thresholds. When you're in nepantla, you're in chaos—tugged between starkly different peoples and worldviews. Your previous theories, your beliefs about life, no longer make sense. You're in free fall—painful, terrifying free fall.

Held in chaotic tension, these oppositional energies can activate transformation. (Here we see opposition, but not a dichotomous form. Nepantla's
multiplicity complicates oppositionality, breaks it out of the binary.) During an Anzaldúan nepantla, individual and collective self-definitions, belief
systems, and worldviews are destabilized as we begin questioning our previously accepted assumptions. Apparently fixed categories—whether based
on gender, ethnicity/'race,' sexuality, religion, or some combination of these
categories and often others as well—are slowly stripped away.[14] Perhaps not
surprisingly, Anzaldúa uses metaphors of awakening and rebirth to describe
nepantla: it's "this birthing stage where you feel like you're reconfiguring your
identity and don't know where you are. You used to be this person, but now
maybe you're different in some way. You're changing worlds and cultures
and maybe classes [or] sexual preferences" (*Interviews/Entrevistas* 225–26). In
short, nepantla is the site of multiple, clashing perspectives and beliefs that
don't seem to make sense, although they coexist with one another. In these
nepantla states, boundaries become more permeable, and begin breaking
down (perhaps transitioning from boundaries to thresholds). This loosening
of previously restrictive categories, perspectives, and beliefs—while incredibly
painful—can create shifts in consciousness and new opportunities for change;
we acquire additional, potentially transformative perspectives, different ways
to understand ourselves, our circumstances, and our worlds. It's as if nepantla
shoves us outside of our existing frameworks, forcing us to change our views.

Some people experiencing these difficult nepantla states choose to become
nepantleras. I underscore the volitional nature of this shift because it's not
easy to be a nepantlera. It's risky, lonely, exhausting work as we live with overlapping, contradictory worldviews, perspectives, and peoples. Never entirely
inside, always somewhat outside, every group or worldview, nepantleras do
not belong entirely to any single location. Yet this willingness to remain with/
in the thresholds enables nepantleras to at least partially break away from the
cultural trance and the binary thinking that has locked us into the status quo.
As Anzaldúa explains in "Speaking across the Divide,"

> Las nepantleras, like the ancient chamanas, move between the worlds. They
> can work from multiple locations, can circumvent polarizing binaries. They
> try not to get locked into one perspective or perception of things. They can see
> through our cultural conditioning and through our respective cultures' toxic
> ways of life. They try to overturn the destructive perceptions of the world that
> we've been taught by our various cultures. They change the stories about who
> we are and about our behavior. They point to the stick we beat ourselves with

so we realize what we're doing and may choose to throw away the stick. They possess the gift of vision. (293)

Living within and among multiple worlds, nepantleras use their frictional existence and discomfort to create alternative perspectives—ideas, theories, actions, and/or beliefs that contain yet exceed either/or thinking. This multiplicity compels them to redefine and thus slip through binary-oppositional frameworks and the dichotomous thinking on which it relies. They invent relational theories and tactics with which they can reconceive and in other ways transform the various worlds in which they exist. Significantly, Anzaldúa's nepantleras do not focus on narrow socially inscribed identity categories but instead forge a much more inclusive planetary vision: "Nepantleras think in terms of the planet, not just their own racial group, the U.S., or Norte América. They serve as agents of awakening, inspire and challenge others to deeper awareness, greater conocimiento, serve as reminders of each other's search for wholeness of being" (293). This planetary vision is post-humanist; as Anzaldúa writes in "now let us shift . . . the path of conocimiento . . . inner work, public acts," it includes but goes beyond all human life, embracing "everyone/everything" (558).

Years before she invented the word *nepantlera*, Anzaldúa was forging the theory in her daily actions, through the unpopular political and personal choices she made. We see an especially good example of the nepantlera's creative nonoppositional resistance in "La Prieta," her 1981 autohistoria, where Anzaldúa draws on her experiences from the previous twenty years and calls for a transformational social-justice movement.[15] During the 1960s and 1970s, she pursued her work as an artist and spiritual seeker while also participating in a number of political-activist organizations, including (but not limited to) the farm workers' movement, the Brown Berets, the women's movement, and the lesbian-gay movement. At a time when separatism was a familiar political strategy among oppositional groups, Anzaldúa maintains her commitments to all of these various movements and peoples. Look, for instance, at the following assertion, where she defiantly reaffirms her connections across differences:

I am a wind-swayed bridge, a crossroads inhabited by whirlwinds. Gloria, the facilitator. Gloria, the mediator, straddling the walls between abysses. "Your allegiance is to La Raza, the Chicano movement," say the members of my race. "Your allegiance is to the Third World," say my Black and Asian friends. "Your allegiance is to your gender, to women," say the feminists. Then there's my allegiance to the Gay movement, to the socialist revolution, to the New Age, to magic and the occult. And there's my affinity to literature, to the world of the artist. What am I? *A third world lesbian feminist with Marxist and mystic leanings.* They would chop me up into little fragments and tag each piece with a label. (45, original emphasis)

Although each particular group adopted an oppositional (and often separatist) approach that made membership contingent on an exclusionary set of demands (a type of sameness, as it were), Anzaldúa maintains her allegiance to all of the groups while rejecting their mono-thinking perspectives, politics, and rules.

Anzaldúa's nuanced response illustrates the relational oppositionality and threshold theorizing I advocate and attempt to develop in *Transformation Now!* By refusing the rules while accepting the people and the groups who impose these rules, Anzaldúa enacts a nonbinary form of opposition. She reaches beyond occidental traditions and defies either/or logic as she embraces apparent contradictions. Addressing the various oppositional activists who have demanded her exclusive allegiance, she exclaims:

> You say my name is ambivalence? Think of me as Shiva, a many-armed and -legged body with one foot on brown soil, one on white, one in straight society, one in the gay world, the man's world, the women's, one limb in the literary world, another in the working class, the socialist, and the occult worlds. A sort of spider woman hanging by one thin strand of web.
>
> Who, me, confused? Ambivalent? Not so. Only your labels split me. ("Prieta" 45–46)

After redefining herself in beyond-binary terms, Anzaldúa shifts her focus from the groups' demands to the underlying framework—the hidden status-quo story and the conventional separatist thinking that undergird these demands and would deny her ability to move among the various groups and worldviews.[16] By thus changing her focus, she acquires additional insights that she uses to examine the divisive roles social-identity labels (and categories) play. Carefully synthesizing acceptance with rejection, Anzaldúa exposes and opposes the labels' limitations and the flaws in the various forms of group-think on which such labels rely. However, she does not reject the people themselves. Nor does she separate herself from the groups. She embraces them all but also exceeds them. By so doing, she attains new insights about the framework that has shaped the many groups to which she partially belongs. She enacts a post-oppositional stance.

Threshold theorizing includes flexible epistemologies and ontologies capable of incorporating contradiction and paradox whenever necessary (*and useful*). Thus, for example, Anzaldúa adopts Marxist, socialist, mystical, and occult beliefs, despite the fact that many Marxists, socialists, and others might insist on these theories' mutually exclusive status. She refuses to choose between them but holds the contrasting beliefs in tension. She sits with the messy complexity. It's this willingness to live with the contradictions that makes nonbinary oppositional work possible. But new insights are not instantaneous, and threshold theories require patience, respectful attention to multiple voices, and the willingness to live with contradictory oppositions. In short, threshold theories require intellectual humility. As explained in more detail in chapter 1, I define intellectual humility as an open-minded, flexible way of thinking that entails the acknowledgment of our inevitable epistemological limitations, the acceptance of uncertainty and the possibility of error, and intense self-reflection. Intellectual humility resembles the "epistemic humility" Lee Hester finds in Choctaw elders' epistemologies. As Hester explains, "When you do not claim to have a correct map of the world, then you do not claim to have the 'Truth.' You are willing to accept that other people have maps that are as good (or as bad) as your own" (331). To borrow Hester's metaphor, threshold theories do not present the "True Map" of the world (or even "True Maps" of smaller regions, ideas, etc.); rather, they remain open to multiple mappings, enabling us to chart additional pathways and possibilities that we can use as we work to build a more inclusionary, socially just world.[17]

Threshold theories invite us to move from binary-oppositional to (*and, possibly, beyond*) relational-oppositional thinking. Anzaldúa illustrates this movement in one of her final essays, "now let us shift," where she draws on her own experiences at the 1990 National Women's Studies Association (NWSA) Conference.[18] During this conference, many women of colors, fed up with the organization's ongoing racism—with its limited attention to their needs, its narrow ('white'-raced, middle-class) definition of "women's issues" and "women's studies," its tokenization, its silencing, and its erasure of their words—walked out. By so doing, they enacted the typical oppositional politics of the time. Deeply wounded by years of dismissive treatment, angered by the ongoing racism they had experienced in U.S. culture and in the NWSA organization, they responded in an oppositional either/or fashion. They entirely rejected the organization. My point here is not to condemn these feminists of colors' actions or to judge them as too narrow to be useful. (*Indeed, had I been at this conference, I might have walked out, too.*) Their reaction was justified and necessary; however, it was not sufficient, in itself, to bring about the radical changes they desired. Along with such binary oppositional acts, radical transformation requires additional perspectives and actions, such as those Anzaldúa provides.

Significantly, Anzaldúa did not deny or discount her colleagues' oppositional perspective. As she explains in an unpublished interview, she fully understood why they felt compelled to leave, and she agreed with their assessment of the organization's deeply embedded racism. However, she also viewed the issue as more complex, with more than two sides. While maintaining full awareness of (*and personally wounded by*) NWSA's ongoing racism and painful actions, she did not entirely reject the organization. Holding these mutually exclusive perspectives in tension, she chose to remain at the conference and work to create opportunities for dialogue that could witness to all sides of the conflict.

This willingness to witness broadly, to all parties, is a dangerous, often unpleasant task. (Indeed, I can't help but wonder if Anzaldúa's work as a nepantlera negatively impacted her health and contributed to her premature death.)[19] However, in order to effect broad-based, lasting progressive transformation, we must move beyond oppositional thinking and take such risks. As Anzaldúa explains in "now let us shift," where she draws on her memories of this conflict-ridden NWSA walk-out as she presents her theory of las nepanteras: "When perpetual conflict erodes a sense of connectedness and wholeness la nepantlera calls on the 'connectionist' faculty to show the deep common ground and interwoven kinship among all things and people. This faculty, one of less-structured thoughts, less-rigid categorizations, and thinner boundaries, allows us to picture—via reverie, dreaming, and artistic creativity—similarities instead of solid divisions" (567–68). As this description indicates, Anzaldúa proposes nepantleras' connectionist thinking as an alternative to the oppositional thought we generally employ. A connectionist approach can be vital during times of fragmentation. When we view conflicts from connectionist perspectives, we try to look beneath surface judgments, rigid labels, and other divisive ways of thinking. We seek commonalities and move toward healing: "Where before we saw only separateness, differences, and polarities, our connectionist sense of spirit recognizes nurturance and reciprocity and encourages alliances among groups working to transform communities" (568). Anzaldúa demonstrates that by thus moving beyond binary thinking, shifts in perspectives, beliefs, and social structures become possible (though not necessarily guaranteed).[20]

Becoming nepantleras: forging complex commonalities, making new connections

I am a nepantlera, torn between theories, divided among worldviews, in love with authors and philosophers who rarely (if ever) speak to one another or even acknowledge one another's work: Ralph Waldo Emerson and Gloria Evangelina Anzaldúa. Engaged Buddhism and Black Feminism. Object-Oriented Ontology and Indigenous Thought. Quantum physics' theory of nonlocality and Womanist theory's LUXOCRACY. The strange couplings continue: Jane Roberts, Seth, and Women-of-Colors Theories. The Paranormal and Social-Justice Work. Spirituality and Activism. Pedagogy and Energy Medicine. Despite their many differences, these divergent academic fields, theories, and worldviews offer potential points of connection. I want to make these connections, draw these disparate worldviews into dialogue, create these synergistic conversations among areas of thought and perspectives that too often are kept far apart. Hence *Transformation Now!* As I make bold and unlikely combinations among fields, theories, and authors generally kept distinct, I simultaneously model and invite others to take similar risks.

Throughout *Transformation Now!* I adopt a relational, dialogic approach and bring strikingly different people, texts, theories, and ideas into convers(at)ion. I bracket the letters "at" in this word to underscore both my hope that these conversations will be transformative and my attempt to embed the transformation deeply within the conversations themselves. Positing interconnections among disparate perspectives, I call for and attempt to enact transformational dialogues—conversations with the potential for conversion. Like Mark McPhail, I believe that "[d]ialogue allows for the recognition of the interrelatedness of positions and propositions that transcends the dualistic essentialism of persuasive discourse, and provides for an understanding of rhetoric as coherence" (*Zen* 80). And so in the following chapters, I stage a series of liminal conversations—boundary collisions and internal disruptions—where unlikely juxtapositions and transformational possibilities occur. Topics range from Ralph Waldo Emerson's individualism, Mary Daly's radical revisionist theology, and mainstream self-help literature to Gloria Anzaldúa's post-Chicana philosophy, Paula Gunn Allen's provocative use of Native American "medicine women" and storytelling traditions, and *This Bridge Called My Back*'s interventions into mainstream feminist theory.

While the specific topics I explore might seem wildly diverse, *Transformation Now!* includes several recurring themes and practices: the importance of enacting *nonoppositional theories and tactics*; the significant, potentially transformative contributions *women-of-colors theorizing* can make to mainstream scholarship and cultural issues; the development of context-specific *relational methodologies* that enable us to forge complex differential commonalities; and the creation of *transformational identity politics* that deeply acknowledge, yet simultaneously move through, existing social identity categories, thus offering a vital alternative to conventional identity politics and postpositivist realism.

These themes are closely related to my larger objectives: First, to encourage scholars and students (of all racial/ethnic/gender/etc. backgrounds) to educate themselves about women-of-colors theories, texts, and perspectives, and to use this work in new ways. Second, to offer viable alternatives to the oppositional forms of consciousness and politics that currently drive social-justice theorizing, activism, and academic disciplines. And third, to generate new commonalities among texts and theories that are generally kept entirely apart. *Commonalities*, as I use the term, is not synonymous with sameness. When I focus on commonalities, I neither deny nor overlook the many differences among us (*defining "us" however you will*). It is, in many ways, almost the reverse: By focusing on potential commonalities among differently situated people, authors, texts, ideas, and/or worldviews, I can develop (*or discover?*) complex points of connection. Commonalities offer pathways into relational investigations of difference—difference defined not as deviation *from* an unmarked norm but as alterations interrelated *with* this norm. In *Transformation Now!* I demonstrate that this nonbinary approach to difference, coupled with (sometimes painful) self-reflection, makes transformation possible, on multiple intertwined levels. As with the threshold theories I describe above, commonalities represent an oscillation between what some might define as mutually exclusive categories. Commonalities are relational and nonbinary. The exploration of commonalities leads to unpredictable discoveries and potentially new modes of interactions with others. I locate these discoveries at least partially in language itself. Language acts.[21] Like Mark McPhail, I believe that language offers untapped possibilities for transformation, possibilities that we can access (*and/or perhaps create*) through self-reflection and open-minded investigation: "As we begin to scrutinize, reconceptualize, and reconstruct our classification systems, we will find forces within the language that will formulate a discourse devoid of domination; one that, in its affirmative approach to language, thought, and action, will be both radical and revolutionary. Such an approach to language will enable critics to engage in a rhetoric that actively recognizes and seeks to transcend the illusory black and white divisions of race, gender, and the language of negative difference" ("Complicity" 12).

Throughout *Transformation Now!* I enact the threshold theorizing I call for. I develop nonoppositional perspectives and relational methods that insist on a politics of hope yet thoroughly acknowledge the existing social disparities and systemic injustices.

Tying up a few loose ends: chapter overviews and text selection

Offering a rigorous analysis of the overlooked theoretical contributions of *This Bridge Called My Back: Writings by Radical Women of Color*, chapter 1, "Beyond Intersectionality: Theorizing Interconnectivity with/in *This Bridge Called My Back*," underscores the importance of women-of-colors theorizing while inviting readers to go beyond intersectional frameworks. A groundbreaking, multigenre collection of writings, *This Bridge Called My Back* has become an iconic text in feminist scholarship and WGS curriculum. However, its impact on contemporary theory and feminist scholarship has been minimal. Although scholars regularly use this book to *illustrate* the diversity and differences among women, they almost never employ the theories within *Bridge* as theory—as part of their own theorizing process. Nor do they integrate contributors' most radical lessons into their own lives and intellectual traditions. In this chapter, I offer another approach to *This Bridge Called My Back*. Drawing on my experiences co-editing *this bridge we call home: radical visions for transformation* with Gloria Anzaldúa (who was also a co-editor for the original *Bridge*), I argue that *This Bridge Called My Back* offers social-justice actors and scholars of all colors innovative tools and theoretical contributions that we still need to learn from, expand on, and implement in our scholarship, teaching, and other forms of activism. With this claim of *This Bridge Called My Back*'s value for *all* people, I also offer an alternative perspective from those who claim that *This Bridge* represents a "safe space" exclusively for women of colors.

Chapter 2 moves sideways through time, connecting my previous work in canonical U.S. literature with my more recent work in U.S. women-of-colors theory.[22] Through a dialogue between nineteenth-century American transcendentalist writers and contemporary women-of-colors authors, "'American' Individualism, Variations on a Theme" investigates and revises conventional models of individualism and personal selfhood. Given the central roles Ralph Waldo Emerson and Henry David Thoreau have played in constructing an "American" self and an "American" literary tradition, canonical transcendentalist texts like Emerson's "Self-Reliance" and Thoreau's *Walden* offer a useful point of departure for this investigation. Although I've been tempted to reject these famous representations of individualism entirely, use their examples as a springboard into a completely different version of individualism, or replace them with an exclusive focus on community and collective identity, I resist these temptations. Working from the inside out, this chapter redefines individualism—including *canonical* versions of individualism—in more relational terms. When we (re)read mainstream versions of "American" individualism and self-reliance through the work of contemporary U.S. women of colors, all parties are transformed: Self-reliance becomes a highly democratic, relational endeavor that simultaneously extends canonical interpretations of personal freedom outward to include previously ignored groups and redefines "American individualism" by reconfiguring the relationship between personal and communal identities.

Building on the previous chapter's explorations of selfhood, identity, and radical self-reliance, chapter 3, "'I am your other I': Transformational Identity Politics," offers an alternative to more conventional versions of identity politics, which I call transformational identity politics. Transformational identity politics represent nonbinary models of identity; differential subjectivities; an expanded, deeply multiplicitous concept of the universal; and relational epistemologies that facilitate the creation of new forms of commonalities. Although identity politics originated in a space of intersectionality that embraced multiple, complex identities, I argue that contemporary uses of identity politics have become too oppositional to effect radical change. However, rather than entirely rejecting identity-based politics and the personalized experiences on which they're based, I redefine identity by anchoring it in a metaphysics of interconnectedness. Through an analysis of Paula Gunn Allen's, Gloria Anzaldúa's, and Audre Lorde's threshold positionings (*their creative use of identity politics, as it were*), I illustrate some of the forms transformational identity politics can take.

Chapter 4 offers a detailed example of how scholars and other readers can use differences to forge commonalities. Focusing on revisionist mythmaking and divergent feminist spiritual traditions, "'There is no arcane place for return': Revisionist Mythmaking with a Difference" puts Mary Daly in dialogue with Gloria Anzaldúa and Audre Lorde; I use this dialogue both to examine the limitations in typical western concepts of the universal and to propose an alternative. While the similarities between Daly, Anzaldúa, and Lorde are at times quite striking, scholars almost never discuss these theorists in conjunction; instead, each is relegated to discrete categories based on genre, culture, and 'race'. Reading Daly in conversation with Anzaldúa and Lorde, this chapter takes a different approach: I demonstrate the possibility of negotiating between the universal and the particular without denying the importance of either. I argue that these negotiations are transformational in (at least) two ways: They enable us to redefine the universal in radically open-ended and inclusionary ways. And, these negotiations between universal and particular alter readers' self-perceptions and collective definitions. This chapter also addresses post-structuralist critiques of origin stories and revisionist mythmaking. While scholars generally ignore Anzaldúa's and Lorde's revisionist mythmaking or dismiss it as a nostalgic desire to return to some prehistorical, utopian gynecentric, Mesoamerican, or Yoruban/Fon community of women, I propose that their revisionist myths are forward-looking and, indeed, visionary.[23] By going "back" to previously erased conventions, they go forward—far beyond "God the Father"—rewriting the past from their present perspectives and inventing new definitions as they go. Their "returns" are performative, not descriptive, and enable them to enact their transformational identity politics.

Reading mainstream "New Age" self-help literature in dialogue with women-of-colors narratives, chapter 5, "From Self-Help to Womanist Self-Recovery," proposes a new genre that I call womanist self-recovery. Womanist self-recovery represents a contemporary transcultural project with several characteristics: the transgression of conventional literary genres; the visionary belief in language's performative power; and the use of non-western cultural traditions (epistemologies, symbols, myths, metaphors, and/or beliefs) to develop inclusionary multicultural communities. The phrase *womanist self-recovery* is intentionally contradictory, juxtaposing womanism's radical liberatory potential with mainstream self-help literature's conservative tendencies. I develop this genre by retracing my troubled engagement with Paula Gunn Allen's *Grandmothers of the Light: A Medicine Woman's Sourcebook*—a provocative book that scholars generally ignore, if they don't condemn outright. After acknowledging my deep concerns about Allen's book, I dive into it and, through my explorations, redefine it as womanist self-recovery. I argue that womanist self-recovery creates communally based, multicultural transformation narratives—stories of self-empowerment that begin with the personal but move outward to encourage and facilitate collective change, stories that synthesize self-love and self-reflection with the quest for social justice.

Drawing on indigenous teachings, recent work in speculative metaphysics, and classroom experiences, the final chapter calls for and attempts to enact alternatives to critical pedagogy. More specifically, in "Pedagogies of Invitation: From Status-Quo Stories to Cosmic Connections," I explore the implications of positing interconnectivity as a framework for invitational pedagogies and relational models of identity. Language, belief, perception, and action are intimately interwoven. The stories we tell ourselves, the stories we learn from our cultures (our families, schooling, religion, friends, the media, etc.) influence our beliefs about ourselves, other people, and the world. Our beliefs affect our perceptions, and these perceptions affect how we act; our actions shape the stories we tell, the stories others tell about us, the ways they perceive us, the ways we perceive ourselves. All too often, however, we (educators and students) assume that our perceptions and beliefs accurately reflect the entire truth about reality and ourselves; such assumptions narrow, limit, restrict our worldviews and inhibit our actions. Take, for example, that well-known story of rugged individualism with its pull-yourself-up-by-the-bootstraps theory of success (explored in chapter 3). My teaching experiences have convinced me that this hyper-individualism is one of the most damaging narratives in U.S. cultures. Seduced by stories of the "self-made man," the majority of my students cannot recognize the co-existence of another story, one of interconnectivity and interrelatedness: What affects others—*all* others, no matter how separate we seem to be—ultimately affects them as well. After examining the crucial role self-enclosed individualism plays in sustaining racism and other forms of social injustice, I use indigenous science and womanist thought to develop transformative pedagogical models, or what I call pedagogies of invitation; invitational pedagogies are nonoppositional and require intellectual humility, flexibility, and an open-minded attitude.

As these brief chapter summaries might suggest, *Transformation Now!* is grounded in women-of-colors theorizing and leans heavily on the work of Paula Gunn Allen and Gloria Anzaldúa. This emphasis is intentional. As I explain above, I believe that women-of-colors theorizing is more intellectually stimulating and useful than any other theories I've encountered. I have been especially influenced by Allen's and Anzaldúa's work. Their writings—more than those of any other theorists, authors, or artists—have inspired and shaped me, encouraging me to take new risks. Gloria Anzaldúa and Paula Gunn Allen are my Gilles Deleuze, my Jacques Derrida, my Judith Butler, my intellectual and spiritual guides. More importantly, Anzaldúa and Allen are two of the most innovative, visionary U.S. theorists of the late twentieth- and early twenty-first centuries. And yet, their most innovative and provocative contributions are generally overlooked. I fear that if we do not attend to these contributions, they might be entirely forgotten, and Anzaldúa and Allen will become far less useful. This loss would be tragic, forcing us (at some point later in the twenty-first century) to reinvent—rather than build on—innovative theories and perspectives.

Although scholars sometimes include Allen's and Anzaldúa's work in ethnic-specific areas of literary studies, women's studies, or lesbian studies, they typically focus on the more predictable elements of their careers—on Anzaldúa's borderlands/new mestiza theory, her Chicana lesbian identity politics, and her oppositional approach in portions of *Borderlands/La Frontera* or *Making Face, Making Soul/Haciendo Caras* and on Allen's discussions of Native feminism and her tendency, at times, to essentialize aspects of Native American and feminine cultures. To be sure, these specific areas are important and should not be ignored; however, they are not the most provocative, potentially transformative dimensions of their work. Indeed, I would suggest that scholars sometimes tend to use (or not use) Anzaldúa and Allen in conservative ways—ways that unintentionally preserve the status quo. Thus, they repeatedly focus on the mid-career Gloria Anzaldúa, the Anzaldúa who can function as a spokesperson for Chicana, Lesbian, and Chicana Lesbian identities, and they rarely examine Anzaldúa's more inclusionary early and late work—her radical challenges to social identities and her visionary calls for planetary citizenship. The avoidance of Allen's work is even broader and more extreme. A founding figure in Native American Studies and one of the first Native-identified women to intentionally and visibly describe herself and her work as feminist (*and lesbian*), Allen produced groundbreaking creative and academic writings that significantly impacted U.S. literary studies and contemporary feminist thought. Why, then, has she been so ignored, and what are the implications of this semi-erasure? Although I return to this question in chapter 5, I would suggest that scholars ignore Allen because she irreverently destabilizes many of our assumptions.

By drawing so extensively on Allen and Anzaldúa—by exploring, applying, and extending the most provocative aspects of their work—I challenge this theoretical erasure and build on their risky theoretical and stylistic innovations. I hope that my example will invite others to explore and apply their work, as well as the work of other women-of-colors theorists. This invitation is an important part of my activism as a scholar.

Postscript and invitation: A few words about my writing style, methods, and aspirations

Although I absolutely love Gloria Anzaldúa's early essay, "Speaking In Tongues: A Letter To 3rd World Women Writers," and can still recall the joy and inspiration I felt when I first read it, I cannot follow her advice to "[t]hrow away abstraction and the academic learning, the rules, the map and compass. Feel your way without blinders. To touch more people, the personal realities and the social must be evoked—not through rhetoric but through blood and pus and sweat" (34). Sure, I'd love to abandon all of my academic training and all those rules and instructions that I learned during my many years in school (*kindergarten through high school, college, graduate school for both a master's and a doctoral degree*). However, despite my optimism and visionary thinking, I can't believe it's really possible to entirely reject, forget, and in other ways "throw away" all of those (*awful, restrictive, spirit-sucking*) rules. They have shaped me, seeped into me (*possibly even at a cellular level*) too thoroughly. And honestly, some of the rules are ok. Punctuation rules, for instance, can be very useful when employed selectively, enabling writers to craft nuanced discussions. Indeed, I don't think that Anzaldúa could follow her own advice; she spent even more years in formal academic training than me (*kindergarten through high school, college, graduate school for a master's degree and extensive doctoral training at two universities*) and she, too, loved playing with language.[24] Nor do I share

Anzaldúa's wholesale rejection of rhetoric. I define *rhetoric* more broadly, to encompass a huge variety of forms, including at least a few that can bleed and ooze from our wounded lives just like the passionate writing she calls for. (*In this instance, perhaps rhetoric embodies that passion.*)

As you'll see when you read the following chapters, although I haven't thrown away all of my academic training, I've twisted it into surprising shapes and sent it spinning off into new directions. Whenever possible, I've replaced standard scholarly conventions (the persuasive arguments, the detached voice, the overly confident assertions, the lengthy refutations, the snarky comments) with questions, contradictions, "declarations of feeling," and other less conventional modes.[25] Rather than persuade, I invite. (*Or, perhaps, I persuade through invitation?*) I've tried to craft flexible invitations; I offer perspectives, theories, and ideas open to being altered and built on—hopefully, by you. Through these gestures, I aspire to enact the intellectual humility necessary for threshold theorizing. Through these words, I offer invitations into additional perspectives, actions, ways of being—possibilities that go beyond what I can currently envision.

I embrace contradiction and poly-vocal meanings. Hence the parenthetical comments, the italics, the italicized parenthetical comments, the questions, the exclamatory statements. Sentences written in the English language are so linear! They march along, word by word, tricking us into logical, organized assumptions, where the meaning builds point by point by point. Parentheses enable me to disrupt this onward movement; they allow me to make two or more (sometimes contradictory) points simultaneously. Take, for instance, this sentence you've just read. By bracketing the words "sometimes contradictory," I can tell you two things at once: (a) The parenthesis enable me to make several points simultaneously; and (b) these simultaneous points might contradict each other. With parenthesis, I can weave opposing ideas together, make them jut up against each other, touch and change each other and themselves. Italics, exclamation points, question marks, and other such feeling-inflected mechanisms give my sentences additional texture, change their tone—marking words differently, calling fresh attention to them. Meaning doubles up, folds back on itself. (*When I really want to double—or even triple—the meaning, offer additional perspectives, or underscore the tentative nature of my claims, I put my words in italicized parenthetical comments.*) Just as these sentences hold the contradiction—the two (or more) meanings, the multiple perspectives—in productive tension, so I invite you to sit with the contradictions, allowing them to jostle each other. These jostlings can be productive, leading to new insights.

In my desire to foster commonalities across disciplinary boundaries and intellectual fields, I rely on epigraphs, subsections, and copious endnotes— formats that enable me to include additional voices and perspectives and, through this multiplicity, foster numerous, overlapping conversations among a wide variety of authors/scholars/texts. (*Or, should I say, conver(sa)tions . . . transformational dialogues?*) By putting these voices and perspectives into dialogue with one another and with myself (*and hopefully with you*), the words, perspectives, theories, and views function synergistically, enabling us (*me, you, and the many writers whose words I borrow and include*) to build on the conversation, to contribute (y)our views . . . . and on we go, creating ideas and perspectives that I (*at best*) only partially envision or control.

If you read my endnotes (*I hope that you will!*), you'll find extra commentary, additional references, and, occasionally, personal opinion. Endnotes hold the overflow. Here, too, I strive for multiplicity and expansive, potentially transformational dialogues. Sharing information, ideas, and texts that have stretched my thinking, I hope that they might stretch yours, as well. Both in the endnotes and throughout the book, I promote the work of authors whose writings have spurred and supported my intellectual-spiritual growth. If you read these brilliant, underread people, their work will have a greater impact, a longer life.

I am now at a place in my life where I can take some additional risks and make suggestions that might strike (at least some) readers as rather crazy— as pretty far out there, out on a limb.[26] I do so both to honor the women-of-colors theorists whose work inspired and emboldened my own and, perhaps, to make things easier for others. I hope that readers can build on my risks, use (some of) my words as shields or platforms or other devises energizing you to take your own risks. I hope that my attempts to rattle the box, to move further, to shift into different spaces, might embolden you to do so, as well. Certainly, this is how women-of-colors theories functioned for me, when I was starting out—fresh from graduate school, sick and tired of the academic rules and constraints. And so, I invite you to take whatever might be useful in the following pages, retool it as helpful for your contexts, and build on it as together we work to enact progressive change—transformation now!

CHAPTER ONE

Beyond Intersectionality

Theorizing Interconnectivity with/in *This Bridge Called My Back: Writings by Radical Women of Color*

> Every generation that reads
> *This Bridge Called My Back* rewrites it.
> Gloria Anzaldúa, "Preface: (Un)natural
> bridges, (Un)safe spaces"

> Much like the language of diversity, the
> language of intersectionality, its very
> invocation, it seems, largely substitutes
> for intersectional analysis itself.
> Jasbir K. Puar, "'I would rather be a
> cyborg than a goddess'"

First published in 1981, *This Bridge Called My Back: Writings by Radical Women of Color* has become a classic of sorts, a frequently cited text in feminist scholarship, histories of U.S. feminism, and women's studies curriculum.[1] Co-edited by Cherríe Moraga and Gloria Anzaldúa, this multigenre collection brought together twenty-nine U.S. feminists from diverse ethnic/racial, economic, sexual, religious, and national backgrounds. I underscore the contributors' feminist politics: *This Bridge Called My Back* reminded readers that feminism was not—and never has been—a 'white'-raced movement. In addition to enacting this more accurate, expansive definition of feminism, *This Bridge* invited women of colors to develop new alliances with one another while, simultaneously, challenging 'white'-identified middle-class women feminists to recognize and rectify their racism, classism, and other biases.[2] In so doing, *This Bridge Called My Back* broke new ground and was instrumental in introducing intersectionality into mainstream feminist discourse.[3] But *This Bridge Called My Back* is even more innovative and visionary than this list would suggest: intersectionality is not only introduced and enacted within its pages; it's also superceded. As I explain later in this chapter, several *Bridge* contributors moved *beyond* intersectionality to offer complex relational perspectives on identity formation and alliance-making—perspectives that feminists and other social-justice scholars have not yet adequately acknowledged or explored.

During the past thirty years, *This Bridge Called My Back* has served as a lifeline for many U.S. women of colors—myself included.[4] I encountered *This Bridge* in a used bookstore back in 1990, near the end of my graduate school education, at a time in my life when I was foundering in a sea of unacknowledged-yet-all-encompassing 'whiteness.' Reading *This Bridge* changed my life, initiating me into a conversion experience of sorts. *This Bridge Called My Back* introduced me, simultaneously and serendipitously, to feminism and to threshold theories; it opened a doorway into a community of like-minded people and spiritual activists—what Gloria Anzaldúa describes as *almas afines* or Toni Cade Bambara calls "potent networks of all the daughters of the ancient mother cultures" (vi). *This Bridge Called My Back* gave me permission to acknowledge and explore both my ancestral heritage and my metaphysical longings and beliefs. More importantly, though, *This Bridge Called My Back* offered me a new way of thinking and a new framework; even as it introduced me to intersectionality, it invited me to move through the intersections, to reach beyond intersectionality and into a metaphysics of interconnectedness.

Building on this framework of radical interconnectedness, in this chapter I argue that *This Bridge Called My Back* contains important lessons for all social-justice actors (scholars, activists, students, and more)—no matter how we identify. While these lessons are, themselves, intersectional, they also point to intersectionality's limitations. Just as *This Bridge* was ahead of its time in illustrating and enacting intersectionality, so can we look at *This Bridge* to find an early enactment of what I call a politics of interconnectivity. This politics, which moves from interconnectivity to inter-relationality, offers a radically inclusionary approach.

This Bridge Called My Back's challenge to status-quo stories

This Bridge Called My Back: Writings by Radical Women of Colors has the potential to alter the psychic landscape of twentieth- and twenty-first-century U.S. feminist thought. Drawing on her personal experiences as a witness to the birth of *This Bridge Called My Back*, Chela Sandoval makes a similar point, noting that

> *This Bridge* was constructed as a mechanism meant to call up and recognize experiences—and to make them matter differently. In 1981, this mechanism changed the authors themselves, who became the very warriors they swore to become through the publication of their words. *Bridge* effected this affirmative transformation in writers and readers alike in much the same way that a contract assures, confirms, promises. The writing or reading of *Bridge* incurred a debt of honor: Its narrative worked in perception in much the same way as a vow, an action that requires a heightened moral consciousness by persons performing it. Through this vow—which was performed as litany, promise, covenant, or guarantee—"radical feminists of color" became women of words, speaking, writing, commanding, directing, giving meaning to silence and, as Anzaldúa writes, . . . transcending the word through code: a password: "I act with my heart in my hand," she explains. We disputed the Logos even as we were after the word. The *post* word. ("Foreword" 22)

As Sandoval suggests, *This Bridge Called My Back* can activate language's performative power, offering new tools and visions for transformation on multiple levels—ranging from individual authors and readers to larger concepts of meaning, or what Sandoval here calls "the Logos." And yet, so much of this "affirmative transformation" remains inert.

Despite scholars' frequent references to *This Bridge Called My Back*, the book's impact on the development and interpretation of twentieth-century feminist scholarship has been much less extensive than its iconic status would suggest. While the book is referenced in order to illustrate a shift in mainstream feminism, it is not used to theorize or to further develop these alterations. As Norma Alarcón observed in 1990, although mainstream feminists often paid reverential respect toward *This Bridge Called My Back* and used it to acknowledge women's diversity, these acknowledgments were casual and superficial, masking a continued focus on gender defined in overly simplified, monolithic terms.[5] Chela Sandoval makes a similar point: "The publication of *This Bridge*

Called My Back in 1981 made the singular presence of U.S. third world feminism impossible to ignore on the same terms as it had been throughout the 1970s. But soon the writings and theoretical challenges by such feminists of color were marginalized into the category of what Allison Jaggar characterized in 1983 as mere 'description,' and their essays deferred to what Hester Eisenstein in 1985 called 'the special force of poetry,' while the shift in paradigm . . . represented in the praxis of U.S. third world feminism, was bypassed and ignored" (*Methodology* 47). In short, during the first two decades of *This Bridge Called My Back*'s life, *Bridge* contributors' important theoretical innovations were almost entirely ignored as mainstream feminist scholars reduced *This Bridge* to eloquent descriptions of the status quo. But what about now? Have things changed in the twenty-first century? Has feminist theorizing (*finally!*) learned from the book's challenges? Do contemporary feminist theorists (of all colors) integrate contributors' most radical lessons into their own lives and build on the book's invitation to consider identity issues in more complex terms?

My desire to explore these questions, coupled with my alienation both from feminist theory and from the academic feminists in my life at that time, compelled me, in the late 1990s, to ask Gloria Anzaldúa if she'd be willing to revisit *This Bridge Called My Back* and co-edit, with me, a follow-up book that we would publish in 2001 to mark *This Bridge*'s twentieth anniversary. I knew, from my previous work with Anzaldúa, that she had been somewhat disappointed both with *This Bridge Called My Back* and with its scholarly reception, that she had envisioned a more transgressive and provocative book.

As Anzaldúa and I envisioned it, our new collection (eventually titled *this bridge we call home: radical visions for transformation*) would not just celebrate *This Bridge Called My Back*. Nor would it be oppositional, condemning the limitations in mainstream scholars' lack of serious critical engagement with the book. Instead, we would take a relational, performative approach and build on earlier work. Our collection would assess feminist progress and invite readers of all colors to develop *Bridge* contributors' insights by creating additional theories and practices designed to enact transformation. In the words of Max Wolf Valerio, a contributor to our book and to the original *Bridge*, we wanted to encourage (*and prod!*) "feminism . . . [to] stretch toward an unseen place" (252).[6]

Our hunch, as we began editing the new *bridge* collection, was that feminist, queer, and other social-justice theories were, in many ways, stuck—circling around a few contentious issues, locked into several theoretical ruts, trapped by their oppositional thinking. We wanted to shake up feminist theorizing and create a radically inclusionary, groundbreaking volume. Key to this desire was our inclusive stance: While *This Bridge* was a product of the mid-twentieth century and thus intentionally and necessarily focused exclusively on women of colors' writings, we wanted to open the gates, so to speak, and invite contributions from a wide array of people—anyone who had been impacted by the ideas in *This Bridge*.[7] We did not view our inclusive invitation as a betrayal or a diminishment of women-of-colors work but rather as an evolutionary development, an infusion of women-of-colors theorizing and perspectives across a broad spectrum of issues, concerns, and peoples. As in *This Bridge Called My Back*, writings by and about women of colors would be foundational. The process of editing our book both challenged and confirmed our hunch that we (U.S. feminist and other social-justice scholars-activists of all colors/sexualities/genders/etc.) have made only limited progress since the early 1980s. Or, as Anzaldúa puts it in her preface to our book, we realized "how much has shifted in the last twenty years, but also how little has changed" ("Preface" 3).

The shifts Anzaldúa refers to are important but not sufficient. To be sure, feminist scholarship and consciousness have experienced remarkable growth since the 1981 publication of *This Bridge Called My Back*. When I see the awareness of intersectional issues expressed by some of my own graduate students or read the powerful assertions of twenty-first-century feminists such as Indigo Violet or Aimee Carrillo Rowe, I have great hope for the future of women's studies and academic feminism more generally. As Violet asserts, describing her own experiences as well as those of her peers, "*This Bridge Called My Back* awakened deep truths for a generation, . . . A new generation of people are taking these lessons to heart, sharing stories with each other, . . . and recognizing the entwined nature of our histories and our existence in America" (486). In her writing and activism, Violet builds on *Bridge* insights to enact new forms of alliance-making that go beyond, without ignoring, conventional social-identity-based boundaries. Thus she describes her coalition of activists, called together in 1997 to challenge the "racism, sexism, and economic exploitation" at the New School for Social Research, as a collection of

> radical women of color, pro-feminist men, and whites. We have been fundamentally transformed by the work of feminists of color who insist that we must contend with the intersections of race, class, gender, sexuality, and nation, teaching us that the personal is inherently political, and that our politics must be holistic—rooted in the erotic, in a sense of the divine. Women-of-

color feminism offers models for building radical solidarity, working vigor-
ously with difference to create coalitional identities of resistance. U.S. Third
World feminism has proposed that we find wholeness in our contradictions
and connection where there is seemingly disconnection. We've been inspired
to mobilize an intuitive, practical, and intellectual knowledge that our togeth-
erness can transport us to new worlds. (486)

Violet and her colleagues create new alliances based on a shared apprecia-
tion of and transformation by women-of-colors feminisms. Without ignoring the many differences among us, these inclusionary alliances insist on
commonalities, or what Violet here describes as "coalitional identities" and
"wholeness in our contradictions."

Similarly, in *Power Lines: On the Subject of Feminist Alliances*, Carrillo Rowe
draws on *This Bridge Called My Back* and other women-of-colors and mainstream feminist scholarship to develop a theory and practice of "transracial
feminist alliances," or what she calls "bridge methodology." This relational
bridge method facilitates new forms of antiracist, multicultural alliances
between women of colors and 'white'-raced women. Like Violet and some
of the original *Bridge* contributors, Carrillo Rowe pays careful attention to
"the intersections and overlaps between our own oppression/privilege and
the conditions of those with whom we seek alliance." Through attentive listening and studious self-reflection, she explores the similarities and differences between "feminists of privilege" and women-of-colors feminists. While
acknowledging the many differences between these two groups, as well as
the internal distinctions within each group, Carrillo Rowe also—simultaneously—works to create complex commonalities.

However, these thoughtful inclusionary approaches are not yet the norm.
At the conferences I attend, in some of the classes I teach, on the Listservs
to which I subscribe, and in most of the publications I read, I still encounter
similar (*or, sometimes, the very same!*) issues to those exposed in *This Bridge Called
My Back*. I still experience the same types of oppositional energies and tactics:
the angry, jumping-to-conclusions debates; the unthinking, knee-jerk judgments and accusations; the rigid, embattled self-naming; the stereotyping;
the hierarchical rankings and "I-am-more-feminist-than-you" positionings;
the restrictive identity politics expressed with unthinking regularity. All too
often, self-identified feminists—no matter how they self-define (whether "of
color" or "white"; whether male, female, or trans; whether lesbian, bisexual,

heterosexual, homosexual, or gay)—continue to judge one another based on appearance and identity labels, and condemn one another without adequately listening or (apparently) trying to understand others' perspectives. It exhausts me! Despite the book's status and its impact on some readers, its most innovative theoretical insights have not been adequately explored and applied. In fact, as I suggest later in this chapter, by ignoring *This Bridge Called My Back*'s approach to intersectionality, we miss out on its most transformative lessons and radical challenges.[8]

These oversights stem at least partially from and thus speak to a more widespread limitation in much progressive scholarship: All too often, feminist and other social-justice scholars remain trapped in what I call "status-quo stories": worldviews that normalize and naturalize the existing social system, values, and standards so entirely that they prevent us from imagining the possibility of change. Status-quo stories contain "core beliefs" about reality—beliefs that shape our world, though we rarely (if ever) acknowledge this creative role. I borrow the term "core beliefs" from Critical Race theorist Reginald Robinson, who in turn borrowed it from psychic and author Jane Roberts.[9] As Robinson explains, "A core belief flows from feelings and imaginations, and ordinary people reinforce this belief through words and deeds. From this core belief, ordinary people co-create their experiences and realities. Core beliefs, experiences, and realities are concentric circles, overlapping and indistinguishable" ("Human Agency" 1370). Generally, we don't even recognize the tentative nature of these core beliefs; we have become entirely convinced that they offer accurate factual statements about all aspects of our reality—ranging from the very small (ourselves and our personal lives) to the very large (other human and nonhuman beings, the planet, the cosmos). Status-quo stories innoculate us into believing that the way things are is the way they always have been and the way they must be. This belief becomes self-fulfilling: We do not try to make change because we believe that change is impossible to make. Status-quo stories both rely on and reinforce a separatist framework and a metaphysics of negative difference. Status-quo stories are divisive, teaching us to break the world into parts and label each piece. These labels solidify, and we read them as natural descriptions about reality.[10]

Look, for instance, at how 'race' functions in U.S. culture: Many of us living in the United States have become entirely accustomed to identifying ourselves and others according to 'race'—based on skin color, physiological features, and other external markers; we assume that the racial categories we regularly employ are factually accurate, unchanging, and homogeneous. But these assumptions—coupled with our daily unthinking references to 'race'—*create* 'race', making it more permanent and inflexible.[11] Similar statements could be made about sexuality, gender, and the other social identity categories that we (often automatically) use as we try to make sense of our world, as well as the concurrent belief in self-enclosed individualism.[12] Trapped by the labels, we cannot fully engage with one another, or with the larger world. As Andrea Canaan explains in her contribution to *This Bridge Called My Back*, when we focus so narrowly on socially-inscribed identities, we "stereotype and close off people, places, and events into isolated categories. . . . We close off avenues of communication and vision so that individual and communal trust, responsibility, loving, and knowing are impossible" (236). This "urgent need" to stereotype and label is extremely widespread and deeply internalized. No matter how sophisticated our theoretical analyses might be, and no matter how we identify—whether as "of color," or "white," as "female" or "male" or "trans," as "lesbian" or "straight" or "bisexual" or "queer"—those of us raised and/or educated in western systems of thought have been trained to read and evaluate ourselves and others according to status-quo stories. We have been indoctrinated into a supremacist worldview—an overreliance on rational thought, scientistic empiricism, and hierarchical binary thinking that creates a restrictive framework that labels, divides, and segregates based on socially defined difference and sameness.

Yet when we automatically label people by color, gender, sexuality, religion, nationality, or any other politically charged characteristics and/or presumed embodied, psychic, political differences, we build walls between ourselves and these others. We isolate ourselves from those whom we have labeled "different." This automatic difference-based labeling process distorts our perceptions, creating arbitrary divisions and an oppositional "us-against-them" mentality that prevents us from recognizing potential commonalities. Status-quo stories about individual and group identity establish and police boundaries—boundaries that push us toward those we've deemed like "us" and boundaries that shove us away from "them"—those whom we assume to be different. These boundaries prevent us from working together to effect radical change. I believe that intersectionality, as too often practiced in contemporary theory and practice, inadvertently draws on and reinforces the types of status-quo thinking I've just described.

Intersectionality and status-quo thinking

Since Kimberle Crenshaw first discussed intersectionality in the context of black women's lives in her 1989 article, "Demarginalizing the Intersection of Race and Sex," references to intersectionality—both as method and as description—have become increasingly common among feminist and other social-justice scholars. All too often, however, these references are used only to signal (rather than actually enact) an inclusionary, deeply multicultural approach. Just as *This Bridge Called My Back* too often functions simply as a convenient way to acknowledge women's diversity while hiding a central focus on gender (defined in narrow monolithic terms), references to intersectionality are often used superficially, to mark difference yet recenter gender. As Jasbir Puar suggests in her discussion of feminist and queer theories, "Much like the language of diversity, the language of intersectionality, its very invocation, it seems, largely substitutes for intersectional analysis itself."[13] In such instances, when *intersectionality* is used as description or reference, scholars stop too soon: although they acknowledge the many differences among people, they use this acknowledgment of difference to stand in for a thorough exploration of these differences. They mark, classify, and divide; they stop with the labels and do not use this labeling process to generate new commonalities. The differences function like walls, not thresholds. Intersectionality, as it is generally discussed and practiced, is too limited. It leads to restrictive understandings of personhood, narrow identity politics, and binary-oppositional tactics. In short, intersectionality can (and often does) reinforce our status-quo stories. My point here is not to condemn intersectionality. It's useful in many ways. Historically, it has offered a crucial lens enabling us to articulate and expose serious (and sometimes painful) differences hidden beneath an unmarked, monolithic norm. But, as with any other application, intersectionality in itself is not enough. We need to range widely. We need multiple stories and multiple tools.

We need new stories, new tactics, and new visions. While I do not advocate nostalgic retreat into a romanticized past, I believe that recursive, thoughtful excavations of our pasts can offer new visions, ancestral knowledge for contemporary times. We go "back" to go "forward." As Renae Bredin suggests, "We have come so far from the bridge, only to find that the way home is a return across that same bridge" (330). And so, I return to *This Bridge Called*

My Back: Writings by Radical Women of Color and find there tools that we can use to build radical visions for transformation; I find in that book theoretical contributions—or what I'm calling lessons—that we still need to learn from, expand on, and implement more fully in our scholarship, our teaching, and other areas of our lives. There are, of course, many lessons in *This Bridge Called My Back*, but in this chapter I focus on only three:

1. Making connections through differences,
2. Positing radical interrelatedness, and
3. Listening with raw openness.

These three lessons offer valuable instruction to those of us who desire to build on intersectionality's lessons by developing and enacting nuanced politics of interconnectivity.

Although it might sound contradictory, in my return to *This Bridge Called My Back*, I go forward. Learning from the contributors' insights and errors, I suggest a few possible directions for feminist/womanist theorizing in the twenty-first century. I hope that my immersion in *This Bridge Called My Back* and my attempts to use the theories in that book to create new theories invites others to do so as well. In this chapter, I develop the lessons. In the following chapters, I investigate and apply them.

Bridge Lesson 1:
Making connections through
differences, seeking commonalities

As I've already mentioned, *This Bridge Called My Back* is especially praised for its attention to differences among women. At its strongest and most provocative, however, *This Bridge* does not simply emphasize difference. Rather, it redefines difference in potentially transformative ways. It illustrates what Anzaldúa describes as "a connectionist sense of spirit" ("now let us shift" 568).[14] While some contributors, like nellie wong, doris davenport, Judit Moschkovich, and Jo Carrillo, rely on status-quo stories that can reinforce self-enclosed identities and rigid racialized/gendered/sexualized differences, others do not.[15] I have been especially struck by Mirtha Quintanales, Andrea Canaan, Audre Lorde, Rosario Morales, and Gloria Anzaldúa. These writers strive to forge alliances and coalitions that do not ignore the differences among women (and, usually, men) but instead use these differences as catalysts for personal and social change—and they do so while acknowledging that at times these differences are so sharp, so profound, and so deep that they seem permanent and impossible to span.

Rather than gloss over or in any other way diminish such enormous differences, Canaan, Quintanales, Lorde, Morales, and Anzaldúa acknowledge and explore them. Risking the personal, they expose (often to themselves as well as to their readers) their own previously hidden fears and desires—fears and desires that have seemed so different, so shameful, that they must be entirely hidden. Thus, for example, in her letter to Barbara Smith, Mirtha Quintanales analyzes the similarities and differences between herself and other women of colors and, through this analysis, creates commonalities. In this short piece, she notes points of possible connection (or what I'm calling "commonalities") by drawing parallels between her experiences as an "essentially middle-class (and white-skinned woman)" immigrant from Cuba (152) and the experiences of women identified as "black," "Third World," "white, poor, and working-class." However, she does not use these commonalities to insist that she and her experiences are the *same* as those of the women she describes. Instead, she demonstrates a type of intellectual humility by acknowledging the limitations in her knowledge. This intellectual humility is remarkable: Quintanales does not hide behind her epistemological limitations; nor does she use them to claim defeat or to indicate some type of unnavigable difference between herself and the women she describes. She acknowledges the gap in her understanding and (rather than retreating) reaches *across* this gap to make connections. Admitting that she "cannot presume to know what it is really like to be a Black woman in America, to be racially oppressed, . . . [or] to grow up American 'White Trash' and destitute" (152), she resists generalizations and stereotypes based on these labels and calls for new forms of unity that acknowledge the differences among us. Instead of denying these differences or claiming that the differences are too enormous to be in any way bridged, she accepts and explores them: She opens herself to the lives of these others, allows herself imaginatively to feel their conflicts and pain, and uses this empathy and openness as pathways to investigate possible points of connection. She negotiates between sameness, similarity, and difference, generating commonalities.

Rosario Morales illustrates other forms that these negotiations among difference, similarity, and sameness might take in her contributions to *This Bridge*. Like Quintanales, Morales acknowledges the complexities (and complicities) in her own social location, and uses this reflection to rethink status-quo stories. Look, for instance, at how she opens her short prose poem, "We're All in the Same Boat":

> *I am not white. I am not middle class.*
> I am white skinned and puertorican. I was born into the working class and married into the middle class. I object to the label white & middle class both because they don't include my working class life and my puertoricanness, but also because "white & middle class" stands for a kind of politics. *Color and class don't define people or politics.* I get angry with those in the women's movement and out of it who deal with class & color as if they defined politics and people. (91, original emphasis)

Morales adopts a nonoppositional approach as she interrogates whiteness and distinguishes between social identity labels, racialization, embodied appearances, and politics. Within the space of two lines, she disidentifies with 'white' as a racial category and yet identifies herself as "white skinned." This ambivalent movement troubles simplistic divisions between women of colors and 'white'-raced women. When we consider her audience and context, this movement becomes even more significant: Morales's refusal to firmly situate herself within a single racial or economic category occurs in a collection of writings by and about women of colors, a collection that in some ways draws stark divisions between these two groups. With this bold refusal, Morales further complicates these issues as she denies the possibility of an automatic one-to-one correspondence between the socially inscribed labels to which we adhere (*or the socially inscribed labels that are thrown at us*) and our politics.

While fully acknowledging the many embodied and socially imposed differences among people and the ways these differences impact our lives, Morales does not view them as permanent barriers to forging connections. Nor does she assume that each difference-based group is homogeneous or in any way predictable; the status-quo stories about social-identity categories should not control us or determine our actions. Look, for instance, at her subtle critique of a type of identity politics that makes facile connections between specific identities and activist beliefs:

> "We know different things   some very much more unpleasant things if we've been women poor black or lesbian or all of those   we know different things depending on what sex   what color   what lives we live   where we grew up   What schooling   what beatings   with or without shoes   steak or

beans   but what politics each of us is going to be and do is anybody's guess. (93, original spacing)[16]

As with the unexpected, rule-breaking gaps in her prose, Morales's politics remain open to the possibility of surprise. She acknowledges that our many embodied and situational differences—differences based on sexuality, color, class, region, upbringing, education, and more—shape our experiences in diverse ways, impacting our knowledge systems and worldviews. Yet she resists the overgeneralizations or stereotyping that would lead her to assume that a person's politics automatically follows hir embodied identity. (*Just because I'm a woman of color, you can't assume that I follow some woman-of-colors agenda—whatever that might be.*) This refusal enables her to remain open-minded and willing to learn from others. (*She doesn't presume to know our politics; she waits to hear us articulate our politics in our own words, on our own terms—whatever those terms might be.*) Like Quintanales, Morales boldly demonstrates an intellectual humility that allows her to make connections among differently-situated people. Through these connections, she insists on shared traits or other commonalities. Look for instance at her narrative's conclusion:

> I'm saying that the basis of our unity is that in the most important way we are all in the same boat   all subjected to the violent pernicious ideas we have learned to hate   that we must all struggle against them and exchange ways and means   hints and how tos   that only some of us are victims of sexism only some of us are victims of racism   of the directed arrows of oppression but all of us are sexist   racist   all of us. (93, original spacing)

Morales's "same boat" represents a complex commonality—a sameness shot through with significant differences. She points to a deep-seated, shared complicity that can take many forms: While our lives and our experiences might be widely divergent, we are all, in various ways, the product of a racist/sexist/oppressive social system, and we have all—to varying degrees—internalized these beliefs. None of us is perfect. None of us has some enormous epistemic privilege that elevates us above the fray, making us the judges of all others. And, because we are all in this "same boat," Morales suggests, we should build additional commonalities and work together—"exchange ways and means hints and how tos"—in order to transform "the violent pernicious ideas" and their material effects.

Delving into—and exposing in print—their personal differences from any type of women-of-colors status-quo, and doing so with intellectual humility and an open-minded willingness to learn from others, Morales and Quintanales use their difference-based explorations to create possible pathways (or bridges) between themselves and their others—no matter who these others might be. They admit the limitations in their knowledge and their complicity in the status quo. They let down their guard. Their intellectual and personal risks, although dangerous, are vital to forging commonalities and generating new forms of community. As Anzaldúa explains in her preface to the twenty-first-century this *bridge we call home*, "To bridge is to attempt community, and for that we must risk being open to personal, political, and spiritual intimacy, to risk being wounded" ("Preface" 3). These risks—particularly for women of colors—are huge, unpredictable, and often quite dangerous. With their questions and bold assertions, Morales and Quintanales exposed themselves to multiple possible woundings. Already isolated both from the dominating culture and from the more conservative (and often patriarchal) portions of their home cultures, they risked further isolation, condemnation, and rejection by women who, in at least some ways, offered a source of potential sisterhood and friendship. How could they possibly know, when they made their assertions in print, if their criticisms of narrow identity politics and narrow versions of feminism would shove them out of feminist women-of-colors communities, mark them as traitors, leave them even more alienated, lonely, and exposed?

Making themselves dangerously vulnerable, Morales, Quintanales, Canaan, Lorde, and Anzaldúa engage in open conversations about differences. They use difference—or, more precisely, the dangerous self-exposure and exploration of differences that this exposure makes possible—to discover and/or create commonalities. Significantly, they forge commonalities without assuming that their experiences, histories, ideas, or traits are *identical* with those of others. As I explain in the introduction, as I use the terms, *"commonalities" and "sameness" are not synonymous*. Rather, "commonalities" indicates complex points of connection that both incorporate and move beyond sameness, similarity, and difference; commonalities acknowledge and include difference. Commonalities enable us to position differences within a larger context, a more visionary framework, one that moves us from oppositional, binary thinking (where "difference" becomes "deviation") into what Chela Sandoval might describe as a spacious "hermeneutics of love" ("Foreword" 26). I cannot overemphasize this point. The attention to commonalities, defined as a woven linkage—a synergistic, alchemical combination between sameness, similarities, and difference—offers us another entry into coalition-building and transformation. When "commonalities" are defined in this complex fashion, the search for and the invention of commonalities can be a potentially transformative methodological approach.

These tricky, complicated negotiations among sameness, similarity, and difference represent a radical departure from conventional dualistic-oppositional practices. Generally, feminists and other social-justice theorists define differences in binary self/other terms: white women/women of color; men/women; black/white; heterosexual/homosexual; and so on. However, these dichotomous configurations inadvertently reinforce an exclusionary (and often invisible, naturalized) norm. This oppositional approach is not surprising; it's the scaffolding for our status-quo stories. As Lorde explains, we have been trained to define differences as deviations from a false standard, or what she terms the "*mythical norm*, which. . . . [i]n america . . . is usually defined as white, thin, male, young, heterosexual, christian, and financially secure" (*Sister Outsider* 116, original emphasis and capitalization). These oppositional definitions of difference distort our perceptions and thus inhibit our ability to forge intricate alliances, for they compel us to define "difference" as "deviation"; to rank these differences hierarchically, in terms of their distance from the unmarked norm (*their degree of deviation, as it were*); and to regard all differences as shameful marks of inferiority. Driven by our shame of difference-as-deviation, we ignore, deny, and/or misname the differences among us.

And then, we sometimes make matters even more complicated and difficult: in our mistaken attempts to demonstrate solidarity, we hide our differences (as well as those of others) beneath a facade of sameness. This desire for connection and community motivates many mainstream feminists or others in some sort of majority position: In their efforts to forge solidarity with others who seem to share some important point of connection (*like gender*), they downplay, deny, ignore, or become oblivious to the differences that co-exist within these shared traits. (*We're all women here; let's unite based on gender. I'm a woman, just like you, so of course I understand you: as you describe your experiences of sexism, I assume that they're just like mine. I nod my head in understanding, but I'm so busy recalling my own experiences [which, I assume, are just like yours because, after all, we're both women—we're the same], that I don't fully hear you.*) I've witnessed a similar dynamic in many of the courses I teach. My students—especially those who by virtue of their gender, color, class, health status, and/or sexuality have been marginalized and occupy only partial versions of the norm—deeply want to create connections with others; but their desire overruns them, and they try to forge their connections by overlooking significant differences between themselves and those with whom they want to connect. It's as if they're afraid that by calling attention to these differences they will create unbridgeable rifts between themselves and others. They want connection!

But of course differences don't disappear just because we ignore, reject, or in other ways deny them. Significantly (*tragically*), our attempts to deny the differences that seem to interfere with our ability to create coalitions have the opposite effect: Denying the differences doesn't bring us together; it pushes us further apart. How ironic! The denied differences grow stronger as we pretend they don't exist by seeking refuge behind stereotypes, monolithic labels, and other false assumptions of sameness. Think, for instance, of the mainstream U.S. women's movement during the 1970s and early 1980s, when gender—defined in simplistic terms—was supposed to trump the many differences among women by creating an automatic (pseudo)universal female bond. As *Bridge* contributors (among many others) demonstrated, this assumption of a homogeneous womanhood created new divisions and in other ways prevented women from generating commonalities and making connections.

In *This Bridge Called My Back*, Lorde, Quintanales, Morales, and several other writers acknowledge, express, and investigate differences, yet—*and simultaneously*—they insist on commonalities. This intertwined acknowledgment of differences and commonalities, coupled with intellectual humility, open-mindedness, and a willingness to risk self-exposure, can revolutionize our approaches to difference. Making themselves vulnerable, these *Bridge* authors draw on their personal experiences to explore the stereotypes and the limitations in identity labels. Their bold explorations challenge assumptions of sameness, demonstrating that it is not differences that divide us but rather our refusal to openly examine and discuss the differences among us. This point is worth repeating because it's so often misunderstood: *Differences are not, in themselves, divisive.* Rather, it's our limited definitions of difference-as-deviation, coupled with our refusal to openly acknowledge, examine, and discuss our differences that divides us.[17]

Anzaldúa offers the boldest, most extensive and potentially tranformative illustration of this nuanced approach to differences in her theory and practice of El Mundo Zurdo, or The "Left-Handed World."[18] This activist theory spans Anzaldúa's career, from the late 1970s until her death in 2004, and in many ways embodies her visionary, inclusionary stance. In addition to titling the last section of *This Bridge Called My Back* "El Mundo Zurdo: The Vision," Anzaldúa defines, explores, and enacts El Mundo Zurdo in her 1981 autohistoria, "La Prieta"; and at various points throughout her career she returned to and expanded on this theory and practice.[19] El Mundo Zurdo represents a spirit-inflected, visionary approach to community building. According to Anzaldúa's theory of El Mundo Zurdo, it's possible (and indeed necessary) for very different people—from diverse backgrounds with a wide variety of needs, politics, experiences, and concerns—to co-exist and work together to enact revolutionary change. As she explains in "La Prieta": "We are the queer groups, the people that don't belong anywhere, not in the dominant world nor completely within our own respective cultures. Combined we cover so many oppressions. But the overwhelming oppression is the collective fact that we do not fit, and because we do not fit, *we are a threat*" (50, original emphasis).

Anzaldúa replaces conventional definitions of difference-as-opposition with a relational approach to differences. She openly acknowledges that the inhabitant-practitioners of El Mundo Zurdo are not all alike; their specific oppressions, solutions, and beliefs diverge and at times even conflict and disagree. She accepts these differences and uses them in nonoppositional ways, to generate new forms of commonality: "these different affinities are not opposed to each other. In El Mundo Zurdo I with my own affinities and my people with theirs can live together and transform the planet" ("La Prieta" 50). Joined by their rejection of the status quo and their so-called deviation from the dominant culture, inhabitants of El Mundo Zurdo enact a planetary citizenship; they create new alliances and use these alliances to transform their worlds.

Anzaldúa's theory of El Mundo Zurdo originated in her daily life when, in the late 1970s, she organized poetry readings as the El Mundo Surdo Reading Series in San Francisco.[20] This series was intentionally diverse and included people of all colors. Unlike many other progressive social-justice activists and theorists of this time period who were uniting into identity-specific groups (*or, we could say, groups premised on some specific type of foundational sameness*), Anzaldúa refused to self-segregate, instead resolutely creating alliances among people from a variety of different social locations. Despite the many differences among them, her El Mundo Surdo participants shared several commonalities, including their personal experiences of alienation, discrimination, and/or oppression; their interest in issues of social justice; their shared rejection of the status quo; their visionary beliefs in the transformational power of imagination and the spoken word; and their work as creative writers and artists.

With her theory of El Mundo Zurdo, Anzaldúa demonstrates that we can seek commonalities without ignoring differences (whether in cultures, experiences, beliefs, politics, and/or desires) among people. As she asserts in her preface to *this bridge we call home*, "Our goal is not to use differences to separate us from others, but neither is it to gloss over them. Many of us identify with groups and social positions not limited to our ethnic, racial, religious, class, gender, or national classifications. Though most people self-define by what they exclude, we define who we are by what we include—what I call the new tribalism" ("Preface" 3). I want to underscore the importance of Anzaldúa's approach to differences. By shifting from exclusionary to inclusionary identity formation, she redefines differences as opportunities, or pathways, enabling us to forge complex commonalities. Anzaldúa grounds this nuanced approach in her metaphysics of interconnectedness—a spirit-infused worldview enabling broader, more inclusive contexts for difference. Defining each individual as part of a larger whole, she insists on a commonality spanning "everyone/everything"; despite our many differences, we "share a category of identity wider than any social position or racial label" ("now let us shift" 558).[21] For Anzaldúa, this shared identity category is foundational, and enables her to replace the rigid boundaries imposed by status-quo stories with a relational approach.

The foundational belief in our interrelatedness is the second *Bridge* lesson I explore. . . .

Bridge Lesson 2:
Positing our radical interrelatedness

Because we are radically interrelated, what we think and do impacts others—*all* others (both human and nonhuman others), no matter how different or distant they might be. This concept of interrelatedness is a key tenet of many Indigenous worldviews—ranging from the Dakota belief expressed in the phrase "all my relatives" (*mitakuye owasin*), which reminds us that we are related to all existence, to the Buddhist teaching of co-dependent arising, to Thích Nhất Hạnh's theory and practice of inter-being. Indeed, interdependence is even partially grasped by some nineteenth-century U.S. transcendentalists such as Ralph Waldo Emerson, Henry David Thoreau, and Walt Whitman. However, I first saw this belief in our interrelatedness embodied and lived out within the pages of *This Bridge Called My Back:* in Rosario Morales's assertion that "we are all in the same boat" (93); in Luisah Teish's belief that "my destiny is infinitely tied with that of everybody else" (Anzaldúa, "O.K. Momma" 223); and in Anzaldúa's bold claim that "[w]e have come to realize that we are not alone in our struggles nor separate nor autonomous but that we—white black straight queer female male—are connected and interdependent. We are accountable for what is happening down the street, south of the border or across the sea" ("Foreword" (1983) n.p.). In each of these statements, the collective is defined so broadly that it includes all human life.[22] Like Morales, Teish, and Anzaldúa, I believe that we are interrelated and interdependent—on multiple levels and in multiple modalities: economically, socially, ecologically, emotionally, linguistically, physically, and spiritually. We are interlinked in every way we can possibly imagine, as well as in ways that we cannot yet fathom. Indeed, our relatedness goes beyond interconnections with all human life to include our radical interconnections with nonhumans. As Inés Hernández-Ávila states in her contribution to *this bridge we call home*, "We are related to all that lives" (532).

Interconnectivity is foundational to *This Bridge Called My Back*. It serves as the inspirational force behind the book and the motivational energy infusing its pages. As an analysis of Anzaldúa's archival materials and published work indicates, her own deeply held belief in our radical interrelatedness was instrumental, motivating her to initiate this collection of writings by women of colors.[23] For Anzaldúa, this interrelatedness goes beyond humans' interconnections to encompass a planetary (and possibly even cosmic) dimension. As she writes in an unpublished draft of her 1983 foreword to the second edition of *This Bridge*, she believes that "[e]very person, animal, plant, stone is interconnected in a life and death symbiosis" ("Second Edition"). While Anzaldúa's desire to edit a collection of writings exclusively by women of colors was very intentional, she did not view this exclusivity as a separatist gesture, creating new borders or in other ways deepening the divisions among women. Rather, she believed that the concentrated focus on women-of-colors voices, with their detailed attention to differences, would generate new connections and conversations among women of all colors (including those racialized as 'white'). Look for example at her response to a *Bridge* contributor who, angry about Anzaldúa's and Moraga's editorial decision to include a quotation by Adrienne Rich (a 'white'-raced, middle-class feminist and well-known poet) in their introduction to *This Bridge*, threatened to pulling her contribution out of the collection. Anzaldúa validates her contributor's concern yet also eschews her separatist politics:

> Spent almost a whole day going over your paper—felt a lot of love toward you. We *want* you in our book. . . . You object to our use of A. Rich's quote. My vision does not exclude white women. I learned from R. She took her work as far as she could coming from a privileged class. We all have our different paths, our different works cut out for us. / It is not politically correct to cite a white woman. But for me it is personally correct. We must not let color or class separate us—there are too many divisions in our lives, too much silence among us. / We went to white schools, read white women's books and some of us marry whites and the guilt we suffer for doing so[.] ("Correspondence," original emphasis)

As both her expression of love and her distinction between political correctness and personal correctness indicate, Anzaldúa responds thoughtfully and in a nonbinary oppositional manner to her contributor's objection. While she rejects separatism's usefulness for herself, she does not try to impose her nonseparatism on everyone, even as she reminds this contributor of the many divisions among us and calls for new bridges. Like Morales and Quintanales, Anzaldúa does not ignore the points of connection between women of colors and whiteness ("We went to white schools, read white women's books and some of us marry whites").

I underscore *This Bridge Called My Back*'s lesson of radical interconnectivity because it's one that we too often ignore or forget. This collection is so often associated with the recognition of differences that it's easy to overlook its equally important points about interrelatedness. Jacqui Alexander makes a similar observation: "in the midst of uncovering the painful fault lines of homophobia, culture, and class within different communities of belonging, [and] advancing critiques of racism within the women's movement, [*This Bridge Called My Back*] did not relinquish a vision of interdependence, of interbeing. . . . Not a transcendent vision, but one rooted in transforming the dailiness of lived experience, the very ground upon which violence finds fodder" ("Remembering *This Bridge*" 97). As Alexander suggests, this "vision of interdependence" is not some abstract belief in an otherworldly reality to which we escape so that we can avoid the difficult conversations about embodied and psychic differences; this vision is, rather, deeply embedded in everyday life and impacts even our most ordinary actions and encounters.

Not surprisingly, then, positing radical interrelatedness has concrete ethi-cal implications. Because we are all interconnected, the events and belief systems impacting others—no matter how different, distant, alien these others seem to be—affect us as well. To borrow Rosario Morales's analogy, we are all in the same boat, floating on the same water, tossed about by the same waves, battered by the same storms: We all rise or sink together. When we view ourselves as interrelated, we must consider our actions' impact on others. On the personal level, then, interconnectivity and accountability are closely intertwined—like two sides of the same coin. Defining and perceiving ourselves as radically interrelated, we react thoughtfully as we engage with others; we learn to pause and self-reflect. We practice a relational ethics that demands a new level of mindfulness: we must carefully think through the implications of our words and deeds before we speak or act.

Recognition of our profound interrelatedness has revolutionized my life in ways I'm still trying to comprehend and embody in my daily actions.[24] (*And I still fail far more often than I succeed.*) In my scholarship and teaching, positing interconnectivity has challenged me to reconsider my use of binary-opposi-tional frameworks. Like many people trained in the academy, I have honed my debate skills; I have learned to think on my feet, to quickly assess and find the weaknesses in opponents' arguments and perspectives. I focus on these weak spots in my opponents' perspectives as I champion my own views. (*Notice my language here: In order to sharpen my arguments, I've defined those not in agreement with me—those who differ from me—as my "opponents."*) Given my progressive politics, as well as my status as a lightskinned woman of color in the academy, this op-positionality has seemed vital for my survival. (*If I don't object and oppose, I'll be erased—swallowed up by the academy's vast 'whiteness,' denied by my sisters of colors.*) However, after living so intimately with *This Bridge Called My Back*, working so closely with Anzaldúa on *this bridge we call home* and other projects, and reflecting on my personal and professional life thus far, I've realized and can (*finally!*) admit that my oppositional politics are not very effective. My oppo-sitional approach has inhibited my growth, damaged my health, threatened my relationships, soured my worldview, and harmed me in other ways.

Ironically, I was hit with this realization while editing *this bridge we call home*. Excited about the book's progress and in awe of the brilliant writers/artists/thinkers/activists participating in our project, Gloria and I decided to create a virtual space where contributors could meet, exchange ideas, and benefit from our collective energy.[25] And so, to facilitate this community building and dialogue, we started a Listserv for all of the contributors. Although many contributors used the Listserv to share insights and express their excitement about our project, a few people reacted violently when they realized that Gloria and I would be including contributions by people who do not identify as "women of color" in the book. The anger was visceral and shocking as several contributors expressed their stunned surprise and intense disappointment that our new book would not provide the same type of "safe" women-of-color-only space as that found in *This Bridge Called My Back*.[26] I still do not fully understand the dynamics, but these reactions morphed . . . from shocked sorrow to aggressive anger—directed not toward the editors (which, in our opinion, was where the anger should have been addressed) but instead toward each other. Rather than expressing their extreme disappointment directly by confronting Gloria and me about our twenty-first-century vision of bridging and our decision to create a radically inclusionary book, the listserv conversation took a strange detour into a volatile debate between a small handful of pro-Palestinian and pro-Israeli contributors. The rhetoric grew increasingly hateful and hostile; each side treated its "Other" with extreme disdain, dehumanizing anyone who held an opposing view, refusing to listen to and try to understand their Other's perspectives. (*The anger in their words jumped through the computer screen, slamming into my body.*) It was a stunning display of oppositional energies, and it made us physically ill. As Anzaldúa writes, "[t]he contentious debates . . . churned a liquid fire in our guts" ("Preface" 2).

This painful clash among our contributors forced me to confront and reflect on my own oppositional politics and energies. As I carefully monitored my initial reactions, I noted my strong desire to react oppositionally, to fight back, to counter the contributors' angry words with my own anger, to meet aggression with aggression, to give what I was receiving. (*Confession: because I've been trained to "win," I wanted to do more than return the opposition—I wanted to draw on my righteous anger and persuade the contributors that their perceptions were incorrect, that their beliefs were WRONG. I wanted to punish them with my righteous wrath.*) Our Listserv—this beautiful space designed to facilitate visionary planning and bonding—had been hijacked by several very angry people, and I was angry in turn. I was hurt, and this wound made me furious! I wanted to point out that the hostility was misdirected and should be directed toward Gloria and me; the angry contributors had been sidetracked. I wanted to scold these contributors; I wanted to remind them of *This Bridge Called My Back*'s radical vision of bridging, bonding, and loving across differences; I wanted to suggest that they adopt the *Bridge* authors' teachings and stop judging each other so harshly; I wanted to tell them to reread our call for papers more carefully. In short, I wanted to respond by attacking those contributors who were slinging hostile words at each other. I was so mad! I composed (but, fortunately, did not actually send) many angry emails, filled with harsh words and strong critiques of the flaws in both sides' perspectives—the stereotyping, the othering, the apparent hatred, the mean-spirited energy. Not surprisingly (given my bottled-up rage), I became physically ill, and (after many discussions and intense soul-searching) Gloria and I decided to shut down the Listserv. (*Perhaps our decision demonstrates that it's not always possible to build bridges and create communities or to enact what, in the following section, I call "listening with raw openness;" sometimes, we must listen to our bodies and withdraw.*)

My illness forced me to slow down and reflect on the angry debate. Through this reflection, ongoing conversations with Gloria, my meditation practice, and my daily swims, I obtained additional insights into oppositional strategies' limitations. Our Listserv experiences illustrated Irene Lara's assertion in "Healing Sueños for Academia": "Standing in rigid opposition is a strategy for survival, but it has also killed us and will continue to sever our souls and assail our hearts. Western binary oppositions wound us in many ways. . . . Feeding the interests of the dominant, these false splits keep us from ourselves, each other, and our visible and invisible world" (434). As I explained in the introduction, because binary oppositions have their source in the dominating culture and support its values and worldviews, our oppositional politics cannot be as transformative as we might assume. Indeed, oppositional politics can become poisonous and subtly self-defeating.

Based on either/or thinking and dualistic ("us" against "them") models of identity, this binary-oppositional approach reinforces the status quo. Oppositional logic reduces our interactional possibilities to two mutually exclusive options: Either our views are entirely the same *or* they are entirely different. In this either/or system, differences of opinion and differing worldviews become monolithic, rigid, and divisive. When we examine the world through this binary lens, we assume that the differences between our views and those of others are too different—too *other*, as it were—to have *anything* (of importance) in common. This assumption of negative difference traps us within our existing ideas and beliefs, for it prevents us from developing new forms of knowledge and new alliances. After all, if we're so busy defending our own views, where is the room for complexity, compromise, and exchange? How can we possibly learn from social-justice theorists who hold views unlike our own?

Positing radical interconnectivity, I am shifting my politics, pedagogy, and daily actions from binary-oppositional to relational approaches. Thus, for example, in my classrooms, interdependence offers alternative epistemologies, ontologies, and ethics and thus serves as a crucial point of departure for teaching about and enacting social justice. Exposing the limitations in status-quo stories about self-enclosed identities, I invite students to examine both our radical interconnectedness and the ways this interconnectivity energizes us and makes us accountable—on multiple levels and in multiple ways.[27] This recognition, when it occurs, encourages us to develop new alliances. As Anzaldúa explains, "[t]he knowledge that we are in symbiotic relationship to all that exists and co-creators of ideologies—attitudes, beliefs, and cultural values, motivates us to act collaboratively" ("Preface" 2).

However, these collaborative actions can only succeed when we (try to) adopt intellectual humility and other spiritual-activist technologies and begin moving beyond binary thinking and dualistic self/other identities, which brings me to the third *Bridge* lesson I explore. . . .

Bridge Lesson 3: The importance of listening with raw openness

We must listen to each other. It sounds so obvious. . . . doesn't it? But we (I'm thinking here of womanist/feminist scholars, educators, and students, but it applies to those in other social-justice disciplines as well) spend so much time coming to voice, talking back, and transform[ing] silence into language and action that we seem to forget the importance of listening—opening ourselves and really *hearing* what others say.[28] This, too, is a lesson found in *This Bridge Called My Back*. As Mitsuye Yamada reminds us, "one of the most insidious ways of keeping women and minorities powerless is to . . . let them speak freely and not listen to them with serious intent" (40). I interpret the phrase "serious intent" to represent a type of deep, self-reflective listening that takes tremendous effort, demands vulnerability, and requires a willingness to be altered by the words spoken. This intention to listen deeply and open-mindedly is crucial to the nonbinary oppositional work I'm advocating in *Transformation Now!*.

Throughout *This Bridge Called My Back*, contributors insist on the importance of listening with serious intent—listening carefully, thoughtfully, and humbly, ready to be changed by what they hear. Judit Muscovitch, for example, challenges her Anglo-American women audience to stop tokenizing Latinas and other women of colors and to do their own homework: they must "*read and listen*" to what women of colors have to say (80, original emphasis). Similarly, in her "Open Letter to Mary Daly," Lorde implies that Daly has not read Lorde's work with an open mind, with the desire to be altered through what she learns. Lorde accuses Daly of a superficial type of reading-for-difference-as-illustration, asking: "Do you ever really read the work of black women? Did you ever read my words, or did you merely finger through them for quotations?" (95). Although these examples, taken on their own, seem to imply a unidirectional approach, where women of colors voice their experiences and concerns as 'white'-raced women silently hear what is said, Muscovitch's and Lorde's words are part of a larger conversation that in many ways had been dominated by 'white'-raced women. Muscovitch, Lorde, and the other *Bridge* contributors had spent years trying to work with their white-raced colleagues, trying to have engaged conversations yet finding themselves repeatedly rebuffed, tokenized, stereotyped, devalued, homogenized, ignored, and in other ways treated as inferior.[29]

Listening with raw openness is multidirectional. We need numerous overlapping dialogues among all types of people (human and nonhuman). We need dialogues where listeners do not judge each other based on appearances, presuppositions, previous encounters, or anything else. We need to engage in risky conversations—potentially transformational dialogues where listeners don't jump to conclusions but just open our minds and listen, with the intention to learn from and, potentially, be changed by what we hear (*while acknowledging that these changes might be painful*).

I describe this deep listening as "listening with raw openness" to underscore both the extreme open-mindedness it demands and its difficult, often painful, dimensions. Listening with raw openness can be dangerous! When we listen with raw openness we make ourselves vulnerable: we risk being wounded. This vulnerability threatens our hidden self-images, our public personae, our self-esteem. Peeling back our defensive barriers, we expose ourselves (our identities, our beliefs, our worldviews, and sometimes even our secret desires) to change. By so doing, we can acquire new, sometimes shocking, insights about ourselves and others. As Anzaldúa suggests, we open "the gate to the stranger, within and without" ("Preface" 3). These insights can compel us to re-examine and revise our most solid truths, our most deeply held convictions.

Listening with raw openness begins with the belief in our interrelatedness and with the subsequent willingness to posit and seek commonalities—defined not as sameness but as intertwined differences and possible points of connection. Listening with raw openness requires that we make space for what Anzaldúa describes as "an unmapped common ground" ("now let us shift" 570). As the word *unmapped* suggests, this commonality cannot be narrowly labeled or described. Resisting the certainty and control (*as well as the limitations!*) a precise definition might supply, our common ground must be created tentatively and (perhaps) temporarily, through our interactions. We posit commonalities and step out on faith; we engage in conversations and investigate what we might have in common as we listen to and explore each other's positions. We remain flexible and open to surprise. As I've already mentioned, *This Bridge Called My Back* has its source at least partially in this faith in an uncharted common ground. Despite the various forms of rejection they had experienced, Anzaldúa and Moraga did not relinquish the possibility of feminist alliances but instead worked with a diverse group of people to create *This Bridge*.[30]

Like most academic sites, feminist and other progressive classrooms, conferences, and Listservs often operate according to the binary-oppositional politics I describe in *Transformation Now!* In these situations, we can be very quick to judge each other—often in negative, extremely harsh terms.[31] Yet these judgments are driven by overly simplistic status-quo thinking based on stereotypes that invite superficial judgments: We look at a person, label her, and categorize her based on these labels. We assume that we fully know her position, motivations, values, and beliefs. We *know* her . . . because of her appearance and the identity groups to which she seems to belong, because of her previous comments, because of her overly assertive tone, or because of other such external signs. How can we be so confident in this knowledge? Even in those situations when we *do* know what she'll say, can we be entirely certain that we fully understand what she means? Do we thoroughly know the history, intentions, and desires behind her words? Of course not! People are far too complex to be reduced to a summary observation or cursive assumption.

My point here: When we assume that we entirely know this other person or this other group, we stop listening "with serious intent." We stop listening, and we simply react. After all, if "I know you," then I don't need to listen to your words. I've heard them already, I've heard them many times, and so I'll just react based on my assumption of what I know you'll say. I will dismiss your words and perspectives while loudly repeating my own views. In fact, rather than listen to your words when you're talking, I'll formulate my reactions as I pretend to hear what you're saying. And so we become frozen, locked into our already-existing views, battling our stale, old perceptions of each other, reinforcing the status quo with each repeated judgment and reaction we make. No wonder change happens so slowly, if at all!

In short, listening with raw openness demands intellectual humility. As I mention in the introduction, I define intellectual humility as the willingness to acknowledge our epistemological limitations; embrace uncertainty, contradiction, and the possibility of error; and engage in intense self-reflection. Our understanding is always partial and incomplete. How could it be otherwise? In this changing, fluid, enormous world—how could we possibly know everything? Life is filled with startling shifts, unexpected changes, unseen energies, and unpredictable complexities. People can surprise us! Each human being is multidimensional and contradictory, with what Avery Gordon describes as a "complex personhood": "Complex personhood means that all people (albeit in specific forms whose specificity is sometimes everything) remember and forget, are beset by contradiction, and recognize and misrecognize themselves and others. Complex personhood means that people suffer graciously and selfishly too, get stuck in the symptoms of their troubles, and also transform themselves. . . . [P]eople's lives are simultaneously straightforward and full of enormously subtle meaning" (4–5).

At the pragmatic level, to ignore this complexity and assume that we already have 100 percent accurate and complete information of and knowledge about another person or situation limits our thinking and stunts intellectual growth. And perhaps when we assume that we entirely know what another person or group will say or do, our expectations subtly limit their options, influence their actions, and prevent them from surprising us (and possibly themselves). When we listen with raw openness, we remain receptive to learning more, to acknowledging the possibility of limitations in our views. Through this acknowledgment, we can expand our views and enhance our learning. In my epistemology, openness to change is one of the primary ways that new knowledge is created.

When extended to those we encounter, intellectual humility demands that we recognize each individual's "complex personhood": every person we encounter has a specific, highly intricate history, an upbringing and life experiences that we cannot fully know. We don't know the forces that shaped her and, at best, we can only partially ascertain her intentions and desires.[32] (*Think about it: we don't even entirely know ourselves! What misguided hubris, then, to think we could completely know those we encounter.*) We will misunderstand, despite our best efforts. Perhaps some misunderstanding is inevitable. Here again *This Bridge Called My Back* is instructive. Despite the editors' desire to create an inclusionary space for all radical women of colors, they did not fully achieve their goal. *This Bridge Called My Back* has absences, gaps, desconocimientos, silences, spaces where marked but invisible others do NOT appear. As Deborah Miranda notes, the collection inadequately represents Native women, and as Nada Elia points out, it totally ignores women of Arab descent. There are other omissions, as well.[33] Even our best intentions can fall short. What might we learn if we could view our errors and those of others—when acknowledged with grace—as pathways for growth, avenues that lead to fuller understanding?

Listening with raw openness, diving into nepantla?

We're living at a nexus point, or what Anzaldúa calls nepantla:

> We stand at a major threshold in the extension of consciousness, caught in the remolinos (vortices) of systemic change across all fields of knowledge. The binaries of colored/white, female/male, mind/body are collapsing. Living in nepantla, the overlapping space between different perceptions and belief systems, you are aware of the changeability of racial, gender, sexual, and other categories rendering the conventional labelings obsolete. Though these markings are outworn and inaccurate, those in power continue using them to single out and negate those who are "different" because of color, language, notions of reality, or other diversity. ("now let us shift" 541)

Nepantla represents an unstable, unpredictable, precarious, transitional space/time/epistemology lacking clear boundaries, directions, or definitions. Nepantla demands intellectual humility and openness to change. During nepantla, our status-quo stories and comfortable self-conceptions are shattered as apparently fixed meanings and categories—whether based on gender, ethnicity/'race,' sexuality, religion, nationality, politics, family, or some combination of these categories and perhaps others as well—unravel. Boundaries become more permeable, and begin breaking down. This loosening of previously restrictive labels, while intensely painful, can create the shifts in consciousness and transgressive opportunities for change that, in turn, push us into threshold theorizing. (*Threshold theories as our last resort.*)

I find this shift in Anzaldúa's own thinking, where she transforms the oppositional politics and intersectional identities found in *This Bridge Called My Back* and her own work from the mid-1980s and early 1990s into increasingly holistic politics and identities in her twenty-first-century writings.[34] Thus in "now let us shift . . . the path of conocimiento . . . inner work, public acts"—her 2002 *bridge* essay written at least partially in conversation with contributors' agonizing reactions to our book's radical inclusivity—she describes conventional social identity categories as "obsolete," "outworn," and "inaccurate." Given the central roles such categories had previously played both in Anzaldúa's personal life and in her public career, this re-assessment is striking.[35] Although Anzaldúa aspired to be a Famous Author—a famous (unmarked) author, like Nathaniel Hawthorne, Arthur Rimbaud, and other unmarked (*read: European-descent*) authors whose work is read long after their deaths—her path to public recognition occurred through her embodied identity: Her work co-editing *This Bridge Called My Back: Writings by Radical Women of Color* was the first step in bringing her to a larger audience. From *This Bridge* to *this bridge*—and beyond—she was asked to speak as a woman of color (and often, more specifically, as a Chicana), about women of color/Chicana issues. This identity authorized her work and her voice, giving her a certain degree of visibility, acclaim, and economic freedom. And yet, by the late 1990s she felt that this definition "pinches like an outgrown shoe" ("now let us shift" 549).[36]

As she investigates the "changeability" in the categories and labels that she herself had previously embraced, Anzaldúa questions and works to transform the clear-cut distinctions between women "of color" and "white," asserting in her preface to *this bridge we call home* that "whiteness may not be applied to all whites, as some possess women-of-color-consciousness, just as some women of color bear white consciousness" (2). I want to underscore the radical nature of Anzaldúa's provocative claim—especially in the context and history of *This Bridge Called My Back*—a book often cited for its strong *distinctions* between these two groups. By emphasizing consciousness, Anzaldúa temporarily shifts from the external (culturally imposed racialized categories) to the internal (self-selected ways of thinking, perceiving, and acting). This shift brings important epistemological and ethical consequences, for it inspires her to envision inclusive communities that simultaneously draw from and move beyond the oppositional politics so beloved, so frequently used, by most academics and activist scholars.

Anzaldúa is not naive about the dangers these radical shifts might provoke. She calls for and works to create inclusive communities, while admitting the risks involved. As she explains in her foreword to the 2002 edition of *This Bridge*, "It is risky to venture outside the confines of our color, class, gender and sexuality, as it is to make alliances with others who do not fit into the categories of our self-identity" (xxxvii). She knows these risks intimately; they are embedded in her body, engraved on her mind. (*And, quite possibly, they contributed to her premature death.*) Drawing on her personal experiences, she lists some of these dangers: isolation, rejection, anger, mockery, and more (xxxvii–xxxviii).[37]

Is it any surprise, then, that so few theorists/activists are willing to take these risks, to blur boundaries, to question our conventional training with its either/or oppositional politics, in such extreme ways? Although we "deconstruct" some of our old worldviews and theories, we still cling to identity-based labels and claim the power of self-naming in the face of erasure. (*Sometimes, the higher we climb, the more status we obtain within the dominating culture's systems [the lair of the beast, the den], the more tempting [the more necessary?] it can seem—to cling to these labels, to use them as our only defense against the oppressive acts, the erasure, the invisibility, the pain.*) LOOK! Even in this chapter, a chapter I've designed to *interrogate* and *erode* these social categories and conventional meanings—I've only somewhat loosened my own grip on them! I've used identity labels repeatedly. I can't seem to let go. And look at how I continually hide my most radical claims behind Anzaldúa's words. I am complicit in this critique I make of other scholars, but in my confession I hope to enact the intellectual humility that moves me through the complicity, opening as-yet-unknown perspectives.

Our collective resistance to such radical change leads me to describe this current theoretical moment as a nepantla opportunity. For me, nepantla also represents a threshold, a crossroads of sorts—a space/time with many uncertain options: We can remain where we are, locked within the narrow safety of status-quo stories, fixed identities, and binary-oppositional politics. We can try to protect ourselves by actively resisting change. (*After all, who knows what the future will bring, if we give up our old worldviews, our fragile homes?*) We can reinforce the existing categories, and perhaps even create a few new ones (*more hybrid, of course, with more attention to difference—difference carefully described, marked on our bodiesspiritsminds*). Or, we can move in an extremely different direction. We can loosen our grip on these status-quo stories, let go of our old worldviews, and step out on faith, attempting to create the world we envision. We can question the barriers that (seem to) divide us. We can risk listening with raw openness—at least occasionally. We can stretch feminism, womanism, and other social-justice perspectives (*and we can stretch ourselves!*) into new spaces, places, theories, belief systems, and times. We can affirm a "twenty-first century hermeneutics," a "methodology of love." We can envision and call for "creative renewal of the planet" (Sandoval, "Foreword" 25).

To be sure, we have no maps, no clear-cut plans, no definitive, absolutely correct solutions. As we wander through these tangled, painful histories and debates, we will make mistakes, possibly hurt ourselves and others. However, I am convinced that these lessons from *This Bridge Called My Back* can assist us along our way, as we forge the paths we (partially) envision. I invite us to consider these lessons:

1. making connections through differences,
2. forging an ethics of radical interconnectedness,
3. listening with raw openness.

These lessons offer guidelines for those of us interested in stretching ourselves and our theories in additional directions, moving beyond intersectionality, taking a few tentative steps into radical interconnectivity.

In the following chapters, I explore some of the forms these movements might take.

CHAPTER TWO

"American" Individualism, Variations on a Theme;

or, Self-Reliance, Transformed!

This society this incredible way of living divides us by
class   by color   It says   We are individual and alone
and don't you forget it   It says the only way out of
our doom   of our sex our class our race is some
individual gift and character and hard work and then
all we get   all we ever get is to change class or color
or sex   to rise   to bleach   to masculinize   an
enormous game of musical chairs and that's only at its
fairy tale Horatio Alger best   that's only at its best

Rosario Morales, "We Are All in the Same Boat"

I open this chapter with three questions.

QUESTION 1

What, if anything, do the following literary figures have in common?

1. RALPH WALDO EMERSON Born in 1803 in Boston, Massachusetts, to a long line of ministers who first came to this continent from England in the 1630s, Emerson rejected his religious vocation after a brief stint as a Unitarian minister and went on to become a popular lecturer and highly respected writer. Although he grew up in relative poverty and attended Harvard on scholarships and nineteenth-century versions of "work-study," Emerson received a considerable inheritance from his first wife (who died after

only sixteen months of marriage) and, through careful investments and hard work, was able to devote his life to his art while supporting himself and his extended family. Viewed by many of his contemporaries as a radical thinker (so radical, in fact, that for almost thirty years he was banned from speaking at Harvard), Emerson is now one of our most beloved, most canonical U.S. authors, standard reading in many high school and university classrooms.

2. SULA PEACE Born in 1910 in the Bottom—a very poor community, located on the outskirts of Medallion, Ohio, and peopled by ex-slaves and their descendants—this title character of Nobel Prize–winner Toni Morrison's 1973 novel, *Sula*, is an artist without a medium: "Had she paints, or clay, or knew the discipline of the dance, or strings; had she anything to engage her tremendous curiosity and her gift for metaphor, she might have exchanged the restlessness and preoccupation with whim for an activity that provided her with all she yearned for. And like any artist with no art form, she became dangerous." A lawless woman, Sula passively looks on as her mother burns to death, rejects marriage and motherhood as too restrictive, declares her grandmother insane and puts her in a nursing home, and thinks nothing of having sex with her best friend's husband—or with anyone else's husband, for that matter. Ostracized by the town for her unwillingness and/or inability to conform to social standards, this fictional character is generally viewed—by other characters in the novel and by readers—as evil.[1]

3. GLORIA ANZALDÚA Born in 1942 in the Rio Grande Valley of south Texas to sixth-generation mexicanos, this sometimes-self-described "Chicana, tejana, working-class, dyke-feminist poet, writer-theorist" was punished in kindergarten for her inability to speak English, yet went on to achieve a bachelor's degree, a master's degree, and a doctoral degree in English-related fields.[2] Although Anzaldúa devoted the majority of her adult life to her writing career (at times subsisting with food stamps and forgoing urgent medical care and dental treatment), until the final decades of her life, her outsider positions—her overtly queer self-positioning, her challenges to conventional identity politics, and her defiance of status-quo thinking—made it difficult for her words to find a wide audience. As an early queer theorist and one of the first openly nonheterosexual Chicana authors, Anzaldúa has played a major role in (re)defining queer, lesbian, and Chicano/a identities. And as co-editor of *This Bridge Called My Back: Writings by Radical Women of Color* and *this bridge*

we call home: radical visions for transformation and editor of *Making Face, Making Soul/Haciendo Caras*, Anzaldúa played an equally vital role in developing an inclusionary feminist movement.

ANSWER

At first glance, it would seem that these three strikingly distinct figures have (*almost*) nothing in common. Perhaps not surprisingly, given the many differences among them—differences that include but aren't limited to historical era, genre, region, gender, sexuality, ethnicity, language, religion, and class (*not to mention the fact that Ralph Waldo Emerson and Gloria Evangelina Anzaldúa were flesh-and-blood human beings, while Sula Peace is a fictional character*), scholars do not examine them together. Instead, each is classified and relegated to his or her own place in U.S. literature: We read Ralph Waldo Emerson in the context of transcendentalism, the American Renaissance, and "mainstream" American literature; Sula Peace in the context of African American and women's literary traditions; and Gloria Anzaldúa in the context of "Chicana/o" and women's writing.

Yet despite their many differences, these three disparate figures share a striking commonality that—borrowing from Emerson himself (*who, after all, made the term famous*)—I will describe as their self-reliance. Take, for example, the following assertions:

> Nothing is at last sacred but the integrity of your own mind.
> —Ralph Waldo Emerson

> "Girl, I got my mind. And what goes on in it. Which is to say, I got me."
> —Sula Peace

> [M]y own / hands whittle   the final work   me.
> —Gloria Anzaldúa

Commonality is not sameness, and these words are not automatically interchangeable. (*Can you imagine Emerson saying to his good friend and fellow transcendentalist, Margaret Fuller, "Girl, I got my mind. And what goes on in it. Which is to say, I got me"?*) Yet each assertion embodies a radical independence—an unwillingness to be controlled or defined by external standards—and a defiant break from society's expectations and values. To again borrow Emerson's words, these three literary figures seem to advocate and live according to the individualist's self-command: "Trust thyself: every heart vibrates to that iron string." Rejecting conventional dictates, Ralph Waldo Emerson, Sula Peace, and Gloria Evangelina Anzaldúa illustrate variations on that most American of themes: individualism.

QUESTION 2

So what happens when we read such extremely different figures in multidimensional dialogue?

ANSWER

Transformation! As I hope to demonstrate in this chapter, when we read diverse literary figures in dialogue—both with each other and with ourselves—transformation can occur in multiple ways and on multiple levels. Through such (apparently) strange juxtapositions and the relational reading strategies they invite, we acquire and create new perspectives enabling us to redefine the boundaries between apparently distinct literary traditions, peoples, and social groups. Boundaries can become thresholds opening up new definitions of U.S. literature and identities that neither erase nor reinforce the many differences among the various texts we read.

QUESTION 3

Okay . . . but what does this focus on multiculturalism, literature, individualism, and multidimensional dialogic reading have to do with the threshold theories and nonoppositional tactics you're exploring in *Transformation Now!*?

ANSWER

Threshold theorizing can occur in a variety of disciplines, and in this chapter I demonstrate its applicability to one specific field. I model a nonoppositional method that employs differences relationally and, through these relational dialogues, produces commonalities that, in turn, generate new (*or previously forgotten*) knowledge about U.S. literary traditions as they intersect with conventional understandings of individualism.

Multiculturalisms (re)defined

It is, by now, a commonplace among many Americanists to acknowledge the multicultural nature of U.S. literature.[3] Generally, the argument goes something like this: Since the 1820s scholars have tried to distinguish "American literature" from British and other national literary traditions.[4] This focus on American exceptionalism led to the construction of a literary canon embodying what was assumed to be a transcendent set of essentially American thematic and epistemological issues and values such as radical Adamic innocence, the conflict between individual and society in which distinct forms of highly subversive American individualism win out, and the belief in unlimited progress and potential.[5] Until fairly recently, then—say around the mid-1970s—"American literature" was defined by a select group of canonized writers, including (but not limited to) Washington Irving, Ralph Waldo Emerson, Henry David Thoreau, Herman Melville, Nathaniel Hawthorne, Walt Whitman, Henry James, T. S. Eliot, Ernest Hemingway, and William Faulkner. Despite the many differences among them, these "major" writers—viewed as most representative of the American self and American culture—share a number of traits, most notably their gender (they are all men), their ethnicity (they are all of European ancestry), and their regional location (nearly all have their "roots" in East Coast, generally New England, culture).[6] Perhaps not surprisingly, this status-quo story about American literature presents a sophisticated form of mono-thinking: a highly complex yet in many ways mono-cultural description that excludes many more people and authors than it includes. U.S. culture is not and never has been monolithic, and the assumption that a particular group of writers and themes can accurately reflect the diversity in American literature and culture has come under intense scrutiny, resulting in numerous attempts to develop a multicultural theory and praxis of U.S. literature.[7] These explorations of the multicultural dimensions of U.S. literature take several interrelated forms, including critiques of the traditional literary canon, attempts to expand this traditional canon by including a more diverse set of writers; and the creation of additional ethnic-, gender-, and sexual-inflected canons (among others).

All too often, however, these attempts rely on various forms of binary-oppositional thought, as well as inadequate understandings of diversity and multiculturalism in which "multicultural" is defined simply as the coexistence of a variety of distinct literary and cultural traditions, or as what Trinh Minh-ha describes as "the juxtaposition of several cultures whose frontiers remain intact" (*Moon* 232). Unlike the frictional juxtapositions that occur in relational frameworks, such as those I explore throughout *Transformation Now!*, these oppositional juxtapositions represent inflexible, impenetrable boundaries dividing each culture from all others. Although explorations of ethnic-specific traditions have been crucial in expanding contemporary views of U.S. literature, they produce limited forms of multiculturalism, or what I call *separatist multiculturalism*.[8]

As I use the term, separatist multiculturalism represents very limited forms of multicultural readings and scholarship that overemphasize dichotomous differences and focus almost exclusively on ethnicity/race—defined according to the status-quo stories I discussed in the previous chapter. Separatist multiculturalists use a rhetoric of cultural authenticity that reinforces the belief in racial purity and self-contained ethnic/racial identities (collective versions of self-reliant individualism, as it were). Rather than develop new forms of identity or new frameworks for social change, this rhetoric of authenticity relies on already-existing assumptions about 'race' that essentialize (and racialize) each text by equating it with an author's cultural-biological "roots." As Gene Andrew Jarrett explains in his discussion of African American literature, this belief in cultural authenticity shapes readers' evaluations and literary expectations: "Since slave narratives were published in the first half of the 19th century, literature written by black people—or, more precisely, by people who are identified or who identify themselves as black— must be 'the real thing,' a window into the black experience, in order to have any aesthetic, cultural, social, political, or commercial value" ("Judging").

Separatist multiculturalism's oppositional frameworks are too limiting. When readers focus almost exclusively on the differences between supposedly distinct cultural identities, they inadvertently reinscribe inflexible boundaries that foreclose possible common ground in the discussion of works by distinct ethnic/cultural groups. Thus, for example, African American literature is associated only with writers of African descent writing about "black culture" and "black themes," while Chicano/a writings are identified only with people of Mexican ancestry writing about "Mexican" topics and themes.[9] Those authors and texts who do not fit into this type of classification system slip away and are often forgotten.[10] Although separatist multiculturalists examine the intersections between these distinct traditions and canonical Euro-American literature, they seldom expand their studies to explore the similarities and differences among the various ethnic-specific traditions themselves. Instead, they create a series of binary-oppositional conversations between ethnic-specific literary traditions and "mainstream" canonical U.S. texts, overlooking opportunities to develop relational dialogues.[11] But this conception of self-contained cultural/racial identities and traditions is far less accurate (*or useful*) than it might seem. If identity is always relational, then it's never self-contained. However, by focusing almost entirely on the differences between cultural identities and literatures, we often overlook their commonalities.

For the past decade, I've been exploring the pedagogical and theoretical implications of establishing transcultural dialogues—alternative approaches to multicultural theory and practice that go beyond recent emphases on ethnic-specific literary texts and identities without becoming immersed in sameness—in benign, "melting-pot" celebrations of "American" identities and themes. (*Like separatist multiculturalism, melting-pot multiculturalism reinforces the status quo.*) I borrow the word *transcultural* from Cuban literary and political movements, where its usage indicates a profound challenge to hegemonic racial discourse. As Nancy Morejón explains, mestizaje transculturation defies static notions of cultural purity by emphasizing "the constant interactions, the transmutation between two or more cultural components with the unconscious goal of creating a third cultural entity . . . that is new and independent even though rooted in the preceding elements. Reciprocal influence is the determining factor here, for no single element superimposes itself on another; on the contrary, each one changes into the other so that both can be transformed into a third. Nothing seems immutable" (23).[12] As I hope to demonstrate in this chapter, dialogic patterns of reading—patterns that shift among sameness, similarity, and difference, forging complex commonalities through their movements—enable us to develop a transcultural understanding of U.S. literature. Through this transcultural dialogic reading practice, we can redefine the boundaries between distinct literary traditions, authors, and texts as thresholds opening up new definitions of "American" literature and identities that neither erase nor reinforce the many differences among the various texts we read and people we encounter.

My goals in this chapter, though, are more modest. I do not provide a fully developed redefinition of American literature (*although at some point I would certainly like to offer a partial redefinition!*). Instead, I invite you to consider one theme ("American" individualism) and a small cluster of writers (Ralph Waldo Emerson, Henry David Thoreau, June Millicent Jordan, Gloria Evangelina Anzaldúa, Paula Gunn Allen) from a transcultural perspective. With this invitation, I hope to accomplish several goals. First, I offer a transformational alternative to conventional forms of multiculturalism and interpretations of these specific authors. Second, I suggest another approach to canonical U.S. literature. Third, I redefine individualism in relational terms that challenge conventional understandings (*or should I say celebrations?*) of the radically independent Adamic American self. And fourth, through this redefined individualism and the relational self-identities that it implies, I lay the groundwork for my discussion of transformational identity politics in the following chapter.

Individualism (re)defined

Perhaps because the American transcendentalists were one of my primary areas of research in graduate school, Leslie Marmon Silko's provocative claim about the connections between the transcendentalists and "Native American views of the world and relationships" resonated deeply with me when I first stumbled across it. As Silko asserts in an interview with June Arnold, "Even to this day, I point to American Transcendentalism as a sign of what the old prophecies say about the strangers who come to this continent. The longer they live here, the more they are being changed. Every minute the Europeans, and any other immigrants from any other place, come on to the Americas and start walking on this land. You get this dirt on you, and you drink this water, it starts to change you. Then your kids will be different, and then the spirits start to work on you" (qtd. in Arnold 9). This suggestion that the land itself works on us all, subtly changing us and opening us to spirit, affirmed my previously held intuitions and gave me permission to reread U.S. literature through this new lens. (*This suggestion also supports my belief that Speculative Realism and the "new materialisms" in academic thought have much to learn from indigenous theories and worldviews.*)What a gift from this highly regarded Native American (Laguna Pueblo/mixed-blood) author. Energized (*and authorized*) by Silko's words, I began to discover and create all sorts of possible connections between American transcendentalist authors and contemporary authors, and I envisioned teaching an entire course designed to facilitate transcultural dialogues between these groups: We'd look at how Emerson, Walt Whitman, Alice Walker, Maxine Hong Kingston, and N. Scott Momaday defined (and enacted) the poet and imagination; how Whitman, Silko, and Walker engaged with landscape and American identities; how Emerson, Thoreau, Kate Chopin, and Ralph Waldo Ellison illustrated self-reliance; how Emerson and Toshio Mori negotiate between the particular and the universal; and so on. While the possibilities are almost endless, in this chapter I focus primarily on the question of individualism. I do so both because individualism is such a classic theme in American literature and in the U.S. cultural imaginary and because this question fits so well with the larger issues I explore in *Transformation Now!*

Given the central roles that Ralph Waldo Emerson and Henry David Thoreau have played in constructing an "American" self and an "American" literary tradition, canonical transcendentalist texts such as "Self-Reliance" and *Walden* offer a useful point of departure for our transcultural explorations. Reading these nineteenth-century classics in conversation with twentieth-century works by June Jordan, Gloria Anzaldúa, and Paula Gunn Allen transforms static, homogeneous, universalized notions of an authentic "American" self into more flexible models of literary and cultural identity, offering alternatives to the monolithic notions of difference and similarity that can occur in separatist and melting-pot multiculturalisms. Let me emphasize: *My goal is not to deny, ignore, or in other ways erase the differences between the various ethnic-specific traditions that make U.S. literature multicultural.* Nor am I trying to demonstrate that Anzaldúa, Jordan, Allen, or other twentieth- or twenty-first-century writers marked by gender, ethnicity, or sexuality "should be" considered contemporary inheritors of transcendentalist traditions and on those terms incorporated into the U.S. literature canon. (*Although, I must confess, this demonstration does have a certain strong appeal.*) However, to make this type of argument would simply replicate the status-quo stories I touched on earlier in this chapter. Instead, I want to develop alternate reading practices—different "dialogical angles" or transcultural convers(at)ions as it were—that avoid separatist multiculturalism's overemphasis on difference without falling into mono-thinking valorizations of melting-pot multiculturalism's sameness.

Despite the many differences among them—differences that include but are not limited to gender, ethnicity, skin color, geographical location, religion, politics, and historical era[13]—the nineteenth- and twentieth-century writers I examine in this chapter share a number of striking similarities: Their willingness to position themselves as outsiders to dominant U.S. cultural standards; their desire to challenge existing social conventions; their faith in each individual human being's untapped potential; their attempts to create nondual metaphysical systems that—by locating the spiritual in material and intellectual life—blur the boundaries between the spiritual, the material, and the psychic; and their confidence in language's agentic, transformational power.

Although each point of similarity between Emerson, Thoreau, Jordan, Anzaldúa, and Allen opens up new areas of exploration facilitating additional definitions of American literatures and identities, I focus primarily on the various ways their quests for independence and self-definition play out in their texts. My reasons for doing so are threefold. First, Emerson and other nineteenth-century transcendentalists have been instrumental in shaping and representing the highly celebrated belief in American individualism. Second, this celebration of self-reliance and personal autonomy is a foundational element of western modernity. As David Theo Goldberg notes, "[t]he philosophical commitment in the tradition of Western modernity is to radical and atomistic individualism—to rational (that is, self-interested), egoistic (self-maximizing), and self-providing individuals" (25). And third, this belief in self-centered, atomistic individualism is deeply ingrained in contemporary U.S. culture and viewed as an essential, uniquely American theme as well as a distinguishing mark of U.S. literary classics. Thus, for example, Joyce Warren argues that the works of Emerson, Thoreau, Melville, and other nineteenth-century Euro-American male writers illustrate what she calls the "American Narcissus," a radically solipsistic subject who denies the existence of other human beings in his quest for complete self-definition and control:

> Emerson and Thoreau were writing in the American tradition, the tradition that glorifies the individual and insists upon the sanctity of the self. Such a philosophy forces the individual to protect himself by projecting a persona that exhibits all of the traits he feels he must live up to. With all of his energies devoted to the development of this inflated self, the American Narcissus can allow no room for the reality of other selves. That Americans have adopted this philosophy wholeheartedly and continue to endorse the writings of Emerson and Thoreau with such enthusiasm indicates how much this belief in the totality of the self remains a part of our culture. (69–70)

In this binary configuration, individualism entails a hierarchical relationship between subject and object, where the individual and society occupy mutually exclusive poles. Warren's American Narcissus converts everything into a subordinate role; to his "inflated self"; the entire natural world, including all other human beings, lack independent existence, serving "only as objects to be ignored or destroyed (if they are undesirable) or to be made use of or absorbed into the self (if they are desirable)" (17).

To be sure, these dichotomous self/other or subject/object frameworks have played a central role in canonical scholarly descriptions of American individualism (*and in U.S. culture more generally!*). As Nina Baym points out, during the 1940s and 1950s, F. O. Matthiessen, Henry Nash Smith, Charles Feidelson, and other well-known scholars constructed a literary canon centered around their own highly individualistic "myth of America." While Baym uses the word "myth" as a synonym for "falsehood," designed to critique and dispel this common view of "America," I would argue that such "myths" have creative power; this story about American individualism became increasingly true for these scholars and those who followed, thus functioning as a powerful status-quo story. This "myth," associated almost exclusively with texts by "white, middle-class, male" writers,

> narrates a confrontation of the American individual, the pure American self divorced from specific social circumstances, with the promise offered by the idea of America. This promise is the deeply romantic one that in this new land, untrammeled by history and social accident, a person will be able to achieve complete self-definition. Behind this promise is the assurance that individuals come before society, that they exist in some meaningful sense prior to, and apart from, societies in which they happen to find themselves. The myth also holds that, as something artificial and secondary to human nature, society exerts an unmitigatedly destructive pressure on individuality. To depict it at any length would be a waste of artistic time; and there is only one way to relate it to the individual—as an adversary. (131–32)

As Baym's analysis of the adversarial relationship between the individual and society indicates, canonical descriptions of American individualism rely on a sharp division between individual and collective identities. In this highly celebrated status-quo story about "American" identity, the individual is viewed as an autonomous, wholly independent human being, alienated from a society that requires repressive, mind-numbing conformity. Like Warren, Baym argues that this literary drive for self-expansion and independence has its source in a restrictive definition of the human individual that excludes far more people than it includes. Although rarely mentioned by name in canonical discussions of American selfhood, women of all colors, African Americans, Native Americans, and all other nondominant peoples have been denied the freedom, independence, and economic opportunities associated with this solipsistic version of American individualism.[14] Grace Kyungwon Hong makes a similar point: "Although ostensibly universal, U.S. national identity has privileged white enfranchisement and property—as mutually constituted through a protected 'private' sphere—and therefore ensured racialized exploitation and dispossession."

While it might be tempting to reject individualism entirely and focus on the other half of this individual/society binary, to do so would simply flip the script, rather than scramble, rewrite, or in other ways transform the entire configuration. And so, in the remainder of this chapter, I adopt a non- or post-oppositional approach that (1) redefines self-reliance and individualism in more relational terms, and (2) uses this relational approach to re-examine Emersonian self-reliance. Like canonical forms of American individualism, these alternate, multicultural forms resist external socially imposed sources of authority and underscore the importance of self-trust, yet they do so without reinforcing narcissistic, self-enclosed concepts of identity. Instead, they replace the monologic belief in isolated individual human beings with a more flexible theory of identity and human nature, where self-development occurs always in the context of others. (*In the words of the Ubuntu proverb, "I am because we are."*) By positing complex interconnectedness between each individual and society, these intersubjective models of individualism offer alternatives to the exclusionary, dualistic divisions between personal and communal identities found in conventional interpretations of an American self and traditional narratives of the national experience. In such instances, self-reliance is not limited to privileged, 'white'-raced men but becomes a highly democratic endeavor that extends canonical interpretations of American individualism outward to include previously ignored groups while, simultaneously, reconfiguring the relationship between personal and communal identities. This reconfiguration escapes the dangers of separatist-multicultural thinking, where individualism is not redefined but is simply extended outward to embrace (a few select members of) previously disenfranchised groups.[15]

Dialogic readings, LUXOCRATIC visions

June Jordan's politics of self-determination—which I describe as a theory and praxis of intersubjective identity formation where self-development occurs in the context of other equally important individuals—illustrates one form these alternate models of subjectivity and individualism can take. Throughout her work, Jordan emphasizes the importance of self-trust as an epistemological and ethical tool by insisting that all human beings must have the freedom to define themselves and choose their own courses of action. In a chapter titled "Civil Wars," for example, she challenges all external forms of authority, including the "professional leadership" guiding the Black Power Movement, the women's movement, and other politicized groups. According to Jordan, no matter how democratic such leadership seems to be, it cannot replace the authority and wisdom she associates with each person's inner faculties and thoughtful, self-reflective guidance: "The only leadership I can respect is one that enables every man and woman to be his and her own leader: to abandon victim perspective and to faithfully rely upon the truth of the feeling that is his or hers and then to act on that, without apology" (*Civil Wars* 186–87). As this emphasis on inner-directed leadership implies, Jordan bases her politics of self-determination on the nonelitist belief that each person has the ability and the wisdom to control hir own life. In this essay and others, she works to awaken and support this belief in her readers. Rejecting any form of victimhood that would deny personal agency, Jordan urges her readers to take responsibility for their own lives. Because she believes that all human beings have a potentially infallible source of guidance located within ourselves, she encourages her readers to self-reflect; explore their hidden beliefs, needs, and desires; and speak out.

In many ways, this insistence on each individual's inner potential resembles canonical versions of self-trust seen, for example, in Emerson's assertion in "Self Reliance" that "Nothing is at last sacred but the integrity of your own mind. Absolve you to yourself, and you shall have the suffrage of the world" (149) or in Thoreau's confident assumption that by simplifying his life and relying entirely on himself he would discover cosmic truths and universal insights about human existence.[16] Like Jordan, these nineteenth-century transcendentalists reject external forms of authority and underscore each individual's ability to think autonomously. Yet in Jordan's politics of self-determination, this belief in intellectual integrity and personal power has a distinctive, highly complex social dimension that readers rarely associate with Emerson or Thoreau.[17]

I want to illustrate this difference by putting two excerpts in dialogue. First, look at Emerson's (in)famous transparent eyeball description in *Nature*, a passage that has become emblematic of Emerson's philosophy. Drawing on his newfound epistemological distinction between "Understanding" (which he defines as a type of scientistic empirical thinking associated with the mind's limited ability to gather and interpret sense impressions) and "Reason" (which he defines as the mind's power to go beyond empirical facts and intuit additional layers of meaning), Emerson narrates his own "return to reason and faith":

Crossing a bare common, in snow puddles, at twilight, under a clouded sky, without having in my thoughts any occurrence of special good fortune, I have enjoyed a perfect exhilaration. . . . Standing on the bare ground,—my head bathed by the blithe air, and uplifted into infinite space,—all mean egotism vanishes. I become a transparent eyeball. I am nothing. I see all. The currents of the Universal Being circulate through me; I am part or particle of God. The name of the nearest friend sounds then foreign and accidental: to be brothers, to be acquaintances,—master or servant, is then a trifle and a disturbance. I am the lover of uncontained and immortal beauty. In the wilderness, I find something more dear and connate than in streets or villages. In the tranquil landscape, and especially in the distant line of the horizon, man [sic] beholds somewhat as beautiful as his own nature. (10)

At the outset, Emerson views his surroundings in Understanding's typical fragmented way: He—Waldo Emerson the individual—sees the puddles, the rising dusk, and the clouds. Suddenly, without warning, transformation occurs: The clouded sky becomes "infinite space" and Waldo Emerson a "transparent eyeball." Reason awakens, and the borders between Emerson and the world disappear. Paradoxically, he is both everything and nothing. He experiences a conversion in consciousness and sees himself as divine; he is "part or particle of God." As "all mean egotism vanishes," he obtains a mystical insight that reaffirms his interconnectedness with all that exists. The transformed consciousness Emerson enacts in this passage does not imply the radical selfishness and autonomy generally associated with canonical versions of American individualism. Indeed, Emerson rejects a type of petty egotism that focuses exclusively on the private self; this petty self dissolves into an apparently contradictory state that is simultaneously "nothing" and "all." As Reason awakens within him, his awareness expands outwardly and personal interests and desires reign no more.[18] Throughout his writings, Emerson insists that Reason provides *all* human beings with a potentially infallible inner epistemological guidance enabling them to reject external authority and experience their own conversions in consciousness like the one he narrates in this passage.[19]

Emerson's radically democratic vision can be described as a nineteenth-century version of what Layli Maparyan names "LUXOCRACY," a foundational component of the womanist idea. LUXOCRACY represents a holistic belief system that posits each human being's innate divinity. This sacred core is the potential source of and guide to wisdom and an ethical, unique life that simultaneously enhances the individual and contributes in meaningful ways to a socially just world for all living beings. As Maparyan explains,

> LUXOCRACY takes as fundamental that all persons are unique manifestations of the One, the All, the Creator, SOURCE. As such, each person's Inner Light guides the manifestation of that uniqueness across the span of a lifetime. The optimal purpose of society is to foster, facilitate, nurture, protect, and coordinate the expression of every person's Innate Divinity simultaneously. In the past, various structures of governance have used the principle of the commons to try to maximize the number of people who can experience such self-expression and development. The principle of the commons, through its goal of maximization, assumed implicitly that the good could not be optimized for all persons. LUXOCRACY, on the other hand, assumes that this right of optimal well-being has now been extended to all and has become universal and categorical. Thus, the principle of the commons has now been transcended to encompass everyone, as LUXOCRACY rests upon the broader concept of commonweal. (*Womanist Idea* 6–7)

As Maparyan's description suggests, LUXOCRACY with its broader, more flexible definition of the individual, leads to (and contains) a more generous definition of community. Unlike previous definitions, which situate community within oppositional frameworks, the community Maparyan describes is radically inclusive; in addition to embracing all human beings, this LUXOCRATIC perspective defines the individual and society in mutually *in*clusive terms.

But perhaps you're wondering why I'm applying Maparyan's theory of LUXOCRACY to Emerson's work. After all, LUXOCRACY—like the womanist idea it inspires, infuses, and represents—has its primary (though not exclusive) source in black women's thought. As Maparyan explains, "Black women have kept this flame of Innate Divinity and the Inner Light eternally lit across history, culture, and geography, as documented in Black women's religious thought, spiritualized social change leadership, and personal spiritual practice" (*Womanist Idea* 7). While black women have played a critical role in its development and proliferation, LUXOCRACY cannot be contained within any single group; it represents a planetary worldview and ethic: "This preservation of the flame of Innate Divinity has not been limited to Black women—indeed, other women of color, and other people of all genders from a variety of backgrounds—have also done so. The *womanist idea* is really about a practice and a perspective more than an ethnic group or a gender, even though it is undeniable that Black women have had a special role to play in its propagation

and promulgation" (*Womanist Idea* 7–8, original emphasis). I use Maparyan's theory of LUXOCRACY to gloss Emerson's epistemology for two reasons.
First, by reading Emerson through this womanist lens, I underscore the wide-
ranging value of women-of-colors theorizing. Like other women-of-colors
theories, womanist thought has broad impact and application. Second, the
theory works. By reading the womanist idea of LUXOCRACY in dialogue with
Emerson's words, I can more fully comprehend and articulate the (unmet)
promise of Emerson's theory of the individual.

Unlike liberal and neoliberal versions of individualism, which define the
individual narrowly and thus rely on what Maparyan describes as the "principle of the commons" (a principle that excludes many people, as well as all
nonhumans), LUXOCRACY extends individualism—and the "right of optimal well-being" to all (defined broadly, to include nonhumans). Although he
lacked the language to refer to it in these terms, Emerson's Reason-inspired
individualism is grounded in this "broader concept of commonweal." As such,
his belief that all people have access to Reason's inner divine faculty should
make it impossible to dismiss his individualism as elitist. Yet because Emerson associates this transformation in consciousness with the *abandonment* of
"the nearest friend" and other private, personal connections (the petty self,
the small ego), such misunderstandings are not surprising.[20]

Contrast this apparent denial of the personal with Jordan's stance in "On
a New Year's Eve," where she insists that abstract concepts like "infinity,"
"the sacred," or even natural beauty are "propaganda" when not embodied
in concrete particular forms, or what she calls "the temporary sacred":

> I have rejected that
> abstraction that enormity
> unless I see a dog walk on the beach/
> a bird seize sandflies
> or yourself
> approach me
> laughing out a sound to spoil
> the pretty picture
> make an uncontrolled
> heartbeating memory
> instead
> (*Naming* 28)

Whereas Emerson, in *Nature*, implies that the transformation of conscious-ness occurs through solitary immersion in his surroundings, Jordan associates transformation with the "disturbance" or "derangement" that occurs during interactions with others. In her politics of self-determination, each and every individual always takes concrete particular form. She maintains that

> but all alive and all the lives
> persist perpetual
> in jeopardy
> persist
> as scarce as every one of us
> as difficult to find
> or keep
> as irreplacable
> as final
> as every one of us
> (*Naming* 29)

Jordan elevates the particularity of each individual person and thing. By thus emphasizing the particular—especially as played out in her encounters with others—she enhances her recognition and appreciation of the sacred and underscores her broad vision of the commonweal.

Jordan enacts a relational individualism. Thus, in "Thinking about My Poetry," she associates the self-trust she requires as a writer with the devel-opment of a personalized yet collective voice, and demonstrates that self-reflection leads to the discovery of new forms of intersubjective identity. Looking within, she looks outward and recognizes her interconnections with others that she then explores in her work. She explains that because she sees herself and other black and women poets as "all of us working on the same poem of a life of perpetual, difficult birth, . . . I should trust myself in this way: that if I could truthfully attend to my own perpetual birth, if I could trace the provocations for my own voice and then trace its reverberations through love, Alaska, whatever, that then I could hope to count upon myself to be serving a positive and collective function, without pretending to be more than the one Black woman poet I am, as a matter of fact" (*Civil Wars* 126). Locating the source of social change within each individual yet acknowledging the ways sociohistorical forces uniquely shape each person's needs and desires, Jordan posits an intersubjective space where self-reflection, self-definition, and the creation of transformational collective identities can converge. Similarly, in "Civil Wars" she associates each individual's ability to think for hirself with the construction of collective identities capable of bringing about radical social change. She maintains that "the ultimate power of *all the people* rests upon the *individual* ability to trust and to respect the authority of the truth of whatever it is that *each of us* feels, *each of us* means" (*Civil Wars* 187, emphasis added).

As this oscillation between individual and communal identities indicates, Jordan's politics of self-determination relies on an intersubjective matrix where personal interests work in conjunction with the interests of others. Again in her aptly titled "Waking Up in the Middle of Some American Dreams," Jordan challenges conventional forms of individualism: "Misbegotten American dreams have maimed us all. And one of these, especially, continues to distort and paralyze our simplest capabilities for cooperation as a species. Beloved, national myths about you and me as gloriously rugged, independent individuals pervade our consciousness. . . . The flipside of this delusional disease, this infantile and apparently implacable trust in mass individuality, is equally absurd, and destructive. Because every American one of us is different and special, it follows that every problem or crisis is exclusively our own, or, conversely, your problem—not mine" (*Some of Us* 15). An aspect of the "American ideology" that Sacvan Bercovitch describes in his analysis of mainstream, canonical U.S. literature, these much-loved beliefs in our rugged individualism equate personal success with the denial of interpersonal connections. But according to Jordan, these "national myths" of limitless autonomy and freedom are far less empowering than they seem: In addition to their unacknowledged silliness ("this infantile and apparently implacable trust in mass individuality"), they inhibit self-growth by preventing us from recognizing the many ways our individualized needs intersect with those of others. Seduced by visions of uniqueness, each person becomes isolated and alienated, unable to recognize our commonalities.

Drawing on the rhetoric of democracy embedded in U.S. culture, Jordan insists that

> our American dreams of 'the first' and 'the only' produce an invariably mistaken self-centered perspective that repeatedly proves to be self-defeating and, even, antidemocratic. *Demos*, as in democratic, as in a democratic state, means people, not person. A democratic nation of persons, of individuals, is an impossibility and a fratricidal goal. Each American one of us must consciously

choose to become a willing and outspoken part of *the people* who, together, will determine our individual chances for happiness, and justice. (*Some of Us Did Not Die* 19, original emphasis)

Jordan does not posit a binary opposition between the individual human being and society. Nor does she reject individualism and deny the validity of each individual's private needs and desires. Instead, she invents new forms of personal agency, acknowledging the interconnections among apparently separate human beings. More specifically, she incorporates a communal dimension into her definition of the personal and establishes a model of identity formation where self-development occurs through the individual's interaction with others. By thus emphasizing the reciprocal, intersubjective nature of each individual's autonomy and self-growth, Jordan constructs an agent-centered collective subjectivity that interweaves inner direction with outward change.

Jordan's self-naming process in her 1989 collection of poetry, *Naming Our Destiny*, illustrates one form this model of interactional identity formation can take. Throughout the poems collected in this volume, she uses her own experiences as a twentieth-century bisexual woman of Jamaican descent to underscore the importance of personal and communal self-determination. As she examines the linkages between her own destiny and the destinies of a wide variety of national and international groups, she rejects restrictive versions of isolated, self-enclosed individualism. By exploring a diverse set of public and private issues—including South African apartheid, the Palestinian crisis, racial violence in Atlanta, homophobia, Black English, and her relationships with female and male lovers—Jordan demonstrates that her own self-determination entails recognizing and affirming both the similarities and the differences between herself and others. For instance, in "Poem about My Rights," a deeply autobiographical poem drawn from her experience of being raped, she shifts between personal, national, and international concerns. By so doing, she illustrates how the specific forms of oppression she experiences as a single black woman living in the United States intersect with South Africa's invasion of Namibia and Angola, U.S. imperialism, sexual violence against women, and unjust rape laws. In this poem and others, Jordan connects personal with communal agency by drawing analogies between her own rights and the rights of all women, colonized countries, and other apparently disparate groups.

As Jordan's willingness to identify herself with a variety of apparently dissimilar peoples implies, this complex self-naming process represents a significant departure from the rhetoric of authenticity found in many forms of ethnic-specific literary and cultural studies, or what I described as separatist multiculturalism. In her politics of self-determination, individual and collective identities cannot automatically be based on ethnicity, gender, nationality, or any other restrictive, naturalized categories of meaning. As Jordan explains in "Civil Wars," "[n]either race nor gender provides the final definitions of jeopardy or refuge. The final risk or final safety lies within each one of us attuned to the messy and intricate and unending challenge of self-determination" (*Civil Wars* 187). Throughout her work, Jordan develops an intricate interplay between similarities and differences that invites readers—no matter how we identify ourselves in terms of gender, 'race,' sexuality, ethnicity, class, religion, and so on—to re-examine our own subject positions. Thus, in "A Short Note to My Very Critical Friends and Well-Beloved Comrades," she enacts a mobile self-naming process that slips through restrictive labeling. After defiantly outlining the numerous ways her well-meaning friends and comrades have tried unsuccessfully to classify her according to color, sexuality, age, and ideology, Jordan confidently reaffirms her ability to define herself as she sees fit:

Make up your mind! They said. Are you militant
or sweet? Are you vegetarian or meat? Are you straight
or are you gay?

And I said, Hey! It's not about *my* mind.
(*Naming* 98)

The implications of this final line are clear. In rejecting restrictive labels and the binary forms of thinking they so often entail, Jordan throws the responsibility back on to her well-meaning questioners: They must re-examine their own desire for fixed labels and static categories of identity. These lines have a similar impact on readers; as Peter Erickson explains, "Having aroused our irritation, the poem dares us to examine it, to probe our discomfort at being unable to pin down the poet's identity" (222). As she oscillates between apparently distinct categories of meaning, Jordan disrupts the boundaries between fixed identity locations. She replaces the conventional, American belief in isolated, self-contained identities with open-ended models of identity formation. Resisting ethnic- and gender-specific collective identities without denying their historic significance, Jordan exposes the limitations in contemporary forms of separatist multicultural thinking.

Like Jordan, Gloria Anzaldúa enacts a variety of to-and-fro movements in which individual and collective identity formation interconnect and occur simultaneously. Throughout her poetry, fiction, and prose she draws on her own experiences as a Chicana growing up in south Texas and uses a highly personalized, assertive voice to invent forms of intersubjective identity that interweave the personal with the communal. Thus, for example, in "Cihuatlyotl, Woman Alone," she explores the difficulties experienced in her attempts to navigate between the extreme autonomy she requires as a writer and the sense of belonging she desires as a member of her familial community. As the title implies, she does not choose between isolation and connection but rather adopts what many might view as a paradoxical position enabling her to choose both: She redefines the personal and communal components of her own self-identity and speaks simultaneously as "Cihuatlyotl"—a precolonial Náhuatl creatrix figure representing the collective, indigenous, ethnic-specific dimensions of her identity—and as a "Woman Alone," representing her highly individualized stance, her chosen solitude and independence, her identity as Author.[21] After exploring the various ways her family and other Chicanos have tried to control her, she boldly asserts her independence without severing all ties to her ethnic-cultural community:

> I refuse to be taken over   by
> things   people who fear that hollow
> aloneness   beckoning   beckoning. No self,
> only race *vecindad familia*.   My soul   has always
> been yours   one spark   in the roar of your fire.
> We Mexicans are   collective animals.   This I
> accept   but my life's work requires autonomy
> like oxygen.   This lifelong battle has ended,
> *Raza.*   I don't need to flail against you.
> *Raza india mexicana norteamericana*, there's no-
> thing more you can chop off   or graft on me that
> will change my soul.   I remain who I am, multiple
> and one   of the herd, yet not of it.
> (*Borderlands* 173, original emphasis)

At first glance, these assertions seem to contradict each other. On the one hand, Anzaldúa underscores her communal identity as she implies that she has been shaped by history, forced into membership within a specific cultural group: Her "soul" belongs to la Raza, and she is "fully formed carved / by the hands of the ancients." On the other hand, she claims her individuality as she asserts her autonomy and defiantly declares that she shapes herself according to her own highly personal needs and desires: "my own / hands whittle the final work me."

In many ways, this bold rejection of social convention resembles the emphasis on nonconformity found in nineteenth-century transcendental writers. Like Emerson, Anzaldúa exposes the paralyzing effects society's dictates have on each individual. And like Thoreau, she openly refuses to live her life according to the codes of behavior established by others.[22] However, by specifying the many various forms these social conventions can take, she adds increasing levels of complexity and sophistication to conventional interpretations of American individualism. More specifically, she uses the conflicts she experiences as an artist devoted to her calling, a Chicana writer—to enact a complex multilayered dialogue between a variety of groups, including the mainstream assimilationist U.S. culture that attempts to impose a single standard on all citizens, the Mexican American community that imposes its own ethnic-specific masculine standard on its members, and her own personal desires that might intersect with these communities but cannot be contained by them. Thus, in *Borderlands/La Frontera: The New Mestiza*, she deliberately breaks with all negative religious and cultural belief systems and boldly declares

> No, I do not buy all the myths of the tribe into which I was born. . . . I will not glorify those aspects of my culture which have injured me and which have injured me in the name of protecting me. So, don't give me your tenets and your laws. Don't give me your lukewarm gods. What I want is an accounting with all three cultures—white, Mexican, Indian. I want the freedom to carve and chisel my own face, to staunch the bleeding with ashes, to fashion my own gods out of my entrails. And if going home is denied me then I will have to stand and claim my space, making a new culture—*una cultura mestiza*—with my own lumber, my own bricks and mortar and my own feminist architecture. (44)

Replacing the monologic, oppositional conversation between the individual and society generally found in canonical interpretations of American individualism with this multilayered discourse, Anzaldúa generates flexible, open-ended forms of individualized-yet-collective identity, or what she sometimes calls the "new mestiza." As the term suggests, Anzaldúa's new mestiza represents a hybrid, a complex mixed-breed who can neither be reduced to a single category nor rigidly classified according to a specific set of traits.[23] The product of several cultures—each with its own distinctive value system—Anzaldúa's new mestiza draws from these various traditions yet redefines, rearranges, and transforms them in context-specific ways. She "learns to juggle cultures. She has a plural personality, she operates in a pluralistic mode—nothing is thrust out, the good the bad and the ugly, nothing rejected, nothing abandoned. Not only does she sustain contradictions, she turns the ambivalence into something else" (*Borderlands* 101).

Anzaldúa's "new mestiza" represents an important critique of conventional western models of selfhood as well as an innovative intervention into separatist multiculturalism and the restrictive forms of identity politics on which it relies. To begin with, by replacing humanist notions of a stable, unified self with a fluid, shifting subjectivity, Anzaldúa can develop new interconnections with others. As she explains in "To(o) Queer the Writer," her "new mestiza queers have the ability, the flexibility, the amorphous quality of being able to stretch this way and that way. We can add new labels, names and identities as we mix with others" (249). She breaks down the boundaries between isolated individuals, allowing new forms of intersubjective connection based on individual and communal needs, affinities, and desires. And, by extending commonly accepted definitions of the mestizo as a (masculinized) member of a specific biologically based cultural group to encompass the experiences of non-Mexican, non-Indian (feminine) peoples as well, Anzaldúa challenges conventional theories of gender, ethnicity, and sexuality.[24] As I explain in more detail in the following chapter, her highly controversial theory of mestizaje draws from yet also rejects biologically based (*and often essentializing*) concepts of identity that rely on blood quantum, physical appearance, or other physical attributes, and replaces the rhetoric of authenticity found in many ethnic-specific traditions with new forms of communal identity based on each individual's experiential knowledge and personal choice.[25]

For Paula Gunn Allen, as well, self-definition occurs always in the context of others. But unlike Anzaldúa and Jordan, who rely extensively on autohistoria (that is, on aesthetic representations of their personal experiences) to create an intersubjective matrix where these new constellations of individual and collective identities can occur, Allen adopts a more conventional scholarly tone (in most of her work) and relies extensively on literature and myth.[26] She builds on the multiplicitious holism she finds in traditional Native cosmologies and invents a transformational model of identity formation synthesizing the personal and communal dimensions of each individual's life. Locating this transformational model within the oral tradition, Allen develops a dialogic theory of tribal literatures enabling her to redefine the individual in culturally specific yet transcultural forms.

Allen provides one of her most extensive discussions of the oral tradition in an early essay, "The Sacred Hoop: A Contemporary Perspective," where she draws from a wide variety of tribal mythic systems, including Cheyenne, Hopi, and Keres, to distinguish between western literature's highly individualistic bias and the communal dimensions she finds in American Indian literatures. Whereas the former generally celebrates solipsistic, self-enclosed forms of possessive individualism leading only to isolation, separation, and loss, the latter does not.[27] Instead, the oral narratives embodied in traditional tribal literatures posit an underlying dynamic intelligence—or what, borrowing from the Hopi, Allen describes as "what lives and moves and knows" (*Sacred Hoop* 61)—enabling us to create communal identities based on a shared worldview. By associating this holistic worldview with language's transformational effects, Allen can insist that the mythic stories conveyed in oral narratives use participatory, performative speech acts to connect individuals with communities and bring about radical change: "The tribes seek—through song, ceremony, legend, sacred stories (myths), and tales—to embody, articulate, and share reality, to bring the isolated private self into harmony and balance with this reality, to verbalize the sense of the majesty and reverent mystery of all things, and to actualize, in language, those truths that give to humanity its greatest significance and dignity. To a large extent, ceremonial literature serves to redirect private emotion and integrate the energy generated by emotion within a cosmic framework" (*Sacred Hoop* 55). As this synthesis of private power and cosmic communal experience indicates, Allen does not reject all forms of individualism. Instead, she locates each being's personal integrity and power within communally based oral traditions, thus destabilizing the binary opposition between the individual and society (here defined broadly to include nonhuman members, such as the land, as well). Like Jordan, she stipulates that in order to achieve *self*-determination, each individual must go *beyond* our narrowly defined self and recognize our interconnections with others.

According to Allen, the oral tradition can trigger this recognition. As she explains in "Whose Dream Is This Anyway? Remythologizing and Self-Definition in Contemporary American Indian Fiction," "entry into the narrative tradition . . . lets people realize that individual experience is not isolate but is part of a coherent and timeless whole, providing them with a means of personal empowerment and giving shape and direction to their lives" (*Sacred Hoop* 100). In other words, when listeners or readers participate in this narrative, they experience an alteration in consciousness that allows them to perceive themselves and their world in relational terms.

Language plays a pivotal role in this transformational individualized-yet-collective process. Allen maintains that

> through language one can share one's singular being with that of the community and know within oneself the communal knowledge of the tribe. In this art, the greater self and all-that-is are blended into a balanced whole, and in this way the concept of being that is the fundamental and sacred spring of life is given voice and being for all. American Indian people do not content themselves with simple preachments of this truth, but through the sacred power of utterance they seek to shape and mold, to direct and determine, the forces that surround and govern human life and the related lives of all things. (*Sacred Hoop* 56)

This passage illustrates two components of Allen's dialogic aesthetics. First, by connecting each person's "singular being" and self-knowledge with "the greater self" and "all-that-is," Allen can insist that the oral tradition provides an underlying intersubjective matrix for individual and communal self-growth. Second, by associating this "balanced whole" (which dynamically blends individual and collective selves) with the spoken word, she draws on language's agentic force and performative effects to generate personal and social change.[28]

In many ways, Allen's discussion of oral narratives' unifying energy resembles Thoreau's discovery of patterned, perpetual rebirth in *Walden* or Emerson's theory of the imagination.[29] Like Allen, Emerson locates the source of each person's individual power within a larger, communal context and a holistic worldview that he associates with Reason (which, in turn, he identifies with and as the imagination). As he explains in "The Poet,"

> It is a secret which every intellectual man [or woman] quickly learns, that beyond the energy of his possessed and conscious intellect he is capable of a new energy (as of an intellect doubled on itself), by abandonment to the nature of things; that beside his privacy of power as an individual man, there is a great

public power on which he can draw, by unlocking, at all risks, his human doors, and suffering the ethereal tides to roil and circulate through him; then he is caught up into the life of the Universe, his speech is thunder, his thought is law, and his words are universally intelligible as the plants and animals. (233)

This "nature of things," these "ethereal tides," this "life of the Universe" point to what Allen has described as the cosmic Source—"what lives and moves and knows" (*Sacred Hoop* 61). Just as Emerson's theory of imagination acknowledges thinkers' access to this "great public power" uniting them with all that exists, Allen's dialogic theory of tribal literatures underscores each individual's interconnections with a communally based "universe of power" (*Grandmothers* 22)—interconnections that we can perceive and engage with only by "unlocking, at all risks, [our] human doors." Both authors posit a metaphysics of interconnectedness and locate all human and nonhuman beings—indeed, all existence—within this matrix.

There are, however, (at least) two important differences between these theorist-poets. First, Allen directly associates this great universal power with very specific material change by maintaining that individuals who attain cosmic power must take more politicized, active roles in social-justice work.[30] Second, she includes an overtly multicultural dimension by emphasizing the particular embodied forms this all-inclusive power can take. Perhaps we could say that Allen translates the "universally intelligible" words of Emerson's poet into a variety of gender- and ethnic/racial/geographic/species-specific forms, converting culturally specific differences into new types of commonality designed to bring about sociopolitical change. She brings particularity to his (over-)generalized language, thus activating the cosmic energy that Emerson, too, describes.

As I explore in more detail in later chapters, Allen provocatively illustrates some of the forms these transcultural dialogues can take in *Grandmothers of the Light: A Medicine Woman's Sourcebook*. This book defies easy classification yet can perhaps be described as a hybrid synthesis of cultural autobiography with self-help; Allen combines indigenous histories and myths with personal anecdotes and storytelling to transform Native oral traditions into a guidebook for contemporary readers. Drawing from "the vast oral tradition of Native America" (xiii), she selects twenty-one stories that she has found most useful in her own life and reshapes them to meet her readers' contemporary needs. In a sense, she universalizes her experience and enacts her belief that the personal and the communal are mutually supportive and interconnected.

Allen's negotiation between the particular and the universal demonstrates that commonalities can occur on at least three interrelated levels. First, commonalities occur within the diverse racial-ethnic category of Native Americans. As in her earlier, more conventional scholarship, Allen insists on the many differences among Native cultures yet simultaneously examines their underlying similarities. Thus she describes the stories contained in her oral tradition as explorations of "the Great Goddess in a variety of guises— Xmucané, Sky Woman, Six Killer (Sutalidihi), Thinking Woman, Changing Woman, White Shell Woman, Tonan, Scomalt, Selu, Iyatiku, Ic'sts'ity, and Nau'ts'ity" (*Grandmothers* xiii). On the one hand, she maintains that these stories are about a single figure, the "Great Goddess." On the other hand— and simultaneously—Allen emphasizes the multiplicity of culturally specific forms this "Great Goddess" takes. Second, commonalities exist between American Indians and other peoples. Allen extends the interplay between commonalities and differences beyond Native traditions by identifying these many culturally specific figures with a worldwide gynecentric cosmic power:

> The basic nature of the universe of power is magic; the name given to the practice of a mage *Ma* (the *m*-syllable again) comes in variants. . . . All are versions of the same morpheme . . . and refer in one way or another to the Great Mother or Great Goddess of the Indo-Germanic tradition. The Goddess . . . was in time demoted and even changed gender over the ages, but she is known even today. . . . She can be discerned in words such as mother, mom . . . mutter. (15, original emphasis)

By locating this cosmic feminine power within commonplace English words, Allen simultaneously universalizes, particularizes, and indianizes her worldview.

Third, commonalities exist among a diverse group of readers. In *Grandmothers of the Light*, Allen attempts to share her indigenous-inflected worldview with a wide, multicultural female audience. She implies that—when read from a mythic perspective—the Native myths she retells function as a guidebook for any woman interested in learning to "walk the medicine path, . . . to live and think in ways that are almost but not quite entirely unlike our usual ways of living and thinking" (3). As she asserts in an interview with Jane Caputi, "[t]he stories are guides and a handbook on how to be spiritual if you want to be spiritual. [*Grandmothers of the Light*] gives you stories you can use like recipes on how to act, what to do. These stories are about being medicine women, . . . they are about being sacred practitioners, Crones, Hags, Maidens" (qtd. in Caputi 66). By fully participating in the "sacred myths" Allen retells, contemporary English-speaking women of any ethnicity or cultural background can become "medicine women" and develop a spiritual mode of perception that empowers them to bring about psychic and material change.

I want to emphasize the radical nature of these claims. Like Anzaldúa's new mestiza, Allen's medicine woman indicates her attempt to create a new form of culturally specific yet transcultural collective identity. She too goes beyond biological categories of meaning to invent volitional identities. And like Jordan, her insistence that these medicine women attain personal and collective agency enables her to reject the rhetoric of victimhood and maintain that each individual can bring about concrete material change. As Allen explains in the preface, the mythic tribal stories she retells demonstrate "the great power women have possessed, and how that power when exercised within the life circumstances *common to women everywhere* can reshape (terraform) the earth" (*Grandmothers* xvi, emphasis added). I explore the trickiness of Allen's claim in chapter 5. At this point, I will simply suggest that she draws on language's performative power to create the commonality she envisions.

Transformed thresholds

In "La Prieta," Anzaldúa positions herself on the thresholds—simultaneously inside and outside a number of what seem to be mutually exclusive groups. While these various groups try to belittle her liminal stance, labeling her "ambivalent" or "confused," she adopts a post-oppositional perspective and rewrites their scripts:

> You say my name is ambivalence? Think of me as Shiva, a many-armed and legged body with one foot on brown soil, one on white, one in straight society, one in the gay world, the man's world, the women's, one limb in the literary world, another in the working class, the socialist, and the occult worlds. A sort of spider woman hanging by one thin strand of web.
>
> Who, me confused? Ambivalent? Not so. Only your labels split me. (45–46)

She develops flexible models of intersubjective identity formation and self-naming that allow her to establish points of similarity and difference among people of diverse backgrounds. Similar comments can be made about Allen and Jordan, as well. Rejecting the belief in self-enclosed identities and the rhetoric of authenticity based on naturalized concepts of ethnicity, gender, sexuality, or other systems of difference, these three authors replace the celebrated versions of American individualism that rely on an authentic, boundaried core self with alternate, more openly relational forms. As they engage in multiple dialogues simultaneously, they enact a series of displacements that confound binary oppositions between personal and communal identities, reshaping traditional notions of American individualism to meet their own personal and collective needs. Shifting among commonalities, similarities, and differences, these relational individualisms illustrate some of the forms transcultural dialogues can take.

In the following chapter, I apply these to-and-from movements to conventional identity politics.

CHAPTER THREE

"I am your other I"

Transformational Identity Politics

> In the spirit of the Mayan philosophy "In Lak
> Ech"—yo soy tú otro yo, I am your other I—I
> offer these words as a prayer for connection.
>
> Irene Lara, "Healing Sueños for Academia"

> Once you have discerned the meaning of a label,
> it may seem to define you for others, but it does
> not have the power to define you to yourself.
>
> James Baldwin, *The Price of the Ticket*

As we search for increasingly effective ways to use language and invent theories that can assist us in creating progressive social transformation, more equitable societies, and modes of living that value all forms of life, scholar-activist theorists in a variety of fields (including contemporary U.S. literary studies, ethnic studies, women's studies, LGBTQ studies, and queer theory) have relied on oppositional terms like "margin/center," "oppressed/oppressor," and "colonized/colonizer," where one half of the binary represents historically disempowered groups and perspectives, and the other half represents those in power. Although this framework has offered a useful lens with which to analyze systemic issues, the words themselves (and the concepts they represent) reinforce a troubling dichotomous structure, thus undermining the goals we seek to achieve. Despite our intentions, we generally use these terms in ways that subtly draw on and replicate our status-quo stories and the existing power structures these stories reinforce. Take, for example, margin/center discourse. If, in a classroom discussion, I draw on the perspectives of a "marginal" author in order to underscore my point, my reference automatically (yet invisibly, silently, insidiously) reasserts the centrality of the (male/heterosexual/'white') invisible norm.[1]

And yet, given the great epistemological authority often granted to personal experiences, this flipped script—where we marginalize the conventional center and center the previous margin—can seem like common sense. Why not flip this script? After all, we can use our marginalized status for good: as we elevate our marginalized perspectives (*our lives on the borders, as it were*), we can claim epistemic privilege (*our previously unacknowledged perspectives and the additional insights we have obtained from these perspectives give us intellectual authority and new knowledge*). With this new knowledge—these additional perspectives—we make strong assertions designed to achieve social justice. Unfortunately, however, the binary margin/center structure we use in this type of margin/center discourse subtly poisons and undercuts the transformation we're trying to achieve. Henry Louis Gates Jr. makes a similar point in his discussion of "'ethnic and minority'" literary studies. According to Gates, theorists adopting this rhetoric of marginality in order to support their claims overlook the fact that their references to "marginalized" and "central" writers and texts reinforce existing literary values and other categories of meaning. Even if they elevate the margin in order to decenter the existing norm, the fact that the center has defined the margin *as* marginal ensures that the margin's "privileged site of cultural critique" is itself authorized by the dominating hegemonic cultural system. And so, the other's marginalized worldview remains locked in a dyadic relationship that unintentionally (and ironically) reinforces existing power structures and social systems. Gates maintains that our attempts to transcend this binary construction have been equally ineffective and result only in a proliferation of margins, "breeding new margins within margins . . . an ever renewed process of differentiation, even fragmentation" (298). And so, the divisive status-quo thinking continues, and the old worn-out stories remain in place.

My questions about the limitations in dichotomous language structures reflect my larger concern, about the political (in)effectiveness of identity politics and other oppositional forms of resistance, especially when applied to writings by contemporary U.S. feminists and other social-justice activists who locate themselves on the margins and speak in the voice of the other(s). If, as Gates suggests, "keeping inside and outside distinct is a means of keeping the other elsewhere" (298), then the "radical openness and power" that marginal theories seem to promise do not provide social actors with an effective location to transform dominant-cultural discourse. Instead, we sit on our elevated margins—margins defined by the center—and, as we authoritatively claim our unique, superior insights, we cannot help but also, simultaneously, reinforce the status quo. Sure—we might chip away at some central concepts, offer additional perspectives, and make a few small changes; however, we remain firmly entrenched in the existing system. Indeed, some of us "marginalized" scholars might benefit from this system, when we are asked to speak as marginal people, when we use our margin as a pulpit to elevate our specific social-justice visions (*and ourselves*).

Identity politics has become increasingly ensnared in this dichotomous framework, making it less effective today than it was in the twentieth century. When I first realized the dangerous limitations in these oppositional identity-based strategies, I wanted to react with wild abandonment. I wanted to entirely reject all forms of identity politics as too narrow, too worn-out, to be effective anymore. However, after trying out this anti-identity-politics perspective in my classrooms, a few conference presentations, and earlier versions of this chapter, I realized that when I entirely reject identity politics, I unintentionally re-activate the oppositional dynamics I'm trying to move beyond. And so, in this chapter I develop a nonoppositional (*or perhaps post-oppositional?*) approach. Rather than reject all references to personal experiences or the knowledge claims we obtain from our daily lives, I consider how we might redefine identity and identity politics, using a metaphysics of interconnectedness. In the following sections, I build on the previous chapter's critique of self-enclosed individualism and propose an alternative to conventional identity politics that I call "transformational identity politics." As I define the term, transformational identity politics is based on a metaphysics and ontology of interconnectedness; takes multiple, open-ended forms; questions monolithic identity categories and static concepts of selfhood; works to create inclusionary identities and communities; enables us to forge commonalities; and reconfigures self/other dichotomies. Unlike conventional types of identity politics—where social actors base their political theories and strategies on their sense of *personal* ethnic, gender, and/or sexual identity—transformational identity politics questions all such notions of self-enclosed, unified, stable identities. Transformational identity politics offers a more subtle understanding of difference. Rather than simply enabling alliances *across* differences, transformational identity politics employs these complex differences (differences that are often shot through with shared traits) to transform identity itself.

This transformative politics of identity relies on relational epistemologies, nondual ways of thinking that destabilize the networks of classification restricting us to static notions of personal and collective identity. In so doing, it opens up psychic spaces where alterations in consciousness and radical shifts in identity can occur. Transformational identity politics generates new and/or previously unacknowledged commonalities; these commonalities compel us to understand difference differently. Identity itself is transformed.

Conventional identity politics: definitions and limitations

Identity politics is a contentious topic with multiple definitions and applications. The term entered feminist and womanist conversations with the Combahee River Collective, a 1970s black feminist lesbian organization in Boston, who developed the concept in order to articulate their belief that in order to develop political action that could be effective for them, personally, they must begin with their particular location and experiences. As they assert in their 1977 statement:

> This focusing upon our own oppression is embodied in the concept of identity politics. We believe that the most profound and potentially radical politics come directly out of our own identity, as opposed to working to end somebody else's oppression. In the case of Black women this is a particularly repugnant, dangerous, threatening, and therefore revolutionary concept because it is obvious from looking at all the political movements that have proceeded us that anyone is more worthy of liberation than ourselves. We reject pedestals, queenhood, and walking ten paces behind. To be recognized as human, levelly human, is enough. (212)

For the Combahee River Collective, "Black women" were not a homogenous group but represented a complex collection of differently situated human beings. Even as they underscored their particularity as black women, and insisted on a politics that developed from their experiences, the members of the collective expressed a shared commonality—a desire "[t]o be recognized as human, levelly human." Because they realized that "the major systems of oppression are interlocking," they called for a multipronged approach that struggles, simultaneously, "against racial, sexual, heterosexual, and class oppression" (210). I want to underscore this emphasis on complexity, because it's an emphasis too often missing from more recent versions of identity politics.

The Combahee Collective's identity politics were complexly experience based; their organization, their recognition of interlocking systems of oppression, and their specific politics grew directly from their personal experiences. As they explain, "as children we realized that we were different from boys and that we were treated different—for example, when we were told in the same breath to be quiet both for the sake of being 'ladylike' and to make us less objectionable in the eyes of white people. In the process of consciousness-raising, actually life-sharing, we began to recognize the commonality of our experiences and, from the sharing and growing consciousness, to build a politics that will change our lives and inevitably end our oppression" (211). This early version of identity politics illustrates how a focus on differences can lead to insights about shared traits. Rather than using their unique differences as black lesbians to create unnavigable divisions between themselves and others, they use their differences to forge commonalities. The Combahee Collective's identity politics valorize self-love, autonomy, and self-determination yet do so without much oversimplifying and without elevating themselves—their unified collective identity—over others. By adopting a language that underscores multiplicity and interlocking connections among various overlapping forms of oppression, they avoid the traps of sameness and separatism so often found in margin/center discourse and other types of identity-based politics. They move from their personal experiences outward, to make connections with others. Similarly, we could say that Gloria Anzaldúa enacts a version of identity politics in her early autohistoria, "La Prieta." Although she begins with her own experiences, she builds outward to develop complex commonalities, and she uses these commonalities to highlight the interconnections among differently situated groups. Indeed, her theory of El Mundo Zurdo and her call for queer alliances and affinities could be described as a form of identity politics. What promise, then, in these mid-twentieth-century women-of-colors identity politics!

All too often, however, identity politics has been defined and enacted in less expansive terms that subtly reinforce the status quo. These more recent versions generally conflate *identity* with narrow self-definitions. Thus, for example, Diana Fuss defines identity politics as "the tendency to base one's politics on a sense of personal identity" (97). In these status-quo versions of identity politics, identity is built from the self-enclosed individualism and the limited concepts of selfhood I described in the previous chapter. Too often, these oversimplified versions of identity politics focus on a single ethnic/racial group (defined in monolithic terms) and/or a single form of oppression. Grace Kyungwon Hong makes a similar point, noting the difference between women-of-colors' identity politics and more recent versions: "Today, we understand identity politics as signifying a process whereby one singular identification—race, class, gender—is prioritized over all else. But identity politics as imagined by women of color feminists was fundamentally critical of a unitary and reified notion of subject formation" (xxvi).

Like margin/center metaphors and discourse, these more recent iterations of identity politics are too limited to bring about radical change. In fact, narrow identity politics can inhibit transformation, for they draw on (and thus inadvertently reaffirm) status-quo stories in several interrelated ways. First, thriving on binary-oppositional energies, they employ a variety of self/other, margin/center, either/or frameworks. Second, their reliance on conventional identity categories and definitions (based on existing ideas about gender, sexuality, race, and so on) reinforces the social structure they are trying to transform. After all, who's *really* doing the naming, if we adopt the names and categories that were imposed on us, used to separate, segregate, and condemn us? Third, because these versions of identity politics overemphasize narrowly defined, boundaried differences, they prevent us from recognizing and/or creating commonalities among differently situated peoples and groups. Fourth, status-quo identity politics impose unity on and demand "mono-thinking" from members. These membership rules police the group, constraining those who embrace the identity to follow a party line, as it were. As Kathy Rudy explains, reflecting on her experiences as a member of the Durham, North Carolina, lesbian community in the late twentieth century:

> For me, it wasn't only the fact that our politics were based solely on essentialized womanhood that was troubling. It was also the related fact that by the mid-1980s my community had become dangerous in its narrowness and policing. The role of a radical feminist was scripted in such a way that many of my own pleasures were denied. Watching detective shows on TV, going to church, eating meat, wearing polyester or high heels, shopping, feeling feminine—these and many other activities had to be hidden from the larger group in order to maintain membership in good standing in the lesbian community. (209–10)

Fifth, their more exclusive focus on *personal* identity inhibits the creation of inclusionary groups and unlikely coalitions, as well as the development of complex collective identities and alliances across difference.

Sixth, an emphasis on oppression can lead to a type of "Oppression Olympics," where multiply marginalized individuals or groups are ranked, and the person or group with the "most oppressions" (*assuming that we could even measure such a thing!*) "wins." Sara Suleri makes a related point in her discussion of postcolonial U.S. feminist theory when she questions the epistemic privilege typically associated with marginal positions—specifically, with self-identified feminists who use their "outsider" status to claim a type of moral and epistemological authority.[2] As Suleri points out, mainstream feminism's automatic acceptance of doubly marginalized feminist voices creates a highly ironic situation: "Even though the marriage of two margins should not necessarily lead to the construction of that contradiction in terms, a 'feminist center,' the embarrassed privilege granted to racially encoded feminism does indeed suggest a rectitude that could be its own theoretical undoing" (758). In other words, the unquestioned authority given to these marginalized experts makes it almost impossible to develop sophisticated analyses of the complex systems of differences and complicity inscribing contemporary social actors. Cultural critique is reduced to "unthinking celebrations of oppression, elevating the racially female voice into a metaphor for 'the good'" (759).[3]

Restricted by the binary-oppositional frameworks and energies that define and direct them, conventional identity politics cannot effect radical transformation. Pratibha Parmar makes a similar point in her assessment of black British women's attempts to develop a cohesive feminist movement. Although she acknowledges the importance of identity politics, she emphasizes its limitations, explaining that "[w]hile the articulation of self-identities has been a necessary and essential process for collective organising by black and migrant women, it also resulted in political practices which became insular and often retrograde" (102). She attributes these limitations to rigid, exclusionary definitions of identity derived from static conceptions of sexuality, ethnicity, and/or class: When feminists relied on "a language of 'authentic subjective experience'" based on narrowed self-definitions, they developed hierarchies of oppression that prevented the establishment of alliances across differences. Moreover, the appeal to authentic experience leads to "a self-righteous assertion that if one inhabits a certain identity this gives one the legitimate and moral right to guilt-trip others into particular ways of behaving" (107).

In short, these status-quo identity politics often base political strategies on humanist notions of stable, unitary identities that fragmented feminist groups from within.[4] My point, though, is not to suggest that we abandon all forms of identity politics as too limited to be effective. Instead, we can re-examine our approach to the identities on which these politics are based. As Andrea Stuart states in her discussion of British feminists' identity politics, "[t]he problem was not, in a strange way, that we took the implications of organising around identity too far, but that we didn't take it far enough. Had we really pushed this debate far enough, we would have come to appreci-ate that we are all oppressor *and* oppressed. . . . Instead of appreciating the interconnectedness of our oppressions we saw all our interests as mutually antagonistic, instead of making alliances we were in competition with one another" (39). Stuart's invitation to recognize our commonalities and inter-connections applies to U.S. identity politics as well.[5] As Barbara Smith, Gloria Yamato, and other feminist theorists point out, racism and racist behavior are so deeply embedded in contemporary U.S. culture that people of all colors have been (mis)shaped by this "patriarchal legacy" (B. Smith 25). This pa-triarchal, white-supremacist legacy makes us all complicit, in various ways and to varying degrees. Similar statements can be made about heterosexism, sexism, and classism. They, too, are the widespread manifestations of a rigidly dualistic hierarchical mode of thought that has unevenly affected us all. This complicity, and the dichotomous thinking on which it relies, offer rich com-monalities that, if acknowledged and explored, could enable us to develop innovative alliances. However, when we rely on overly simplified versions of identity politics and other binary-oppositional forms of discourse, we can't acknowledge this complicity in potentially transformative ways. We remain locked in our narrow self-defined frameworks.

Instead of rejecting identity politics entirely, I suggest that we develop and enact identity politics in new ways, or what I call transformational identity politics—politics that rely on and propose expansive, inclusionary defini-tions of individual and collective identity and use these identities to evoke transformation. Through an analysis of writings by Paula Gunn Allen, Glo-ria Anzaldúa, and Audre Lorde, I explore some of the forms that transfor-mational identity politics might take. I focus on these authors because they take up, destabilize, transcend, and tactically explode the ways they have been positioned (and sometimes position themselves) within conventional identity categories. Moreover, they forged their complex identities at a time (the mid- to late twentieth century) when separatism and other restrictive versions of identity-based politics were widely accepted. As self-identified lesbians of color, Allen, Anzaldúa, and Lorde could be considered *triply* or even quadrupally marginalized.[6] While at times they use their multiply marginal positions to center their bold assertions and alternative perspectives, they do not convert these marginalized centers into the authoritative types of (centered) margins that Suleri and Gates criticize. Instead, they transform their marginalized identities into liminal, threshold identities. To borrow Victor Turner's phrase, they become "threshold people" who "elude or slip through the network of classifications that normally locate states and positions in cultural spaces" (95). Although the specific classifications and spaces each writer "slips through" and the liminal identities she invents are usually (*though not always!*) particular to her regional, ethnic, and economic background—as well as other differences such as native languages, religion, education, health, and skin color—Allen, Anzaldúa, and Lorde enact their liminality in similar mobile ways. They use their "privileged" identity-based knowledge sites performatively to negotiate diverse sets of socially constructed spaces.

These liminal negotiations are, potentially, transformative—both for readers and for the authors themselves. As Allen, Anzaldúa, and Lorde translate their "threshold" identities (their multiple, shifting positions) into their writings, they engage in *tactical (re)naming*. I bracket the prefix to underscore the contradictory, complicated nature of this naming process. When we engage in tactical (re)naming, we claim new names yet also (often simultaneously) redefine the old. Tactical (re)naming represents the construction of differentially situated subjectivities that, deployed contextually, trouble and destabilize oppositional categories from within. Although threshold identities sometimes resemble what Gayatri Chakravorty Spivak has famously described as "strategic essentialism," I describe this (re)naming process as tactical, rather than strategic, to underscore the temporary, plural, transformational nature of their maneuvers.[7] Engaging in multiple conversations simultaneously, Allen, Anzaldúa, and Lorde enact a series of displacements that confound pre-established divisions between margin/center, self/other, and additional forms of binary positioning and dichotomous thought. To borrow Trinh T. Minh-ha's words, because their struggles are "multiple and transversal—specific but not confined to one side of any border war" (*Moon* 18), they shift between margin/center, oppressor/oppressed, and self/other, complicating clear-cut divisions. Although they might begin on the margins, they move elsewhere; they "use marginality as a starting point rather than an ending point . . . cross[ing] beyond it towards other affirmations and negations" (*Moon* 19).

Allen, Anzaldúa, and Lorde invent differential subjectivities that they use to establish commonalities—points of similarity—among readers of diverse backgrounds. Instead of limiting herself to a single-voiced discourse on one specific topic (such as sexism or racism or homophobia, and so on), each writer draws from her personal-collective experiences and adopts a series of complex speaking positions enabling her to explore issues crossing (and complicating) ethnic, sexual, national, and economic lines. This flexibility provides an important challenge to readers' status-quo thinking, which relies on and reinforces stable notions of self-enclosed personal identity and difference-based social categories. As Trinh asserts, "Essential difference allows those who rely on it to rest reassuringly on its gamut of fixed notions. Any mutation in identity, in essence, in regularity, and even in physical place poses a problem, if not a threat, in terms of classification and control. If you can't locate the other, how can you locate your-self?" (*Moon* 73). In various ways, and to varying degrees, Allen, Anzaldúa, and Lorde destabilize our status-quo stories about ethnic, cultural, gender, and sexual identity; in so doing, they demonstrate the limitations of our fixed sociocultural inscriptions. By disrupting the restrictive networks of classification that inscribe us as racialized, engendered subjects, they develop nonbinary identity models that open psychic spaces where alterations in consciousness can occur. I locate transformational identity politics in (and as) these psychic thresholds.

Tactical (re)naming, creating commonalities

Lorde's shifting positionality throughout the essays and lectures collected in *Sister Outsider* illustrates some of the forms that tactical (re)naming can take. More specifically, Lorde uses potentially essentializing self-definitions tactically. As Gloria Hull points out, "Lorde's seemingly essentialist definitions of herself as a black/lesbian/mother/woman are not simple, fixed terms. Rather, they represent her ceaseless negotiations of a positionality from which she can speak. Almost as soon as she achieves a place of connection, she becomes uneasy at the comfortableness (which is, to her, a signal that something critical is being glossed over) and proceeds to rub athwart the smooth grain to find the roughness and the slant she needs to maintain her difference-defined, complexly constructed self" (155–56). Although I agree with Hull's assertion that Lorde defines herself through her differences from others, I believe that an equally necessary part of Lorde's "difference-defined, complexly constructed self" is the way she uses these differences performatively, to generate commonalities among differently situated readers. Consider, for example, how her shifting self-descriptions in "Age, Race, Class, and Sex: Women Redefining Difference" deconstruct binary oppositions between oppressor and oppressed. In the opening paragraphs, Lorde describes herself as multiply marginalized: Her identity as a "forty-nine-year-old Black lesbian feminist socialist mother of two, including one boy, and a member of an inter-racial couple," ensures her membership in a number of subjugated groups (*Sister Outsider* 114). While she draws on her personal experiences of oppression to discuss racism, heterosexism, and other forms of discrimination, she does not use her epistemic privilege to turn these marginal positions into an oppositional center. Instead, she blurs the boundary between oppressors and oppressed by locating herself, as well as her audience, in both groups. She enacts epistemic privilege not to reinforce but to *challenge* the status quo.

Rather than use her experiences of multiple-marginalization in U.S. culture to make knowledge claims that would separate her from (and elevate her over) others, Lorde extends her experiences outward to include, potentially, anyone—regardless of color, sexuality, gender, age, or class—who does not fit this country's "mythical normal." Significantly, Lorde does so without denying the differences between herself and others. Rather than deny these differences, she transforms them from obstacles into creative tools for communication and community building:

> Certainly there are very real differences between us of race, age, and sex. But it is not those differences between us that are separating us. It is rather our refusal to recognize those differences, and to examine the distortions which result from our misnaming them and their effects upon human behavior and expectation. . . . Too often, we pour the energy needed for recognizing and exploring difference into pretending those differences are insurmountable barriers, or that they do not exist at all. This results in a voluntary isolation, or false and treacherous connections. Either way, we do not develop tools for using human difference as a springboard for creative change within our lives. (*Sister Outsider* 115)

Lorde does not build a new center for herself but instead exposes and critiques the existing center, the invisible norm, as well as the epistemological mechanics that continually reinforce this unstated norm. Thus, in the following passage, she focuses on this norm's underlying mechanics, or what we might call an epistemology of sameness that encourages us to automatically reject any types of human difference we encounter: "Institutionalized rejection of difference is an absolute necessity in a profit economy which needs outsiders as surplus people. As members of such an economy, we have *all* been programmed to respond to the human differences between us with fear and loathing and to handle that difference in one of three ways: ignoring it, and if that is not possible, copy it if we think it is dominant, or destroy it if we think it is subordinate" (*Sister Outsider* 115, original emphasis). In this statement, Lorde uses our mutual complicity in this limited form of thinking to create commonalities among differently situated people.

Tactical (re)naming is an ongoing, flexible process. The shifts Lorde enacts in this essay and elsewhere in her writings are context-specific and temporary, illustrating Trinh's contention that, in order to resist stasis and closure, "the challenge has to be taken up every time a positioning occurs: for just as one must situate oneself (in terms of ethnicity, class, gender, difference), one also refuses to be confined to that location" (*Moon* 229–30). Throughout her work, Lorde carefully positions herself in relation to the specific audience she addresses and the particular social issues she confronts. This willingness to take up a variety of self-positions enables Lorde to avoid binary-oppositional frameworks that define difference as deviation. By rejecting simplistic labels and by addressing multiple issues simultaneously, she demonstrates that the recognition of differences can, paradoxically, create commonalities that serve to unite, rather than divide, apparently disparate groups.

Although Allen's tactical (re)naming takes different forms, she too explores complicated ethnic-, sexual-, and gender-related concerns simultaneously and locates herself within these concerns in context-specific, flexible (or sometimes even contradictory) ways. In academic essays such as "Where I Come from Is Like This" and "Something Sacred Going on Out There: Myth and Vision in American Indian Literature," Allen uses her formal training as a literary scholar, as well as her personal knowledge of Laguna Pueblo traditions, to examine issues that she believes affect all Native Americans, American Indian women, lesbians, mixed bloods, and contemporary U.S. feminists of all colors. There is, however, a significant difference between Allen's and Lorde's self-positioning. Whereas Lorde draws on different elements of her experiences in different contexts and self-defines in various ways (sometimes as "Black feminist," sometimes as "Black lesbian feminist," sometimes as "woman," and so on), Allen generally draws on her Native ancestry and self-defines as a half-breed/mixed-blood American Indian woman. As Elizabeth Hanson puts it, "Allen remains for herself and for us (*at least as she wishes us to know her*) the quintessential 'breed'" (15, emphasis added).

Yet Allen's "breed" identity is no more static than Lorde's shifting positionality for, as Hanson's comment indicates, Allen's (re)naming process is performative and context-specific, not just descriptive. In other words, Allen is not reinforcing status-quo stories about mixed-blood peoples; instead, she uses her self-naming process to enter these status-quo stories and alter them from within. By so doing, she challenges readers to rethink conventional identity categories. For example, by describing herself as the "confluence" of numerous, sometimes conflicting identities, Allen destabilizes our notions of a unitary self. As she explains in an interview, "I am Lebanese-American, I am Indian, I am a breed, and I am New Mexican and they have a lot to do with how I act and what I think and how I interpret things. I was raised in a family and in a world that was multicultural, multiethnic, multireligious, and multilinguistic, with a number of social classes involved. . . . And then I have a kind of overlaying or underlaying American or Anglo culture that I mostly picked up in school. It is all me. It sometimes comes into conflict with itself, but it is all me" (qtd. in Eysturoy 103). Given this complex background, it's probably not surprising that Allen resists any type of unitary self-identity. As she states in another interview, she contains, within herself, a complex multiplicity; her Laguna/Sioux/Lebanese/Scotch/German ancestry makes her "split, not in two but in twenty, and never . . . able to reconcile all the *places* that I am" (qtd. in Bruchac 18, emphasis added). However, by portraying herself as the convergence of apparently irreconcilable places, Allen subtly underscores the indigenous elements of her identity while giving her marginal status a central role in U.S. culture.[8]

Significantly, Allen does not reify this indigenous-inflected centrality, developing yet another oppositional (*colonized/colonizer*) framework, but instead creates a fluid, permeable, shifting center. Thus, for example, she maintains that "half-breeds" function as catalysts for cultural change (*threshold people, nepantleras, as it were*): "We have a mediational capacity that is not possessed by either of the sides. What we are able to do is bridge variant realities because everybody is pissed off at us and we are pissed off at ourselves. What we are able to do is move from flower to flower, so to speak, and get the pollen moved around among each of our traditions. Then we can plant back into them" (qtd. in Bruchac 19). Allen does not use her mobile marginalized status to acquire an epistemic privilege that reinforces already existing categories of meaning. Instead, she employs her marginality (and the epistemological authority it implies) to *challenge* such categories; she enacts a to-and-fro movement that takes up yet disrupts conventional interpretations of Native American identities. She stages a fluid, indianized self-definition and worldview that she invites her readers—no matter what their biological/cultural backgrounds—to adopt.[9]

The title character in Allen's novel, *The Woman Who Owned the Shadows*, illustrates this invitational indianized perspective. A mixed blood cut off from tribal traditions and educated at Catholic schools, Ephanie Atencio must painfully discover the ways her identity has been (mis)shaped by Native American, Mexican, and Anglo cultures. Like shadows, which involve (as it were) a nonoppositional interplay of light and dark, Ephanie represents the mingling of apparent opposites.[10] When she recognizes that her mixed heritage prevents her from aligning herself with a single group, she works to establish new connections between and among diverse peoples. As Allen points out, at the novel's conclusion Ephanie "goes back to teach white people. So her resolution is that this is not about race; this is about vision. *The people who live on this continent are Indians*, that is to say, they live on the Indian continent, and what we must do is teach them how to live here. We tried and they kept killing us. That was then; but now maybe there are people here, lots of them, who are ready" (qtd. in Eysturoy 105, emphasis added). Allen's intriguing distinction between race and vision, as well as her compelling claim that all of us living on this (North American) continent are Indian, speaks to the performative dimensions of her own tactical (re)naming process.

Allen, like Ephanie, teaches "white people" how to live respectfully on this continent—how to live like (some) Indians. Yet Allen takes this educational process even further, for her lessons are designed to teach North American "white people" that they *can become* "Indians." Throughout her scholarly writing, Allen draws on her mixed-blood heritage to authorize her position as "spokesperson within the scholarly community" (Hanson 14). Readers are tricked by this self-positioning and generally assume that she functions as a native informant (an insider to cultural secrets) who simply reveals previously hidden aspects of American Indian life. Indeed, Allen herself often reinforces this interpretation by presenting her literary and cultural criticism under the guise of *explaining* Native American traditions to "outsiders." (*She is such a trickster!*) Yet Allen is at least equally concerned with developing and presenting alternative gynecentric "Native American" traditions capable of transforming her readers as well as herself.

In other words, Allen does not simply attempt to explicate the intersection of gender and ethnicity in Native American texts. Instead, she uses her gendered/ethnic identity performatively in order to alter her readers' self-perceptions, as well as their views of tribal cultures. Thus, in the scholarly essays collected in her groundbreaking book, *The Sacred Hoop: Recovering the Feminine in American Indian Traditions*, Allen reinterprets the historic and mythic beliefs of indigenous North American peoples from a twentieth-century feminist perspective and develops a highly distinctive woman-focused tradition. Similarly, in *Grandmothers of the Light: A Medicine Woman's Sourcebook*, Allen combines theory, myth, and story to construct a twentieth-century feminist pan-Indian worldview that she invites her readers to adopt. She implies that—read from the proper mythic perspective—the Aztec, Cherokee, Navajo, and other Native American stories she retells function as a guidebook for any woman interested in learning to develop her own shamanic powers and "walk the medicine path" (3). By fully participating in the "sacred myths" collected in her anthology, contemporary English-speaking women of any ethnicity or cultural background can develop a spiritual mode of perception that empowers them to bring about psychic and material change. (*No wonder contemporary scholars so often avoid Allen's work! Her bold claims and radical invitations veer dangerously close to appropriation, commodification, and other forms of theft. While Allen's intentions might be brilliantly progressive, she opens herself to potentially dangerous misinterpretations and misappropriations.*)[11]

For Anzaldúa as well, identity and related issues offer pathways into complicated, potentially transformational conversations between herself and her readers. Throughout her career, from *This Bridge Called My Back: Writings by Radical Women of Color* to *this bridge we call home: radical visions for transformation*, Anzaldúa aspires to develop transformative dialogues among people of diverse backgrounds. Like Lorde, she converts simplistic oppressor/oppressed dichotomies into complex interconnecting fields. Within the space of a single passage in *Borderlands/La Frontera: The New Mestiza*, for example, Anzaldúa identifies herself with both the "oppressed" and the "oppressors"—with the "Chicano, indio, American Indian, mojado, mexicano, immigrant Latino, Anglo in power, working class Anglo, Black, [and] Asian"—as she describes the psychic struggles facing all twentieth-century peoples and calls for the development of larger commonalities, insisting that "we need to meet on a broader communal ground" (109). And like Allen, Anzaldúa uses the epistemic privilege obtained through her marginal status to undermine status-quo stories and redefine socially imposed and sanctioned identity categories. Consider, for example, her discussion of "new mestiza queers" in "To(o) Queer the Writer," where she redefines and combines queer and mestiza identities: "the new mestiza queers have the ability, the flexibility, the amorphous quality of being able to stretch this way and that way. We can add new labels, names, and identities as we mix with others" (249). As I suggested in the previous chapter, Anzaldúa's new mestiza represents a hybrid, a complex mixed breed who can neither be reduced to a single category nor rigidly classified according to a specific set of traits.[12] The product of two or more cultures—each with its own value system—Anzaldúa's mestiza is in a "state of perpetual translation" as she attempts to reconcile, rather than reject, the many voices in her head.

Anzaldúa's expansive theory of mestizaje represents at least two significant departures from its earlier usage. First, by replacing the masculine-inflected "mestizo" with the feminine-inflected "mestiza," Anzaldúa offers an important in(ter)vention into the twentieth-century Chicano literary and theoretical movements that, as Ramón Saldívar and many others have noted, have been dominated by "male-centered themes and values" (39). Second, by extending conventional definitions of the mestizo as a member of a biologically based cultural group, Anzaldúa de-essentializes and pluralizes culturally specific notions of identity. As Marcos Sanchez-Tranquilino and John Tagg explain, Anzaldúa's theory represents an innovative shift from earlier views: "Her interpretation goes beyond the traditional concepts of mestizaje. For Anzaldúa, that concept cannot ever again be thought of as a simple mixing of blood or cultures but rather that what has always been in effect of mixing of identities many times over—beyond the old dualities be they gender, historical, economic, or cultural, etc." (568).

Anzaldúa takes her theory of mestizaje even further in her post-*Borderlands* writings. Look, for instance, at "now let us shift . . . the path of conocimiento . . . inner work, public acts," where, using the second-person voice, she retraces her own complicated identity formation:

> You examine the contentions accompanying the old cultural narratives: your ethnic tribe wants you to isolate, insisting that you remain within race and class boundaries. The dominant culture prefers that you abandon your roots and

assimilate, insisting that you leave your Indianness behind and seek shelter under the Hispanic or Latino umbrella. The temptation to succumb to these assimilationist tactics and escape the stigma of being Mexican stalls you on the bridge between isolation and assimilation. But both are debilitating. How can you step outside ethnic and other labels while cleaving to your root identity? Your identity has roots you share with all people and other beings—spirit, feeling, and body comprise a greater identity category. The body is rooted in the earth, la tierra itself. You meet ensoulment in trees, in woods, in streams. The roots del árbol de la vida of all planetary beings are nature, soul, body. (560)

I've quoted this passage at length because it beautifully illustrates Anzaldúa's nonbinary approach to the oppositional identity issues so often found in status-quo stories (or what Anzaldúa here calls "the old cultural narratives"). Confronted with two mutually exclusive options (either separate or assimilate), Anzaldúa avoids this either/or status-quo thinking that would compel her either to accept one of the two options or to reject them both. She neither entirely accepts nor fully rejects these limited options but instead acknowledges both their appeal and their restrictions. She embraces them and then reinterprets their implications from within her metaphysics of interconnectedness. Positing "a greater identity category," Anzaldúa moves beyond the human to align herself with a transhuman, planetary citizenship. Then, using this extreme identity position, she revisits her previous identity questions and further redefines her concept of mestizaje, creating her theory of "new tribalism": "you 'grow into' an identity of mestizaje you call the new tribalism by propagating other worldviews, spiritual traditions, and cultures to your árbol de la vida. You pick and choose views, cultures with transformational potential—a partially conscious selection, not a mestizaje imposed on you, but one whose process you can control. . . . A retribalizing mestizaje becomes your coping mechanism, your strategy of resistance to both acculturating and inculturating pressures" ("now let us shift" 560–61). Anzaldúa's spirit-inflected, radically inclusive new tribalism goes far beyond status-quo concepts of identity (which generally focus on biological and familial traits) to include belief systems and cultural perspectives; it is intentional yet open to unexpected changes.[13]

Indeed, Anzaldúa's "retribalizing mestizaje" offers one of the most provocative expansions of status-quo identities I've yet encountered. She redefines individual identity so extensively that it can startle even very progressive thinkers. Look, for instance, at her discussion of nepantleras in "now let us shift." As I explained earlier in *Transformation Now!*, Anzaldúa drew on her own experiences as a complex mediator (*or, we could say, as a threshold person*) among feminists of color and 'white'-raced feminists to develop this theory. Anzaldúa's nepantleras fluidly and lovingly challenge exclusionary practices. These challenges have their source at least partially in the nepantleras' relational self-definitions, their belief in "an unmapped common ground" that makes self and other entirely intertwined: "We are the other, the other is us" ("now let us shift" 570). This reconfiguration enables nepantleras to move beyond conventional identity categories and "recogniz[e] that some members of a racial or ethnic group do not necessarily stay with the consciousness and conditioning of the group they're born into, but shift momentarily or permanently. For example, some whites embody a woman-of-color consciousness, and some people of color, a 'white' consciousness" (570).

What a challenge to social inscriptions! Anzaldúa posits a cosmic, planetary identity component that makes each human being interconnected with all existence. Her claim is enormous and, if thoroughly understood and carefully followed, could profoundly alter the terrain of twenty-first-century social-justice movements.

Differential subject formation . . . becoming you, becoming myself

Beginning with their own embodied lives and context-specific experiences, Anzaldúa, Allen, and Lorde transform rigid, boundaried concepts of self-identity into transcultural, transgendered networks of subjectivity. As they resist rigid self-categorization, define themselves in relational terms, and explore their interconnections with (*or, possibly, as*) others, they enact threshold identities, illustrating what Trinh T. Minh-ha might call the "Inappropriate Other/Same":

> Not quite the Same, not quite the Other, she stands in that undetermined threshold place where she constantly drifts in and out. Undercutting the inside/outside opposition, her intervention is necessarily that of both a deceptive insider and a deceptive outsider. She is this Inappropriate Other/Same who moves about with always at least two/four gestures: that of affirming "I am like you" while persisting in her difference; and that of reminding "I am different" while unsettling every definition of otherness arrived at. (*Moon* 74)

Like other threshold people, Anzaldúa, Allen, and Lorde use these shifting, relational identities to develop multilayered conversations. Their complex dialogues generate commonalities (*not sameness!*) by inviting us to recognize both the differences and the similarities between and among apparently dissimilar peoples. In their writings, "self" and "other," "me" and "you," mingle and blur . . . subtly shifting readers' perspectives and self-definitions. Look, for instance, at Lorde's collective self-positioning in "Between Ourselves," where, after critiquing black nationalism's restrictive identity politics and self-definitions, she replaces the demand for sameness with a reminder that we share complex commonalities: "we are all children of Eshu . . . / and we each wear many changes / inside of our skin" (*Black Unicorn* 114). Here, commonalities and differences work together. Lorde exposes the limitations in the desire for racialized ideological sameness and warns readers that until we recognize these many different faces as our own and "stop killing / the other / in ourselves / the self that we hate / in others," we remain blinded by our own self-denial and unable to create alliances among people of diverse backgrounds (*Black Unicorn* 114). As Cheryl Clarke notes, "The speaker rejects unitary blackness as the only signifier of community. . . . She exposes the reduction of racial heritage to 'easy blackness' by offering the narrative of her great grandmother who was sold into slavery by a black man. Rejecting race as the sole basis of affinity and unity, she refuses the fictions used to justify this longing for racial purity" (159–60).

Although Lorde here focuses on black nationalism, her invitation has implications for everyone—no matter what our politics are or how we identify. Her challenge, that we acknowledge the "many changes" within "our skin" and discover "the other / in ourselves," represents an important departure from some of our most deeply held status-quo stories about self-identity, and points to an important tactic in transformational identity politics. She reminds us that each person's self-identity—our core self, our subjectivity, our sense of selfhood—is complex and multifaceted, containing "many changes." And, by blurring the boundaries between self and other, Lorde destabilizes the binary-oppositional frameworks that keep us apart. As she encourages readers to recognize the other(s) within ourselves and, simultaneously, to recognize ourselves within our so-called others, she redefines personal identity in nondual terms, replacing typical self-other divisions with an interwoven self-other constellation.

Lorde illustrates a model of differential subject formation that resonates with Chela Sandoval's theory of "differential consciousness." According to Sandoval, self-splintering—which she describes as a "violent shattering of the unitary sense of self"—leads to the development of differential consciousness, a flexible epistemology and ethics. Like transformational identity politics, differential consciousness requires a radical alteration in self-identity that leads to an ethical shift—a change in how we act. This alteration in self-identity, this "violent shattering," does not represent a *negation* of one's selfhood; it is, rather, an opening up, an expansion, a transformation.[14] Thus Sandoval uses the term "*differential consciousness*" to represent both this expansive shift in self-identity and the nonbinary oppositional tactics effectively deployed by U.S. women-of-colors feminists in their efforts to confront simultaneously racism, sexism, and other forms of oppression. As she explains in *Methodology of the Oppressed*,

> Differential consciousness is composed of difference and contradictions, which then serve as tactical interventions in the other mobility that is power. ... Entrance into this new order requires an emotional commitment within which one experiences the violent shattering of the unitary sense of self as the skill that allows it mobile identity to form takes hold. As Bernice Reagon has written, "most of the time you feel threatened to the core and if you don't, you're not really doing no coalescing" ("Coalition Politics: Turning the Century"). Within the realm of differential consciousness there are no ultimate answers, no terminal utopia (though the imagination of utopias can motivate its tactics), no predictable final outcomes. Its practice is not biologically determined, restricted to any class or group, nor must it become static. (196)

Sandoval outlines a "four-phase hegemonic typology" of traditional oppositional ideologies and describes differential consciousness as a fifth form that enables social actors to use already existing binary oppositional strategies in a new ways. It's this use—rather than rejection—of oppositionality that makes differential consciousness distinctly post-oppositional.

Differential consciousness is not oppositional in any conventional sense of the term. Unlike oppositional forms of resistance, which rely on exclusionary mechanisms and dichotomous categories, differential consciousness represents a fluid, sometimes-contradictory both/and approach. And yet, differential consciousness does not entirely always *reject* all conventional forms of opposition; rather, differential consciousness draws from binary oppositional modes selectively, in context-specific ways. By enabling us to move "between and among" traditional oppositional strategies, differential consciousness "permits functioning within yet beyond the demands of the dominant ideology" ("U.S. Third World Feminism" 3). In short, differential consciousness converts binary oppositions into a context-specific pluralistic approach. As Sandoval explains, differential consciousness represents "a new subjectivity, a political revision that denies any one ideology as the final answer, while instead positing a tactical subjectivity with the capacity to recenter depending upon the kinds of oppression to be confronted. This is what the shift from hegemonic oppositional theory and practice to a U.S. third world theory and method of oppositional consciousness require" (*Methodology* 58). When we employ differential consciousness, we might use conventional oppositional readings of culture, but we do so selectively and creatively. The selective, context-specific, imaginative nature of these oppositional readings liberates us from the dichotomous energies that would otherwise limit our options.

Although Sandoval attributes the development of differential consciousness to U.S. women of colors (or as she says, "U.S. third word feminists"), she does not associate it exclusively with this group but insists on its "accessibl[ity] to all people." Indeed, she maintains that Anzaldúa, Lorde, and other twentieth-century self-identified U.S. third-world feminists have demonstrated that differential consciousness provides the most effective form of resistance for *all* contemporary social actors. Whereas conventional "hegemonic" oppositional theories "rigidly circumscribe what is possible" by establishing binary categories between dominant and subordinate groups and by demanding an internal consistency that eventually fractures resistance movements from within, differential consciousness remains flexible and acknowledges its partial containment in hegemonic power structures ("Feminism and Racism" 60).

I've discussed Sandoval's differential consciousness in detail for several reasons. First, I believe that it beautifully illustrates the non- and post-oppositional forms of theorizing that I call for and try to enact in *Transformation Now!* Second, and more importantly for my argument in this chapter, the differential movement among binary-oppositional frameworks is analogous to transformational identity politics' relationship with conventional social identity categories. Transformational identity politics does not move us entirely *beyond* identity, into some post-identity future world. Rather, transformational identity politics enables us to enter into and yet also see beyond these conventional social identities, as well as the unitary versions of individualism on which such social identities rely.

Transformational identity politics invites us to recognize our interconnections with others. We, too, can affirm our shared identity with all existence. As we live out the implications of this extreme interconnectivity, we can move through and beyond the status quo, envisioning alternate modes of identification and affinity, new possibilities for social justice and for our daily lives.

CHAPTER FOUR

"There is no arcane place for return"

Revisionist Mythmaking with a Difference

Let us begin with what a myth is not: a myth is not a lie or a false statement to be contrasted with truth or reality or fact or history, though this usage is, perhaps, the most common meaning in casual parlance. . . . In its positive and enduring sense, a myth is a story that is sacred to and shared by a group of people who find their most important meanings in it.

Wendy Doniger, *The Implied Spider*

For too long, in both popular and academic vernacular, myth and history have been deployed as an imposed taxonomic framework, wherein myth and history are constructed as diametric opposites. History is viewed as disciplinary and approaching objectivity while myth lacks the necessary epistemological truth claims validated by a strict methodology. Notably, these delineations mark and mask power relations. . . . [T]his juxtaposition and bifurcation of myth and history was an imposed Eurocentric taxonomy and continues to be a critical force in maintaining the legacies of colonization. Not recognizing indigenous epistemologies and systems of record-keeping, European colonization ascribed myth to the cultural narratives of native peoples.

Lee Bebout, *Mythohistorical Interventions*

While revisionist mythmaking was a common strategy among many twenti-eth-century feminist and ethnic-nationalist authors and social-justice actors, it seems to be less often employed or examined by contemporary authors and scholars.[1] Perhaps this limited attention has its source at least partially in our restrictive definitions myth. After all, in the English lexicon the word *myth* has practically become a synonym for *falsehood* or *lie*. In this context, revisionist mythmaking seems pointless—why replace one untruth with another? (*Lies upon lies upon lies—why bother?*) Or perhaps revisionist mythmaking has fallen out of favor thanks at least in part to twentieth-century post-structuralist critiques, where cultural feminists' calls for female images of the divine were dismissed as regressive, essentializing strategies that inadvertently rein-state normative gender roles, stereotypes about women, and other harmful (*backward!*) practices. However, as the epigraphs to this chapter indicate, this dismissal of revisionist mythmaking, as well as the conflation of "mythic stories" with "lies," is too simplistic and overlooks the crucial roles mythol-ogy plays in shaping our material realities and other dimensions of our lives.

I'm not ready to give up on revisionist mythmaking! Because mythic sto-ries embody a culture's deep-seated, often unacknowledged (and therefore unquestioned) assumptions about human nature, revisionist mythmaking offers an important tool to effect transformation on multiple levels—rang-ing from our psychic lives to our social structures—and beyond.[2] Revisionist mythmaking can take a variety of forms: we can entirely reject the existing stories, rewrite portions of them, retell them from different perspectives, recover alternative versions that have been lost (*or that never before existed*), and create new myths. After exploring some of the underlying issues that have prompted the semi-erasure of revisionist mythmaking, I explore the possibility of developing transcultural, difference-inflected universals. Like Anna Lowenhaupt Tsing, I believe that, despite the dangers in universal ideas, images, and claims, we cannot simply reject all universals. As Tsing notes, "The universal offers us the chance to participate in the global stream of hu-manity. We can't turn it down. Yet we also can't replicate previous versions without inserting our own genealogy of commitments and claims. Whether we place ourselves inside or outside the West, we are stuck with universals created in cultural dialogue" (1). Through this chapter's analysis of revisionist mythmaking, I engage in this "cultural dialogue."

Post-structuralist debates over the (in)effectiveness of gynecentric origin stories are part of several larger debates concerning the possibility of posit-ing, from within our current social and symbolic systems, universal categories of meaning and radically inclusionary "beyond(s)": Can we affirm the "feminine" yet arrive at representations of "Woman" that are really universal and *qualitatively* different from phallocratic descriptions? Perhaps more importantly, can we do so without erasing or in other ways ignoring the many material and cultural differences between real-life women? And what do we mean by "women," anyway? Can this category include transpeople? Must it include all biologically female-bodied people? Could it also perhaps include some who identify as men, or who slip through gendered categories? On the one hand, terms like "Woman" and the "feminine" can be misleading and divisive when they prevent us from recognizing that, because gender intersects with historical, economic, ethnic, sexual, national, regional, religious, and many other axes of difference in complex ways, it is an unstable category with multiple meanings.[3] But on the other hand, to refuse all references to sexual difference, "Woman," and/or "women" risks reinstating the pseudo-universal human subject defined exclusively according to masculinist standards. Moreover, to ignore or actively deny the "feminine" (*however we might define this troubling word*) perpetuates dichotomous either/or thinking and the oppositional frameworks on which it relies. As Drucilla Cornell reminds us, "the repudiation of the feminine is part of the very 'logic' of a patriarchal order" (*Beyond Accommodation* 5). These options (to entirely accept or entirely reject) are too limited. We need additional possibilities; we need context-specific, tactical forms of mythmaking. Or perhaps, to borrow Jasbir Puar's words, we need "cyborgian-goddesses."[4]

And so, rather than entirely reject revisionist mythmaking's universal categories and broad, sweeping claims, I adopt a relational approach that puts Mary Daly in dialogue with Gloria Anzaldúa and Audre Lorde. By so doing, I hope to offer additional perspectives on revisionist mythmaking and transcultural universals. Among other things, then, Lorde's and Anzaldúa's revisionist mythmaking becomes a vehicle for the transformational identity politics I discussed in the previous chapter.

Back to the mother?
Post-structuralist critiques
of revisionist mythmaking

This section's title reflects a contentious twentieth-century debate among some feminists: the political (in)effectiveness of prepatriarchal origin stories and other forms of gender-specific revisionist mythmaking. (*Indeed, even the term* prepatriarchal *seems suspect to post-structuralist theorists!*) According to radical theologian Mary Daly, accounts of woman-centered creation stories can empower women in several interrelated ways. First, by positing a time *before* male-dominant, patriarchal societies, prepatriarchal feminist origin stories suggest the contingent nature of female oppression and thus can motivate women to challenge restrictive social systems. In Daly's exuberant words, women are inspired to "transcend the trickery of dogmatic deception," reject the "distorting mirror of Memory," and "recognize the Radiance of our own Origins" (*Pure Lust* 113). Second, by depicting nonpatriarchal egalitarian communities of women, these stories offer a new teleological perspective—alternative possibilities for how we might envision future social systems. And third, by replacing the (male) "God" with a (female) "Goddess," feminist revisionary myths reject the hierarchical worldview that elevates men (who are made in God's image) over women (who are not).

Perhaps not surprisingly, Daly associates her revisionist mythmaking with the importance of reclaiming and transforming language. Thus, for example, in *Beyond God the Father: Toward a Philosophy of Women's Liberation*, she argues that genuine selfhood—which she defines as each individual's ability to name the self, God, and the world—has been "stolen" from women. By defining God as "the Father" and human beings as "mankind," conventional language has effectively silenced women; it has denied their existence. She maintains that in order to move from silence and "nonbeing" to self-affirmation and speech, women must establish a new relationship to language, one acknowledging their presence by recognizing their "Female/Elemental divinity" within.

Many other twentieth-century theorists were far less sanguine about the usefulness of these attempts to move beyond "God the Father."[5] (*Indeed, if the limited scholarly references to anything related to religion or spirituality is a clue, this reluctance continues today; most contemporary feminist theorists would prefer to entirely ignore this issue, as well as others related to religion, spirituality, spirit, or the sacred, and focus only on so-called secular concerns.*)[6] For many post-structuralist theorists, subversive strategies that imply an "irrecoverable origin" (Butler 78) in a prehistorical past or an "innocent and all-powerful Mother" (Haraway 218) are far less effective than Daly and other radical feminists suggest. Judith Butler, Donna Haraway, and other feminist theorists have argued that mythic accounts of a maternal origin are exclusionary, divisive, and politically conservative, for they lead to simplistic identity politics based on restrictive, ethnocentric notions of female identity. Butler, for example, maintains that although feminist origin stories might be taken up and used in order to destabilize the dominant representational system, they generally replicate existing conditions: "The postulation of the 'before' within feminist theory becomes politically problematic when it constrains the future to materialize an idealized notion of the past or when it supports, even inadvertently, the reification of a precultural sphere of the authentic feminine. This recourse to an original or genuine femininity is a nostalgic and parochial ideal that refuses the contemporary demand to formulate an account of gender as a complex cultural construction" (36). In other words, feminists' attempts to recover or re-create "prepatriarchal" forms of women-centered communities inevitably rely on existing (which, for Butler, means phallocentric) definitions of "woman"; consequently, these revisionist-mythmaking feminists reject conventional gender categories only to establish other (equally restrictive) heterosexist binary oppositions between women and men. They remain trapped in status-quo thinking and therefore cannot address the ways gender is socially constructed in culturally specific ways. Moreover, Butler maintains that focusing on a time supposedly prior to or beyond contemporary socioeconomic-political conditions is escapist, and inhibits feminist analysis and action in the present.

Teresa de Lauretis takes a similar position. According to de Lauretis, there's no "going back to the innocence of 'biology'" or to biologically based descriptions of gender. She rejects essentialist definitions of women's identity, arguing that because gender is produced by a wide range of discursive practices, it cannot be described as a "natural" attribute, as "something originally existent in human beings" (2–3). Like Butler, she maintains that such descriptions draw on and thus strengthen normative phallocratic definitions of "woman," as well as the hierarchical male/female binary system. She, too, critiques what she dismissively describes as "some women's belief in a matriarchal past or a contemporary 'matristic' realm presided over by the Goddess, a realm of female tradition, marginal and subterranean and yet all positive and good, peace-loving, ecologically correct, matrilineal, matrifocal, non-Indo-European, and so forth; in short, a world untouched by ideology, class and racial struggle, television—a world untroubled by the contradictory demands and oppressive rewards of gender as I and surely those women, too, have daily experienced" (20—21).

Donna Haraway seems even more scornful of feminists' revisionist mythmaking in her classic essay, "Manifesto for Cyborgs." Rejecting the essentialist language and metaphysical assumptions often found in feminists' revisionary myths and religious-spiritual discourse, she claims that in our fragmented, postmodern world, "[i]t's not just that 'god' is dead; so is the 'goddess'" (81). She insists that all such "transcendental authorizations" lead to restrictive political agendas based on totalizing and imperialistic identity politics that prevent feminists and other social-justice activists from constructing effective coalitions in the sociopolitical, historical present. According to Haraway, "There is nothing about being 'female' that naturally binds women." Haraway takes her critique even further, to challenge our assumptions about biological sex: "There is not even such a state as 'being' female, itself a highly complex category constructed in contested sexual, scientific discourses and other practices" (72). Like de Lauretis and Butler, she challenges us to reject all naturalized identities and develop temporary strategic alliances based on situational choices.

As I demonstrated in the previous chapter, I, too, mistrust any version of identity politics founded on exclusionary accounts that elevate and homogenize "women's experience." Like Butler, de Lauretis, and Haraway, I question the political effectiveness of rallying around normative concepts of "Woman," or mythic-monolithic images of "*the* Goddess"; all too often such representations inadvertently reinstate phallocentric descriptions of "Womanhood" and reproduce heteronormative, racist, oversimplified gender systems.[7] To be perfectly honest, I cringe when I hear or read references to "*the* Goddess."[8] I avoid these types of feminist revisionist mythmaking, with their enormous sweeping statements about "women," their dichotomous gender structure that focuses exclusively on women—ignoring many, if not all, of the differences among women and entirely rejecting (at times even condemning or vilifying) men; their monolithic references to patriarchy; and so on. (*"I do not belong to these groups!" I want to shout. "Leave me out! You're not talking about me or my gods."*)

But to reject and condemn this revisionist mythmaking would be hypocritical—given my desire to develop nonoppositionality as a legitimate, valued scholarly approach. Moreover, I know from personal experience that the recognition of female and other nonmale gods can be empowering. To assume that we can (or even *should*) reject *all* origin myths, along with *all* references to "Woman," "goddess," or the "feminine," seems dismissive—not to mention highly unlikely. These categories have become so deeply ingrained in our personal and cultural meaning systems (*and possibly in our hearts, psyches, minds, and bodies*) that we cannot automatically reject them. Nor should we, because to do so simply reintroduces the binary thinking that locks us into various iterations of the status quo. And so, in this chapter I take a different, non-oppositional (*or semi-oppositional?*) approach.

Rather than entirely reject revisionist mythmaking, I adopt a relational perspective that sets Mary Daly in dialogue with Gloria Anzaldúa and Audre Lorde. The similarities between their discussions of feminist spiritualities and revisionist mythmaking are, at times, striking. Yet scholars almost never discuss these three people—one labeled "white" and the others "Chicana" and "Black"—in conjunction; instead, each is relegated to discrete categories of feminist thought based on genre, culture, academic discipline, and 'race'. At most, scholars use Lorde's well-known "Open Letter to Mary Daly" to criticize or dismiss Daly's attempt to invent new images of female identity as too eurocentric and therefore exclusionary to be effective. However, a relational approach offers us another, more generous lens with which to interpret Daly's work; this relational lens simultaneously enables us to re-examine Lorde's and Anzaldúa revisionary myths and thus more fully appreciate their innovative contributions. My goal is not to redeem Daly. (*She's not lost, not in need of redemption.*) Nor am I trying to say that Anzaldúa and Lorde are somehow "better" than this radical theologian. (*Although I do prefer them.*) Instead, I use this chapter as a laboratory, an experiment in relational dialogue, a hypothesis of sorts: I posit that revisionist mythmaking can demonstrate the possibility of writing the "feminine" in open-ended, nonexclusionary ways that revise previous notions of the universal. Rather than reject the possibility of universals, I hope to redefine (*or possibly enact?*) the universal in open-ended fluid ways. By so doing, I suggest and try to model another way of forging commonalities while enacting post-oppositional thought.

Locating themselves in the present yet going "back" to their indigenous Mesoamerican and West African mythic origins, Anzaldúa and Lorde invent new myths that both illustrate and extend Daly's call to move beyond "God the Father." Like Daly, Anzaldúa and Lorde redefine the past from their present perspectives, replacing patriarchal male-centered mythologies with self-affirming images of female identity. They develop metaphoric representations of Woman that neither erase culturally specific definitions nor erect rigid barriers between disparate racialized groups. Instead, their writings enact and in other ways affirm fluid, transcultural universals—ongoing cultural transmutations that they incorporate into their mythic metaphors of Woman. Just as the mestizaje transculturalism and the transcultural dialogues I discussed in chapter 2 represent profound, nonoppositional alternatives to hegemonic racial discourse and other forms of mono-thinking, so transcultural universals offer post-oppositional alternatives to the static, monolithic forms universals generally take. (*Rather than entirely reject all notions of the universal, I enter them, I occupy them from within.*) Flexible, open-ended, and polyvocal, transcultural universals enable us to redefine previously fixed pseudo-universals in context-specific ways.

Drawing on the dialogic elements of verbal art, Anzaldúa and Lorde use metaphoric language's performative effects and invite their readers to live out the "feminine" in new ways. They develop nondual epistemologies and embodied metaphysics that disrupt conventional boundaries between writer, reader, and text. Their transcultural affirmations of the "feminine" challenge readers to rethink our status-quo stories, the dominant-cultural sociopolitical inscriptions, the labels that define each person according to gender, ethnicity, sexuality, class, and other systems of difference. Destabilizing the restrictive networks of classification that inscribe us as racialized, engendered subjects, their transcultural universals open up psychic spaces where alterations in consciousness can occur. They create what Trinh Minh-ha describes as "a ground that belongs to no one, not even to the 'creator'" (*Woman* 71). Unlike conventional identity politics' foundationalist justifications, this "ground" represents nonessentialized, shifting locations where new forms of identity can occur. (*Transformational identity politics, as it were.*)

Language matters,
poet-shaman aesthetics

For Gloria Anzaldúa, metaphoric language has very specific physical, material effects.[9] In her metaphysics-aesthetics, words and matter are so deeply intertwined as to be inseparable. Thus in her brief introduction to the final section of *This Bridge Called My Back*, she asserts that "The change evoked on these pages is material as well as psychic. Change requires a lot of heat. It requires both the alchemist and the welder, the magician and the laborer, the witch and the warrior, the myth-smasher and the myth-maker" ("El Mundo Zurdo" 196). Words do not simply represent or point to externalized material reality in some correspondence-type mode. Words neither serve merely as a veil between ourselves and a more real (i.e., more tangibly material) world nor create our reality in some post-structuralist approach (i.e., the "linguistic turn" so frequently criticized in early-twenty-first century writings).[10] As do indigenous practitioners, Anzaldúa grounds herself in a metaphysics and ontology positing that words, images, and material things are intimately interwoven; the performative power of specific, carefully selected words *shifts* reality. Stories and metaphors are as real as tables, chairs, lightning, doorknobs, Kansas, the book you're holding in your hands, Catholicism, houses, rain, and rocks.[11]

Anzaldúa draws on mythic metaphors embedded in culturally specific oral traditions as she develops her transcultural universals. Thus she identifies her task as a writer with that of the Aztec *nahual*, or shaman: She is a "shape-changer" who uses language to reinvent herself, her readers, and her world. In *Borderlands/La Frontera* and again in her preface to *Making Face, Making Soul/ Haciendo Caras*, she insists that each reader is "the shaper of [her] flesh as well as of [her] soul."[12] Like Daly, Anzaldúa does not rely exclusively on academic arguments or western philosophical discourse to validate her truth claims concerning writing's transformational potential. Instead, she uses this ancient Náhuatl proverb and the relational worldview it represents to authorize, develop, and present her argument—an argument based on embodied metaphysical power, where the inner and outer dimensions of life are so intimately related as to be inseparable. For Anzaldúa, this interrelationship implies that all creative endeavors include a "spiritual, psychic component: synthesizing body, soul, mind, and spirit" ("Haciendo caras" xxiv). She describes writing as "making face, making soul" to underscore language's transformational power, its ability to alter the material-spiritual-psychic dimensions of reality.

Revisionist mythmaking plays an important role in Anzaldúa's transformational theory of language.[13] Look, for instance, at her discussion of Coatlicue, an ancient Mesoamerican creatrix, in *Borderlands/La Frontera* and "now let us shift." By (re)claiming and (re)interpreting this figure, Anzaldúa invents a mythic narrative where historical and contemporary issues of gender, culture, sex, nationalism, and class converge: As she traces the shifts in Coatlicue's story, from her high status in pre-Aztec myth—where she was depicted as an all-encompassing, multigendered divine being—to her current status as the demonic Serpent Woman, Anzaldúa charts the transition to increasingly male-dominated, hierarchical social structures that occurred when the indigenous Mesoamerican peoples were conquered by the Aztecs and Spaniards. Stripped of her all-inclusive cosmic powers, this god/dess[14]—who originally "contained and balanced the dualities of male and female, light and dark, life and death"—was doubly divided, first feminized then split into two: As Tlazolteotl/Coatlicue, she was banished to the underworld, where she became the embodiment of darkness, materiality, and female evil; and as Tontantsi/ Guadalupe, she was purified, christianized, "desexed," and transformed into the holy virgin mother (*Borderlands* 49).

As my use of the words "(re)claiming" and "(re)interpreting" with their bracketed prefixes suggests, Anzaldúa's revisionist mythmaking does not represent an attempt to be historically authentic. It is, rather, inventive. Anzaldúa is not digging through history (*and pre-history!*) in an effort to recover an accurate, factual representation of an ancient mythic figure worshiped centuries ago. Her description of Coatlicue's mythic transition (or, in biblical language, we might say "Fall") should not be read as the nostalgic desire to return to a utopian, gynecentric state of epistemological innocence—to what Haraway might skeptically dismiss as "a once-upon-a-time wholeness before language, before writing, before Man" ("Manifesto" 93). Nor does it imply what Butler might describe as a deterministic trajectory that authorizes the existing unjust conditions, "a necessary and unilinear narrative that culminates in, and thereby justifies, the constitution of the law" (*Gender Trouble* 36). Instead, Anzaldúa adopts and revises this Náhuatl mythic being in order to invent a multidimensional symbol—an autobiographical and culturally specific yet transcultural, transgendered figure synthesizing social critique with the invention of new ways of thinking: She develops a complex narrative that she calls the "Coatlicue state," associating Coatlicue's loss of elemental power both with the double consciousness she experiences as a non-Anglo woman in contemporary U.S. culture and with the hierarchical division between reason and intuition found in Cartesian-based knowledge systems.

At the personal level, Anzaldúa associates the Coatlicue state both with her own ambiguous position in contemporary U.S. culture and with her health crisis. As she explains in *Borderlands/La Frontera*, the opposing Mexican, Indian, and Anglo worldviews she has internalized lead to self-division and shame. On the one hand, she is drawn to nonrational Native traditions that validate the psychic, supernatural events she's experienced throughout her life; on the other hand, she has been trained to rely solely on reason and to dismiss such beliefs (as well as her personal experiences) as "pagan superstitions." These two modes of perception—"the two eyes in her head, the tongueless magical eye and the loquacious rational eye"—seem to be mutually exclusive; they are separated by "an abyss that no bridge can span" (67). Eschewing binary either/or thinking, Anzaldúa maintains that her willingness to embrace, rather than reject, the cultural ambiguities and immerse herself in the Coatlicue state activates an alternate mode of perception that synergistically combines rational and nonrational thought. Anzaldúa describes this synergistic energy as a "third element," which she names "mestiza consciousness." Drawing on her own experiences of alienation in the various cultures she interacts with, she explains that the new mestiza learns to live with conflicting Indian, Mexican, and Anglo worldviews "by developing a tolerance for contradictions, a tolerance for ambiguity. . . . She has a plural personality, she operates in a pluralistic mode—nothing is thrust out, the good the bad and the ugly, nothing rejected, nothing abandoned. Not only does she sustain contradictions, she turns the ambivalence into something else" (101).

Similarly, in "now let us shift" Anzaldúa uses her theory of the Coatlicue state to represent both events in her life and an agonistic stage in her theory of knowledge, which at this later point in her career she calls "the path of conocimiento."[15] Mixing autobiographical details with epistemological analysis, she narrates the chaotic reactions she experienced when diagnosed with type 1 diabetes. Self-denial, anger, and a willed unawareness, or "desconocimientos," battle themselves out within her, pushing her more deeply into despair. Significantly, she reacts nonoppositionally. Through conscious attention and mindfulness to this growing depression, she slowly achieves the glimmer of new insights within the abyss of anger and self-loathing:

> During the Coatlicue phase you thought you'd wandered off the path of conocimiento, but this detour is part of the path. You bodymindsoul is the hermetic vessel where transformation takes place. The shift must be more than intellectual. Escaping the illusion of isolation, you prod yourself to get out of bed, clean your house, then yourself. You light la virgen de Guadalupe candle and copal, and, with a bundle of yierbitas (ruda y yerba buena), brush the smoke down your body, sweeping away the pain, grief, and fear of the past that's been stalking you, severing the cords binding you to it. (554)[16]

As in *Borderlands/La Frontera*, Anzaldúa uses Coatlicue to develop her relational epistemology, a complex, holistic way of knowing that synergistically combines the physical and intellectual dimensions: "You realize you've severed mind from body and reversed the dichotomy—in the beginning you blamed the body for betraying you, now you blame your mind. Affirming they're not separate, you *begin* to own the bits of yourself you've disowned, take back the projections you've cast onto others, and relinquish your victim identity" (554, emphasis added). Significantly, Anzaldúa does not describe this insight as a final destination for her epistemology. The Coatlicue state is only one stage within a recursive, nonlinear seven-stage process.

Anzaldúa's fluid, mobile epistemology requires intellectual humility and the willingness to embrace uncertainty and change. Thus, in *Borderlands/La Frontera*, Anzaldúa indicates that mestiza consciousness does not represent a systematic, fully structured alternative to existing theories of knowledge. Instead, it offers new pathways that open up *within* our existing epistemological systems. For Anzaldúa, mestiza consciousness is not a final destination; it is, rather, an invitation to invent new forms of thought. She maintains that "[a] massive uprooting of dualistic thinking is the *beginning* of a long struggle" (102, emphasis added). Similarly, in "now let us shift," Anzaldúa describes conocimiento as an ongoing, spiraling process that cannot be charted in any definitive way. Its movement is unexpected, complicated, and, at times, quite messy:

> In all seven spaces you struggle with the shadow, the unwanted aspects of the self. Together, the seven stages open the senses and enlarge the breadth and depth of consciousness, causing internal shifts and external changes. All seven are present within each stage, and they occur concurrently, chronologically or not. Zigzagging from ignorance (desconocimiento) to awareness (conocimiento), in a day's time you may go through all seven stages, though you may dwell in one for months. You're never only in one space, but partially in one, partially in another, with nepantla occurring most often—as its own space and as the transition between each of the others. (545)

In Anzaldúa's epistemology, there is no single intellectual trajectory; no unitary correct form of thinking; no fixed, static Truths; no monolithic Universals. Both mestiza consciousness and conocimiento are permeable and open-ended; they include recursive movements among existing categories of meaning that defy fixed boundaries and final goals. The nondual energy Anzaldúa describes indicates an ongoing transformational process that continually breaks down the rigid, unitary elements in any new paradigm we construct. (*This process is painful, as "now let us shift" attests.*)

Anzaldúa associates her transformational epistemology with culturally specific oral traditions. In *Borderlands/La Frontera*, for example, she reinterprets Náhuatl metaphysical beliefs from her contemporary perspective and incorporates them into her theory of writing. This partial movement beyond "western" practices serves two interrelated purposes. First, by insisting that tribal cultures' shamanic traditions represent the development of sophisticated, well-integrated aesthetic, religious, and political systems, Anzaldúa exposes and resists the ethnocentric bias that dismisses native peoples' belief systems as "mere pagan superstition." According to Anzaldúa, precolonial Mesoamericans believed that art should be "metaphysical" yet communal, participatory, and intimately related to everyday life (89). Consequently, art played a vital role in people's social and spiritual existence by validating their lives and empowering them to bring about individual, collective, and cosmic change. Second, by incorporating this dialogic, performative tribal perspective into her theory of writing, Anzaldúa emphasizes (and authorizes) language's transformational role, its ability to revitalize individual and communal identities. Thus she describes her own work as "acts encapsulated in time, 'enacted' every time they are spoken aloud or read silently . . . as performances and not as inert and 'dead' objects (as the aesthetics of Western culture think of art works). Instead, the work has an identity; it is a 'who' or a 'what' and contains the presences of persons, that is, incarnations of gods or ancestors or natural and cosmic powers" (89). As "both a physical thing and the power that infuses it" (89), Anzaldúa's written texts are, as it were, a complex mixed breed; just as the new mestiza (*and, later, the nepantlera*) mediates between diverse cultures, her art synthesizes past, present, and future perspectives by mediating between political, personal, psychic, and spiritual dimensions of reality. Through this synthesis of apparently distinct categories of meaning, Anzaldúa insists on writing's transformational power. She describes her own work as a series of mind/body-altering processes, or "[t]hought shifts, reality shifts, gender shifts: one person metamorphoses into another in a world where people fly through the air, heal from mortal wounds. I am playing with my Self, I am playing with the world's soul, I am in dialogue between my Self and el espíritu del mundo. I change myself, I change the world" (93).

As these highly metaphoric descriptions of writing suggest, Anzaldúa draws on indigenous North American oral traditions and employs metaphors of shape-shifters and shamanism to support her contention that writing and other forms of art can physically, materially, psychically, and in other ways impact both writers and readers. Like the Aztec shamans whose interaction with unseen forces enabled them to transform themselves and their people, she explains, the mestiza writer is "nahual, an agent of transformation, able to modify and shake primordial energy and therefore able to change herself and others into turkey, coyote, tree or human." She describes her own writing practice as "carving bone . . . creating [her] own face, [her] own heart—a Náhuatl concept" to emphasize the ways in which writing enables her to redefine herself and her interactions with others (96–97). Similarly, in "Haciendo caras" she adopts a Náhuatl saying—"'[U]sted es el modeador de su carne tanto como el de su alma. You are the shaper of your flesh as well as of your soul'"—to emphasize her readers' ability to attain personal and collective agency (xxv).

By associating her theory of writing with the Aztec shamans' ability to negotiate and transform the apparent boundaries between spiritual and material worlds, Anzaldúa develops a theory of hybrid metaphors that unites visionary language with political intervention, creating a type of poet-shaman aesthetics.[17] She maintains that because "the spirit of the words moving in the body is as concrete as flesh and as palpable," metaphoric language can bridge the apparent gaps between writer and reader (*Borderlands* 93). In "Metaphors in the Tradition of a Shaman," she describes writing as a fluid process between the writer's body and the reader's mind. She explains that writers "attempt to put, in words, the flow of some of [their] internal pictures sounds, sensations, and feelings and hope that as the reader reads the pages these 'metaphors' would be 'activated' and live in her" (122). As in "Haciendo caras" and *Borderlands/La Frontera*, Anzaldúa defines herself as a "poet-shaman," a cultural healer or agent of change who uses metaphoric language to fight the diverse forms of oppression existing in contemporary North American societies. She describes the negative images, destructive stereotypes, and false information concerning oppressed groups as "dead metaphors" (122).

"Deadly metaphors" might be a better term, because these negative metaphors have powerful, deeply destructive personal and socioeconomic effects when they work their way into our self-images and worldviews, as they so often do. As psychologists' scholarship on stereotype threat has demonstrated, people who see themselves (or people in the social groups with which they identify) continually referred to in derogatory terms internalize these negative images and begin acting them out. The terms themselves can trigger the negative stereotypes. The stereotypes seep into us, poisoning our self-worldviews, subtly compromising our performances.[18] Anzaldúa insists that writers can replace such debilitating beliefs with "new metaphors": "Because we use metaphors as well yierbitas and curing stones to effect changes, we follow in the tradition of the shaman. Like the shaman, we transmit information from our consciousness to the physical body of another. If we're lucky we create, like the shaman, images that induce altered states of consciousness conducive to self-healing" (122). The poet-shaman Anzaldúa describes takes this transformational process even further: She makes what she thinks materialize in her readers. She "listen[s] to the words chanting" in her *own* body and attempts to inscribe them in the bodies of others (90).

According to Anzaldúa, then, metaphors can literally—physiologically and psychically—transform us; images communicate "with tissues, organs, and cells to effect change" ("Metaphors" 121). Words can transform our bodies, altering our physical states. As her phrase "making face, making soul" implies, she displaces the boundaries between spiritual, material, and textual worlds and destabilizes their conventional meanings. In her poet-shaman aesthetics, the rigid borders between writer, reader, and text dissolve: words have concrete physiological, ideological, and psychic effects as physical bodies are transformed into texts and texts into bodies. Not surprisingly, Anzaldúa views the writing process as multilayered conversations between author, world, readers, and text. In the introduction to her edited collection, *Making Face, Making Soul/Haciendo Caras*, for example, she describes her writing process as a "constant dialogue" between her selves, her readers, and the words on the computer screen: "Ultimately alone with only the hum of the computer, accompanied by all my faces (and often yours as well), the monitor's screen reflects back the dialogue among 'us.' I talk to myself. That's what writers do, we carry on a constant dialogue between language and hands and images, one or another of our identities trying desperately to get in a word, an image, a sound" (xxiv).[19]

In many ways, Anzaldúa's conversation between writer, readers, and text resembles the "journey of women becoming" (*Pure Lust* 1) that Daly enacts in her works. Take, for example, how she describes her use of language in her 1990 preface to *Gyn/Ecology*: "[T]he emergence of *Hag*-related words, as well as such Names as *Crone, Spinster, Harpy, Fury* and other New Words, was an integral part of the writing process, and when I spoke these aloud to women I was committing Acts of Be-Speaking. I was speaking the words into be-ing. Nor was I alone in this process. Wild women Heard me into Be-Speaking, and together we were forging a Metalanguage that could break through the silence and sounds of phallocratic babble" (xx, original emphasis). As Daly's emphasis on language's creative power indicates, she too insists that words can have concrete, shape-shifting material effects.[20] She rejects the conventional western dichotomy between language and action as inaccurate and maintains that there is "no authentic separation" between them. Similarly, in *Pure Lust*, she associates metaphoric language—or what she describes as "Be-Witching metaphors" (405)—with alternate modes of perception that she invites her readers to share. She explains that the images she employs "stir the atmosphere E-motionally, awakening ancient connections not only with each other, but with winds, waters, rocks, trees, birds, butterflies, bats, cats, stars" (405). When readers are moved by these "Be-Witching metaphors," they experience a transmutation in consciousness that dissolves mind/body, human/nonhuman, and self/world divisions. No longer confined by the paralyzing implications of patriarchal language, they "break out of linguistic prisons" (26) and begin defining reality for themselves.

Both Daly and Anzaldúa use metaphoric writing to activate language's performative effects, its ability to bring about individual and collective change. Yet it's easy to overlook the performative dimensions of Daly's writing. Focusing on the specific metaphors she employs, scholars generally assume that she attempts to change only individual words—not underlying structures; thus, they conclude that her linguistic tactics are ultimately ineffective. For example, Meaghan Morris argues that Daly replaces one form of (phallocentric) hierarchical thinking with another, equally hierarchical form (31–35). Such accusations, while understandable, oversimplify Daly's tactics, and Daly herself cautions readers against this superficial use of language. Both in her "Original Reintroduction" to *Beyond God the Father* and again in her "New Galactic Introduction" to *Gyn/Ecology*, she insists that it's not enough to replace the word "God" with "Goddess."[21] In order to be effective, this shift must occur in a larger context, which she describes as a "profound alteration of consciousness and behavior—that is, of the *context* in which words are spoken" (*Beyond*, xix, original emphasis). For Daly, this new context is postpatriarchal and entails a twofold process: first, the recognition that existing forms of discourse have been (mis)shaped by male-dominated pseudo-universal interests; and second, each woman's decision to begin naming reality for herself. As she explains in *Beyond God the Father*, "To exist humanly is to name the self, the world, and God. The 'method' of the evolving spiritual consciousness of women in nothing less than this beginning to speak humanly—a reclaiming of the right to name. The liberation of language is rooted in the liberation of ourselves. . . . [T]he liberation of language from its old context implies a breakthrough to new semantic fields" (8).

Perhaps not surprisingly, however, Daly's exclusive focus on the gendered implications of this contextual shift can prevent her critics from recognizing the "new semantic fields" that Daly tries to enact with her words. Her claims can seem so large, so universal, and so literal, that scholars (when they do not ignore her entirely), stop too soon and react to the words' surface-level meaning (*which is often reinforced through the many capital letters and bold inflexible claims*). Here's where reading Daly in dialogue with Anzaldúa can be useful. At a local level, by putting these theorists into conversation, we can appreciate (*or at least speculate on*) the performative dimensions of Daly's language. At a larger, more theoretical level, by comparing Daly's universalized noncultural references to women with Anzaldúa's culturally specific universalizing claims, we obtain additional insights into the possibility of creating transcultural universals.

By repeatedly incorporating a marked, culturally specific dimension into her theory of metaphor, Anzaldúa more persuasively demonstrates the radical possibilities opened up by performative language. Look, for instance, at her use of mythic metaphors to emphasize the transformational dimensions of her own writing process. In *Borderlands/La Frontera* she draws on revisionist myth to underscore the intense self-exploration she requires as a writer. When she writes, she explains, she must "jump blindfolded into the abyss of her own being and there in the depths confront her face, the face underneath the mask" (96). By identifying this hidden "face" both as the "alien other" and as her own "inner self, . . . the godwoman . . . Antigua, mi Diosa, the divine force within, Coatlicue . . . Coatlalopeuh-Guadalupe" (72), Anzaldúa displaces the conventional boundaries between inner/outer, subject/object, and self/other. She locates the "alien other"—the objectified outsider—within herself and dissolves writerly/readerly/textual borders. Writing becomes a series of perpetual rebirths in which her "soul . . . is constantly remaking and giving birth to itself through [her] body" (94).

Anzaldúa's equation of writing with perpetual physical/spiritual self-(re) birth is disruptive. As Trinh observes, "a subject who points to him/her/itself as a subject-in-process . . . is bound to upset one's sense of identity—the familiar distinction between the Same and the Other, since the latter is no longer kept in a recognizable relation of dependence, deviation, or appropriation" (*Woman* 48). By disassembling the image of a monolithic self and destabilizing the boundaries between writer, reader, and text, Anzaldúa's transcultural revisions challenge readers to redefine their own borders and begin (re)writing themselves. Because she believes that "[n]othing happens in the 'real' world unless it happens in the image in our heads" (*Borderlands* 87), Anzaldúa develops metaphoric configurations of psychic and political power such as the Borderlands, mestiza consciousness, "putting Coyolxauhqui together," and the Coatlicue state itself.[22] These graphic metaphors are performative; they push readers to imaginatively reconstruct their worldviews and envision alternate ways of living.[23]

Using mythic metaphors that "concretize the spirit and etherealize the body" (*Borderlands* 97), Anzaldúa builds a new culture, una cultura mestiza, el mundo surdo. Her words incite us to actively create a complex mixed-breed coalition of "queers"—outsiders who, because of ethnicity, gender, sexuality, class position, nationality, religion, or whatever, attempt to transform dominant cultural inscriptions. Although Daly's new culture is not as inclusive as Anzaldúa's, she too uses mythic metaphors that break down the boundaries between the spiritual and material realms and invites readers to create revolutionary communities.[24]

Mythic women and redefined selves

Like Anzaldúa, Audre Lorde draws on precolonial mythic figures and wisdom traditions, associating her belief in writing's transformational power with her own culturally specific nonwestern worldview.[25] In her interview with Claudia Tate, she defines art pragmatically, as "the use of living," and explains that, whereas a European worldview would depict life as a series of conflicts, "African tradition deals with life as an experience to be lived. In many respects, it is much like the Eastern philosophies in that we see ourselves as part of a life force. . . . We live in accordance with, in a kind of correspondence with the rest of the world as a whole" (qtd. in Tate 112).[26] As Lorde herself points out, this approach to life is not uniquely African (*and let's not forget that "African" itself encompasses many diverse peoples and cultural traditions*). Yet by attributing her holistic worldview to her African ancestry she subtly emphasizes the political implications of her work. According to Patricia Hill Collins, black U.S. women activists' (re-)creation of African cultural traditions has enabled them successfully to resist the dominant society's attempts to destroy their sense of community: "By conserving and recreating an Afrocentric worldview women . . . undermine oppressive institutions by rejecting the anti-Black and anti-female ideologies they promulgate" (*Black Feminist Thought* 144). I see Lorde's revisionist mythmaking as an important dimension of this political activism. As she incorporates Yoruban and Dahomean orisha, or spiritual forces, into her poetry, fiction, and prose, Lorde simultaneously reclaims and invents a gynecentric tradition that has been almost entirely erased by Judeo-Christian and Euro-American cultural beliefs.[27]

This mythological erasure parallels the experiences of historical and contemporary African American women who are dehumanized—both by the dominant U.S. culture and by their local communities—through a series of overwhelmingly negative stereotypes (or what Anzaldúa would call "dead metaphors") such as the matriarch, the welfare mother, and Jezebel (the sexually promiscuous woman).[28] As Collins notes, although these doubly oppressive images make each woman "invisible as a fully human individual," many African American women have transformed their status as "invisible Other" into a source of tremendous inner strength (94). By developing a "private, hidden space of . . . consciousness," they have successfully defied the externally imposed labels and maintained their authority to define themselves (92–93). Indeed, one of Collins's main arguments throughout *Black Feminist Thought* is that African American women's ability to create unique self-expressed standpoints, or ways of knowing based on their personal experiences as black U.S. women, has been essential to their survival. However, because they often use a doubled consciousness and mask their inward resistance with outward conformity, this inner dimension of their lives has received little recognition (91). As Collins suggestively notes, "far too many black women remain motionless on the outside . . . but inside?" (93, original ellipses).

Lorde uses revisionist mythmaking to embody and in other ways externalize the "inside ideas" Collins describes as a hallmark of black U.S. women's resistance to dominant groups. In Lorde's work, West African mythic images function as vehicles for her transcultural vision, enabling her to establish new definitions of womanhood, definitions that affirm personally and culturally specific components of her own black female identity yet go beyond this affirmation to offer all women (*and quite possibly some men*) alternative models of subject formation. By drawing on her personal experiences and expressing her own self-defined standpoints through the figures of Aido Hwedo, Seboulisa, and other Yoruban/Fon orisha, Lorde critiques previous images of womanhood modeled on European beauty standards and social roles, creates positive role models for other black women, and offers readers of all cultural/ ethnic backgrounds new ways to perceive themselves and new ways to act. It's this trajectory from "inside ideas" to outer forms that Lorde refers to in the interview with Tate when she describes her attempt to develop a voice "for as many people . . . who need to hear what I have to say—who need to use what I know." When she writes, she explains, she "speak[s] from the center of consciousness, from the *I am* out to the *we are* and then out to the *we can*" (qtd. in Tate 105, original emphasis).

Lorde's "we" is performative; it enables her to establish a personal/collective voice and an intensely self-reflective, relational epistemology she invites her readers (*of any color, culture, sexuality, gender, etc.*) to adopt. In her well-known essay, "Uses of the Erotic," Lorde locates this "nonrational knowledge" in a "deeply female and spiritual plane" and describes it as "the erotic—the sensual—those physical, emotional, and psychic expressions of what is deepest and strongest and richest within each of us" (*Sister Outsider* 56). Like Anzaldúa's theories of mestiza consciousness and conocimiento, or Daly's Realizing reason, Lorde's theory of the "erotic" represents a nondual, transformational mode of thought that works with language's agentic power and performative effects to bring about personal, collective, and societal change. Lorde maintains that those who acknowledge their "erotic knowledge" gain access to a previously unrecognized source of wisdom, "an incredible reserve of creativity and power" with which to transform themselves and their world (*Sister Outsider* 37, 56). As she explains in the interview with Tate, the erotic serves an interpretive function enabling us to develop new frameworks for self-definition and social transformation—"new ways of understanding our experiences. This is how new visions begin, how we begin to posit a future nourished by the past. This is what I mean by matter following energy, and energy following feeling. Our visions begin with our desires" (qtd. in Tate 107). As this transition from feeling to energy to matter implies, Lorde's theory of the erotic represents an attempt to interweave material and nonmaterial dimensions of life. Just as Anzaldúa's mestiza consciousness/conocimiento and Daly's Realizing reason enable them to synthesize spiritual, political, and material issues, Lorde's theory of the erotic enables her to integrate her Afrocentric spirituality and a vibrational metaphysics with social protest and cultural change.[29]

Lorde's theory of the erotic represents an innovative epistemological process that subverts status-quo stories by affirming previously devalued ways of knowing. This synthesis of emotional energy with rational thought implicitly challenges the Cartesian mind/body dualism, the commonly accepted belief that ideas and insights arise exclusively from mental processes. Like several contemporary post-structuralists, Lorde replaces this binary knowledge system with an embodied theory of knowing that posits an affective foundation for thought.[30] In her epistemology, "thinking" represents an intimate, indivisible connection between body and mind. Ideas and insights have their source in physical, as well as intellectual, experiences. Locating this emotionally charged mode of perception within every individual, Lorde develops a complex theory of relational autonomy and personal agency. She maintains that

> when we begin to live from within outward, in touch with the power of the erotic within ourselves, and allowing that power to inform and illuminate our actions upon the world around us, then we begin to be responsible to ourselves in the deepest sense. For when we begin to recognize our deepest feelings, we begin to give up, of necessity, being satisfied with suffering and self-negation, and with the numbness which so often seems like their only alternative in our society. Our acts against oppression become integral with self, motivated and empowered from within. (*Sister Outsider* 58)

As this synergistic trajectory between deep feeling and external action indicates, Lorde associates her theory of the erotic with an agent-centered collective subjectivity fluidly uniting inner direction with outward change.

Lorde uses revisionist mythmaking to create and convey her transformational epistemology. By identifying herself with Yemanja, Oshun, Oya, and other Yoruban/Fon orisha, she creates new-yet-old myths enabling her to embody her erotic way of knowing into a complex self-naming process that combines the rejection of negative images with the invention of new individual and communal identities.[31] In "October," for example, she calls on Seboulisa to infuse her vision with power (*Chosen Poems* 108). By aligning herself with this Yoruban orisha, Lorde synthesizes language with action and memory with myth. She replaces the destructive stereotypes of Jezebel with an African-inspired tradition of strong women capable of transforming themselves and their world. Again in "The Winds of Orisha" Lorde borrows from Yoruban myth to invent new images of female power. In this poem, she uses revisionist mythmaking to affirm her identity as a black woman warrior poet and lover of women. She creates an extended family of divine female figures, including Yemanja, mother of all the orisha; Oshun, orisha of beauty and love; and Oya, orisha of destruction and change, who Lorde describes as both her sister and her daughter. By aligning herself and her work as a writer in such intimate fashion with these West African spiritual forces, Lorde underscores the importance of her task, as well as her own creative power. Like Oya, whose power can erode and destroy huge segments of land, Lorde's words are forceful, transformative, and dangerous. And, by describing a sexual interchange between herself and Oshun, she affirms her own lesbian-identified, embodied erotic knowledge: "the beautiful Oshun and I lie down together / in the heat of her body truth my voice comes stronger." As this fluid shift from the orisha's "body truth" to the poet's voice suggests, Lorde's revisionist myth enacts the erotic. She depicts an embodied, transformational way of knowing where "[i]mpatient legends speak through [her] flesh / changing this earths [*sic*] formation / spreading" (*Chosen Poems* 48–49).

As she reinvents strong female images drawn from Yoruban and Fon mythic systems, Lorde invests her personal insights with collective, ethnic-specific meaning. Karla Holloway makes a similar point in her study of West African and African American women writers' use of nonwestern mythic material. As Holloway demonstrates, by incorporating metaphoric ancestral and goddess figures into their work, contemporary black women writers can create gendered, culture-specific self-definitions and worldviews. In their work, West African mythology becomes a cultural-linguistic bridge and foundation, a "meta-matrix for all uses of language and the primary source of a literature that would recover a historical voice that is at once sensual, visceral, and real" (107). Given the brutal history of colonization and enslavement, women writers of the diaspora cannot physically reclaim the diverse African cultures—the "language[s], religion[s], political independence, [and] economic polic[ies]"—violently ripped away during the Middle Passage and slavery; however, their revisionary myths enable them "spiritually" to re-member and reconstruct their cultural pasts (20).

Although Holloway seems to imply a literal recovery of the past (*which, I contend, would be impossible*), her emphasis on the interconnections between mythic metaphors, voice, and "spiritual memory" (20) offers a useful lens with which to examine Lorde's poetry and revisionist mythmaking more generally. In *The Black Unicorn*, Lorde's collection of poems thematically unified by references to Yoruban and Dahomean orisha, mythology functions as a "meta-matrix" of sorts, which Lorde uses to invent culture- and gender-specific voices. In the first section, Lorde reshapes West African myth to define herself as a black woman warrior poet. Throughout the remaining sections, she enlarges this original definition and encompasses a network of mythic, historic, contemporary, and imaginary women and men extending from the Yoruban orisha—through the ancient Dahomean Amazons, her family, friends, and female lovers—to the "mothers sisters daughters / girls" she has "never been" (48). Her use of Yoruban and Dahomean myth enables her to create what Holloway might describe as a basis for "the community's shared meanings [and] interactions with both the spiritual and the physical worlds" (31). With these revised West African mythic figures, Lorde challenges and in other ways intervenes in existing systems of gendered meaning and dichotomous self/other thought.

Throughout *The Black Unicorn*, Lorde uses revisionist mythmaking both to critique existing mainstream and black-nationalist definitions of Woman and to invent new definitions that more accurately reflect her own experiences as a woman of African descent and her own future desires. Replacing European-based, masculine images of a benign Mother Goddess with metaphors of Yoruban/Fon orisha, she exposes the limitations in western ethnocentric concepts of womanhood, challenges nationalist concepts of Black identity, and develops alternative models of female identity formation that begin with a specific cultural location yet move outward. Lorde's revisionist mythmaking challenges other negative status-quo stories about female identity, as well. In "A Woman Speaks," she spurns the image of "womanly" power as a gentle nurturing force and warns readers that she is powerful, "treacherous," and angry, filled with "old magic" and "new fury" (5–6). And, like Daly's "Unfolding Nature" (*Pure Lust* 336), Lorde's metaphoric women combine transcendence with immanence. In "The Women of Dan Dance with Swords in Their Hands," she subverts the dualistic notion of a transcendent deity—a disembodied spiritual power that exists elsewhere, in a nonphysical, supernatural place—by declaring that her power, although divine, is neither otherworldly nor natural: she "did not fall from the sky," nor does she descend gently "like rain." Instead, she likens herself to an Amazon warrior woman, dancing with a sword in her hand (*Black Unicorn* 14–15).

For Daly, as well, revisionist mythmaking offers a vehicle for the invention of alternative models of individual and collective female identity. Take, for example, her discussion in *Pure Lust* of the Archimage, or "the Muse within" (90). According to Daly, "The true *Archimage behind* the simulators/reversers . . . is the Great Original Witch, who is in women and all Elemental creatures. As an Original Act of Exorcism, of dis-spelling the archi-magi's bad magic, Lusty women can reclaim the name *Archimage*, Naming the fact that she is the Witch within our Selves. She is a verb, and she is verbal—a Namer, a Speaker—the Power within who can Name away the archetypes that block the ways/words/ of Metabeing" (86–87, original emphasis). In many ways, this Archimage functions analogously to Lorde's erotic, for it provides women with an inner source of transformative power enabling them to rename themselves and their world. Thus Daly insists that when women gain access to their inner "Great Original Witch," they acquire new forms of personal and communal agency empowering them to transcend patriarchal culture's "dogmatic deceptions" (113) and reestablish cross-cultural communities of women, or what she describes as "a Cosmic Commonality, a tapestry of connectedness which women as Websters/Fates are constantly weaving. The weaving of the tapestry is the Realizing of a dream, which Adrienne Rich has Named 'The Dream of a Common Language'" (26–27). According to Daly, this "Dream" is already a reality—the "Real Presence—that shines through appearances" (113). But she stipulates that in order to recognize this already-existing "Real Presence," women must awaken this Archimage—the "root of connectedness in the female Elemental Race" (87)—within themselves.

There is, however, an important difference between the Archimage Daly describes and Lorde's mythic women: Daly's metaphoric Woman seems almost to eschew the culturally specific dimensions found in Lorde's work. As her references to "female Elemental Race" and "Cosmic Commonality" imply, Daly often uses highly generalized singular terms (*and lots of Capital Letters*) in her attempt to create cross-cultural communities of women, or what she describes in her "New Intergalactic Introduction" to *Gyn/Ecology* as "biophilic Bonding with women of *all races and classes,* under *all the varying oppressions* of patriarchy" (xxxi, emphasis added). Significantly, Daly's statement seems to indicate that she does not intentionally *ignore* differences among women. Indeed, at times she seems to intentionally acknowledge these differences. Moreover, her "Great Original Witch" could even be seen as a culturally specific mythic image, tied to earlier Celtic traditions; however, Daly herself does not underscore this possible connection. Rather, she uses this Witch as an unmarked category to unify all women into a single originary "Elemental Race," a gynecentric form of "Metabeing" that supersedes the many differences among women; it is "a metaphysical way of Naming forth and Naming faith in this common bonding of Lusty women. For *Metabeing* names the Elemental participation in Powers of Being which is the source of authentic female bonding" (*Pure Lust* 27, original emphasis).

Daly's work demonstrates that the desire to forge commonalities, when expressed through overly generalized statements or images (*sameness!*), can backfire and create divisions rather than connections. (*How ironic! How sad.*)

By erasing the cultural specificity of this image, Daly inadvertently normalizes the generic ('white') norm and thus erases other types of cultural specificities. My point here is not Daly's choice of mythic figures. The problem is not that her "Great Original Witch" has its roots in European traditions but rather that Daly does not openly associate her Witch specifically with these or with any other culturally specific traditions. In her attempt to include all women, she begins with and relies too heavily on an unmarked universal. She might be trying to embrace all women; however, she inadvertently closes out those who cannot identify with an unmarked ('white') norm (*as well as those who react negatively to the extreme exclusion of men*). This attempt to generate commonalities among all women by positing versions of sameness resembles the misguided efforts I discussed in chapter 1. Attempts to create commonalities fail when *commonality* is confused with *sameness* and, in the desire for community, gives only superficial acknowledgement to difference.

Although Lorde (like Daly) works to create transcultural communities of women, her approach is quite different. She begins with the culturally specific (such as Yoruban/Fon belief systems) and moves outward, remetaphorizing female identity and womanhood in ways that are culturally specific yet nonexclusive. Thus, for example, in her letter to Daly she associates Mawulisa, Yemanja, and other orisha with "the female bonding of African women" but maintains that these "old traditions of power" are available to "*all* women who do not fear the revelation of connection to themselves." She invites Daly to acknowledge this connection, to "re-member what is dark and ancient and divine within yourself that aids your speaking" (96–97, emphasis added). Though it might seem contradictory, it's these culturally specific contexts that enable Lorde to go beyond the particular and create transcultural, transgendered communities that neither ignore nor reinforce the many differences among us.

Similar statements can be made about Anzaldúa. She, too, uses culturally specific mythic metaphors that destabilize monolithic conceptions of female identity and create transcultural, transgendered communities.[32] But how do these movements from the particular to the transcultural occur? And what makes Anzaldúa's and Lorde's broad, potentially universalizing claims more effective for many readers than Daly's? After all, Anzaldúa, Daly, and Lorde *all* employ universalizing discourse to generate new bonds among women from diverse backgrounds, yet only Daly has come under intense criticism for creating exclusionary, pseudo-universal concepts of female identity.[33] Although these issues require far more detailed exploration than I can provide in this chapter, we find important clues in the various forms their universalism takes.

Transcultural universals

By definition, the term *universal* should be all-inclusive; for example, if we talk about universal attributes of humankind, we should be talking about attributes shared by all human beings—everyone, from all times, locations, and so on. However, as a number of scholars have observed, all too often such supposedly broad universals are defined too restrictively, in culturally, regionally, and/or historically specific ways. Take, for example, how the concept of a universal reason—defined in Enlightenment-based terms as an unbiased, objective intellectual faculty and method of thought potentially available to all human beings—facilitated colonialism, where Europeans defined this supposedly universal mode of thinking as superior to all other epistemologies and used it as a lens and measurement (*a battering ram of sorts*) with which to justify their exploitation and conquest of non-European peoples and regions, who they defined as intellectually (and therefore culturally) underdeveloped and inferior. As Anna Lowenhaupt Tsing explains in her ethnographic study of global connections, "In the context of colonial expansion, universalism was the framework for a faith in the traveling power of reason: Only reason could gather up the fragments of knowledge and custom distributed around the world to achieve progress, science, and good government. In the matrix of colonialism, universal reason became the mark of temporally dynamic and spatially expansive forms of knowledge and power. Universal reason, of course, was best articulated by the colonizers. In contrast, the colonized were characterized by particularistic cultures; here, the particular is that which cannot grow" (9). This "universal reason" was less all-encompassing than the European colonizers could have assumed, for it was shaped by the experiences and values of its creators—elite European men (*and, possibly, a few women*).[34] I describe these narrow versions of the universal as "pseudo-universals," in order to underscore the extremely limited nature of their universalizing claims.

Like the self-enclosed individualisms I explored in chapter 2, pseudo-universals generally have their source in an unacknowledged ethnocentric definition of the human that excludes far more people than it includes.[35] (And, of course, these definitions stop with the human and seem not even to consider the nonhuman world!) Pseudo-universals are monologic, imposing one standard on all human beings and positing (*insisting on!*) a narrow, singular, absolute Truth. Rather than represent a shared category embracing all people, pseudo-universals cannot account for the many differences among us. Such restrictive concepts of the universal are not benign (*just ask the many peoples decimated by the überreasoning European colonizers*), for they dehumanize and in other ways delegitimize those whose epistemologies do not fit.

While it's tempting to reject all forms of universalism as too dangerous and limited to be liberatory or in any other ways useful for social-justice goals, to do so would be short-sighted. Such automatic rejection just flips the script and thus reinforces the oppositional structures that undergird the status quo. More specifically for my argument in this chapter, to reject all universals overlooks the possibility that some universals might do useful (*progressive, transformational, bridge-building*) work in the world. Universals are a necessary (non)fiction. As Ernesto Laclau argues, the universal represents "an empty but ineradicable place," a never attainable yet always necessary space that mobilizes social actors, providing them with new horizons of the possible (157). Universals do not exist—if we define them in monolithic, absolute, all-encompassing, one-size-fits-all fashion, like the conquering universalizing reason described above. Yet sometimes we need the energy and vision universals can provide. Of course, the universals we really need are more fluid, contextual, and therefore malleable—or what Tsing describes as "hybrid, transient, and involved in constant reformulation through dialogue" (9). As Tsing notes, universalisms do important work in the world:

> Liberal universals mix and meld with the universals of science, world religions (especially Christianity and Islam), and emancipatory philosophies including Marxism and feminism. Moreover, the embrace of universals is not limited to just one small section of the globe. The West can make no exclusive claim to doctrines of the universal. Radical thinkers in Europe's colonies long ago expanded Enlightenment universals to argue that the colonized should be free, thus establishing doctrines of universal freedom at the base of Third World nationalisms. . . . This brings to light a deep irony: Universalism is implicated in both imperial schemes to control the world and liberatory mobilizations for justice and empowerment. (9)

The transcultural universals I explore in this chapter are in many ways analogous to the inspirational universalisms Tsing describes. They are contextually specific, flexible, and open to change.

In their attempts to develop inspirational, transcultural universals, Anzaldúa, Daly, and Lorde use revisionist mythmaking (*among other tactics*). By appropriating and subverting Enlightenment-based concepts of the (masculine) universal, they invent new universals that they invite their readers to adopt. Yet Daly's universals stop too soon. Her universalized representations of Woman can be so abstract, so sweeping in their claims, so ahistorical, and so absolute—so monolithic and unitary, as it were—that they strip away meaningful context and thus function to exclude many women (*not to mention all men!*).

I attribute the limitations in Daly's universalizing attempts to the limitations in her engagements with differences among women, her exclusionary binary-oppositional gendered framework, and her ethnocentric lens. Unlike Anzaldúa and Lorde, who often focus on the differences among women (*and, sometimes, men*) but define these differences in non-oppositional terms (as differentials), Daly seems to define *difference* as *deviation* and, consequently, overlooks the role that differences among women can play in redefining our understanding of the universal. She uses references to specific ethnic/cultural traditions too casually, only to highlight what she sees as all women's shared "Elemental" power, a universal gynecentric form of sameness transcending the many differences between women.[36] To be sure, Daly does not entirely ignore the differences among women. However, she seems to regard these differences as obstacles to community building and transformation. Thus, for example, in *Pure Lust* she gives a general (*and rather abstract*) acknowledgment of the many differences among women, but she quickly leaps over these differences to focus on what she sees as women's sameness: "it is clear that Lusty women are profoundly different from each other. Not only are there ethnic, national, class and racial differences that shape our perspectives, but there are also individual and cross-cultural differences of temperament. . . . But there is also above, beyond, beneath all this a Cosmic Commonality. The word *Metabeing* is a metaphysical way of Naming forth and naming faith in this common bonding of Lusty women. For *Metabeing* names the Elemental participation in Powers of Being which is the source of authentic female bonding" (26–27, original emphasis). In this passage, differences among women might be profound, but they are much less important than the "Cosmic Commonality" (*which for Daly seems to function more like a Cosmic SAMENESS*). Ironically, then, Daly's universality, with its primary focus on women's commonality-defined-as-sameness, can function in exclusionary ways, for it compels readers to undergo a potentially restrictive process of normalization. It can be difficult for those readers who do not define themselves as part of the unmarked norm to identify with Daly's universalized woman.

This normalizing process goes beyond external behavior and requires individuals to see themselves in a specific way. As Etienne Balibar explains, "Normality is not the simple fact of adopting customs and obeying rules or laws: it means internalizing representations of the 'human type' or the 'human subject' (not exactly an essence, but a norm and a standard behavior) in order to be recognized as a person in its full right, to become *présentable* (fit to be seen) in order to be represented" (63, original emphasis). To enter Daly's "Cosmic Commonality," each woman must identify with Daly's "Lusty women" and relinquish or in other ways downplay any claims to the particular that do not conform to the universal feminine Daly describes. Those who cannot or will not fit into her description are excluded or exclude themselves. In short, Daly's universalism interpellates readers into a singular subject position. Perhaps motivated by a strong desire to create connections among all women, Daly downplays the ways differences shape women's identities and implies that gender, in itself, offers women an adequate grounds for "authentic female bonding." Her assertion of an undifferentiated "*Metabeing*" prevents dialogue and revision: the common ground already exists; there is no space to redefine it according to individual desires and needs.[37] Daly forces gender to do too much work; however, gender is shot through with differences, which she too often overlooks.

Whereas Daly relies on a gender-specific universal that transcends differences among women, Anzaldúa and Lorde do not. Instead, they create transcultural universals that negotiate between sameness, particularity, and commonality. This negotiation serves two purposes. First, it enables them to redefine the universal in context-specific, open-ended, potentially dialogic ways. Although they incorporate the culturally specific into their universals, they do not simply universalize the particular (which is, in a sense, what Daly does as she leans too heavily on unacknowledged European-based myths and ideas). Instead, they pluralize the universal, creating a variety of culturally specific forms that coexist in dynamic tension and interaction. This dynamic co-existence makes further change—further transformations of the universal—possible. By moving partially outside western, Eurocentric symbolic ,and mythic systems, Anzaldúa and Lorde acquire additional material that they use dialogically, as they develop their complex aesthetics, ethics, metaphysics, ontologies, and epistemologies. To borrow Lorde's words, in their writings difference becomes a "creative force for change" (*Sister Outsider* 45–46). Second, their negotiations between sameness, particularity, and commonality offer readers a variety of subject positions within their transcultural universals. If we don't identify with one version, we'll probably identify with another. They create inclusionary communities of women (and often men). Individual women can acknowledge their sense of differences(s) from others without feeling excluded. It is, in fact, almost the reverse: They can use differences(s) to redefine the existing universal.[38]

Anzaldúa's and Lorde's transcultural universals and revisionist mythmaking illustrate some of the additional forms that transformational identity politics can take. By highlighting and inventing gynecentric, culturally specific traditions, they redefine ethnic/racial categories.[39] And, by incorporating these redefined categories into their marked representations of female identity and power, Anzaldúa and Lorde create potentially transformational metaphors that can redefine and in other ways alter their readers' ethnic/racial identities, as well. If, as a number of contemporary theorists suggest, each subject is composed of multiple parts and located at the intersection of diverse—sometimes overlapping, sometimes conflicting—discourses, no identity is or ever can be entirely stable and fixed. As Chantal Mouffe states, there is always "a certain degree of openness and ambiguity in the way the different subject-positions are articulated" (35). This potential openness to redefinition makes personal and collective change possible. However, radical social change requires radical transformation, not simply different combinations: "If the task of radical democracy is indeed to deepen the democratic revolution and to link together diverse democratic struggles, such a task requires the creation of new subject-positions that would allow the common articulation, for example, of antiracism, antisexism, and anticapitalism. These struggles do not spontaneously converge, and in order to establish democratic equivalences, a new 'common sense' is necessary, which would transform the identity of different groups so that the demands of each group could be articulated with those of others according to the principle of democratic equivalence" (43). While I question the long-term effectiveness of organizing new subject-positions around *anti*-based oppositional movements, as Mouffe seems to suggest, I share her belief that political unities must be consciously developed through a process of articulation.[40] We—no matter who "we" are—do not automatically unite on the basis of shared "natural" traits. Instead, shared identities must be created.

Through their revisionist mythmaking Anzaldúa and Lorde invent new forms of ethnically-marked-yet-transculturally-shared identities. Their focus on particularity—seen, for example, in their use of culturally specific female mythic images—energizes this transformational process. In psycholinguistic terms, because their representations of Wo/man occur within metaphor, on an imaginary level, they potentially destabilize readers' ego-ideal identifications, the master signifiers or symbols that shape each person's self-conceptions in pivotal ways. When western readers (of any background or gender) identify the "feminine" in ourselves with the "feminine" in Coatlicue, Yemanja, or the other mythic figures Anzaldúa and Lorde employ, we can experience a "metaphoric transference."[41] That is, we encounter a slippage within our current definitions of gendered identities, like "Woman" and the "feminine," as we recognize a gap between what *is* and what *could* or *should be*. This slippage between competing definitions invites us to act out the "feminine" differently. More specifically, because "Woman" and the "feminine" function as master signifiers in identity formation, this recognition produces a shift in self-perception. As Mark Bracher explains, "[W]hat happens to our sense of being or identity is determined to a large degree by what happens to those signifiers that represent us" (25).[42] To be sure, this slippage can also occur when readers encounter Daly's metaphoric Woman. However, because Daly does not seem to value or openly incorporate cultural specificity into her mythic metaphors, the effect is quite different. Whereas Anzaldúa and Lorde often foreground cultural and ethnic markers, Daly strips them away, inadvertently creating the illusion of a single gender-specific subject position that seems simply to replicate already-existing master signifiers of the "feminine." By mexicanizing or africanizing the master signifiers that represent "us" women, Anzaldúa and Lorde mexicanize or africanize their readers as well: they invent a variety of subject positions that they invite their readers to adopt.[43]

As they excavate and re-create culturally specific gynecentric myths, Anzaldúa and Allen take to new levels Daly's injunction to move "beyond God the Father." They replace Judeo-Christian traditions with Náhuatl, Olmec, Yoruban, Fon, and other worldviews and develop new myths to transform themselves and their readers. I want to emphasize the highly inventive nature of the new myths they enact: Anzaldúa and Lorde do not provide readers with authentic, postpositivist standpoints. Their epistemologies are performative, not descriptive; and the effect is radical transformation. They stage fluid, transcultural narratives that they invite their readers—whatever our cultural backgrounds—to adopt. Instead of recovering precolonial mythological systems erased by patriarchal structures, they invent ethical, *artificial* mythologies: These new myths are *ethical*, because their new metaphors of Woman offer imaginary alternatives to contemporary western definitions of the "feminine"; they're *artificial*, because the "feminine" they affirm does not (*yet?*) exist.

Their revisionist mythmaking illustrates what Drucilla Cornell calls "ethical feminism," or what I would describe as the use of performative speech acts to disrupt status-quo stories and the prevailing (*phallocentric*) sociosymbolic order. Significantly, Cornell's ethical feminists are not oppositional; they do not simply reject contemporary definitions of the "feminine" and replace them with alternate definitions that more accurately reflect the truth of women's experience. Instead, these ethical feminists speak from "the utopian or redemptive perspective of the 'not yet'" by using allegory and myth to *imaginatively* reconstruct the "feminine" (*Transformations* 59). Ethical feminism occurs in the subjunctive, in a liminal space between past, present, and future definitions. Or as Cornell explains, ethical feminism "explicitly recognizes the 'should be' in representations of the feminine. It emphasizes the role of the imagination, not description, in creating solidarity between women. Correspondingly, ethical feminism rests its claim for the intelligibility and coherence of 'herstory' not on what women 'are,' but on the remembrance of the 'not yet' which is recollected in both allegory and myth" (59). In other words, ethical feminism reclaims and rereads already existing stories and myths of the "feminine" but interprets and (re)invents them.

A redemptive myth

As this point I want to adopt Cornell's ethical feminism and apply my own "redemptive perspective" to a reading of Daly's origin myths. Despite Daly's apparent comments to the contrary, I suggest that her discussions of a female Elemental Race, women's ancestral memories, or the Radiance of our own Origins, "should be" read performatively, as potentially transformational metaphors. In other words, these metaphoric images do not represent accurate descriptions of an authentic female identity; nor do they indicate the recovery of women's essential inner nature. Such literal interpretations are far too limiting and lock us into status-quo stories, for they lead to restrictive definitions of the "feminine" and confine women's experiences to a predetermined set of characteristics. More importantly, if we read Daly's metaphoric language descriptively, we deny its performative effects and overlook the visionary, ethical dimensions of her work.

As do Anzaldúa and Lorde, Daly uses metaphoric language performatively, to change her readers. She too invents an ethical, artificial mythology and a potentially fluid identity that she invites her readers to adopt. In her revisionary myths, representation and creation become blurred. Her celebration of women's "Female/Elemental divinity" indicates an ongoing creative process that involves what Cornell might describe as the recovery of the "feminine" as an imaginative universal. According to Cornell, this recovery "feeds the power of the feminine imagination and helps to avoid the depletion of the feminine imaginary in the name of the masculine symbolic. This use of the feminine as an imaginative universal does not, and should not, pretend to simply tell the 'truth' of woman as she was, or is. This is why our mythology is self-consciously an artificial mythology; Woman is 'discovered' as an ethical standard. And as she is 'discovered,' her meaning is also created" (*Beyond Accommodation* 178).[44] As Cornell's oscillation between creation and discovery indicates, this use of the "feminine" as an imaginative universal draws on the rhetoric of authenticity yet goes beyond existing definitions to emphasize the artificial, inventive nature of these mythologies of Woman. I want to underscore the open-ended possibilities in this use of the "feminine" as an imaginative universal. Because the "discovery" of Woman as an ethical standard occurs within mythic metaphors, it defies literal, monologic interpretation, thus enabling a proliferation of meanings, meanings that must be invented and lived out by each reader. But by phrasing her new definitions in the language of discovery, origins, and excavated pasts, Daly (like Anzaldúa and Lorde) authorizes her words. Revisionist mythmaking plays an important role in Daly's newly authorized "discoveries," for mythic images are open to multiple interpretations. As Cornell points out, "It is the potential variability of myth that allows us to work within myth, and the significance it offers, so as to reimagine our world and by so doing, to begin to dream of a new one" (*Beyond Accommodation* 178).

Not surprisingly, however, Daly's critics generally don't recognize the "potential variability of myth" in her work. How could they? As I've already suggested, this nonrecognition has its source at least partially in the ways Daly downplays differences and overemphasizes sameness. Perhaps disciplinary (mis)interpretations also play a role in scholars' oversight. Because they classify her primarily as a philosopher or theologian, they might evaluate her according to conventional disciplinary-specific scholarly standards and thus overlook the creative, performative dimensions of her revisionary mythmaking. By reading Daly in dialogue with Anzaldúa and Lorde,—who are generally viewed in somewhat binary terms as creative writers who produce poetry, fiction, and essays but not scholarly philosophical work (*although, as I suggest earlier in this book, they should be viewed as philosopher-theorists as well!*)—I have attempted to suggest another perspective for Daly's work. Like these racially marked writers, Daly uses language performatively, to create a reality that does not—yet—exist. She too draws on (*and creates!*) oral traditions as she attempts to inspire her readers.

In various ways and to various degrees, all three writers use revisionist myth to invent new forms of identity and new social actors. Their origin stories and prepatriarchal creatrix figures do not indicate a nostalgic desire to return to some prehistorical, utopian, gynecentric community of women. By going "back" to previously erased conventions, they go forward—far beyond "God the Father"—rewriting the past from their present perspectives and inventing new definitions as they go. As Trinh asserts, "the return to a denied heritage allows one to start again with different departures, different pauses, different arrivals" (*Woman* 14). These "returns" are performative, not descriptive, and enable them to construct nondual epistemologies that destabilize the boundaries between writer, reader, world, and text. They engage in to-and-fro movements that take up yet disrupt status-quo stories. These disruptive oscillations invite readers to go beyond conventional feminist identity politics, opening up new thresholds, textual and psychic locations where transcultural identifications and radical interconnections can occur.

CHAPTER FIVE

From Self-Help to Womanist Self-Recovery;

or, How Paula Gunn Allen Changed My Mind

> For those raised in the rationalist world where
> the linear mind reigns supreme, distinctions are
> mighty. In it there is no possibility—other than
> imaginary or "psychological"—of being seated
> amidst the rainbow. To rationalists, giants, like
> "little people" (and like their contemporary counter-
> parts, the extraterrestrials), are clearly figments
> of overactive imagination and "mass hysteria."
> Yet traditional people insist that conversations
> with animals and supernaturals—little people, gi-
> ants, immortals or holy people—are actual. They
> tell many stories about women or men being
> changed into bears, about Antelope Spirit girls
> playing with a human girl, about Ogre Women—
> huge and terrifying—abducting children, about
> meetings with Thunderbirds, Dlanua, katsinas,
> goddesses, and gods.
>
> Paula Gunn Allen, *Grandmothers of the Light*

I've been intrigued with and yet troubled by Paula Gunn Allen's *Grandmothers of the Light: A Medicine Woman's Sourcebook* for years. This curious text represents a startling departure from her earlier academic work in Native American Studies. As in *The Sacred Hoop: Recovering the Feminine in American Indian Traditions*, her groundbreaking collection of scholarly essays, Allen uses an indigenous-inflected, feminist lens to examine Native cultures, mythic worldviews, gender identities, and historical themes. But in *Grandmothers of the Light* she offers distinctly nonacademic perspectives on these topics (as well as others) and makes a number of puzzling claims—claims so puzzling that at times they can be almost embarrassing to read. (*No "almost" about it.*) Allen shares her personal experiences and beliefs, linking them with theory, history, story, anthropology, and myth, to construct a contemporary multicultural-feminist, Indigenous-based worldview, which she invites readers (of any cultural/ethnic/racial background) to share.

This invitation indicates a startling shift in Allen's work and seems to contradict the sharp distinctions she draws between Native and European-American peoples and worldviews in *The Sacred Hoop* and other writings. Indeed, only two years prior to *Grandmothers of the Light*'s publication, Allen directly challenged Leslie Marmon Silko's inclusion of sacred Laguna Pueblo clan stories in her classic novel, *Ceremony*, insisting that to do so violated "native ethics," endangered the people's lives, and could lead to other "appalling consequences" ("Special Problems").[1] Allen's criticism of the scholarship on *Ceremony* is even more pronounced: "I believe I could no more do (or sanction) the kind of ceremonial investigation of *Ceremony* done by some researchers than I could slit my mother's throat. Even seeing some of it published makes my skin crawl." As this strong language indicates, Allen draws strict lines between Native and non-Native cultures, emphasizing that "the white world has a different set of values, one which requires learning all and telling all in the interests of knowledge, objectivity and freedom" ("Special Problems"). And yet, only a few years later, with the publication of *Grandmothers of the Light*, Allen seems to be stepping over (*if not entirely erasing*) these lines and playing into this relentless hunger for knowledge by sharing sacred stories with outsiders. (*At this point, I have not yet found the story that can help me explain Allen's extreme shift.*)

Shaped by her belief in the "magical" power of thought and targeted at a wide, multicultural female audience, *Grandmothers of the Light* can easily be (mis)interpreted as a mainstream self-help book heavily influenced by "New Age" thinking.[2] And indeed, Allen makes a number of assertions that strike many readers (*especially academic and scholarly readers*) as outrageous:

- She relies on "direct communication from [her] own spirit guides" for information concerning the stories she retells (xiii).

- She insists on the total reality of the "spirits, the supernaturals, god-desses, gods, . . . holy people" (xvii), "extraterrestrials" (5), "little people," and "giants" (6).
- She speaks respectfully of the "channeled information" she received from the "Crystal Woman" (195).

When I picked up *Grandmothers of the Light: A Medicine Woman's Sourcebook* for the first time back in the mid-1990s, I was willing to be energized by Allen's bravery even as the book's title gave me pause. (*It freaked me out!*) While the first phrase, "Grandmothers of the Light," resonated with my understanding of a type of innate divinity or what Layli Maparyan terms LUXOCRACY the second phrase, with its reference to a singular "Medicine Woman," resonated only with romanticized stereotypes.[3]

I admired Allen's bold references to spirit people and her insistence on the reality of metaphysical, multidimensional nonhuman beings. I was grateful that someone of her academic stature would defy the positivism, post-structuralist skepticism, and humanism that dominates scholarly thought. At a time when academics were so careful to hide their fringe metaphysical beliefs, Allen's claims were refreshing. As a closeted womanist spiritual activist, I secretly hoped that I could borrow from and build on Allen's spirit-based metaphysics.[4] I wanted to channel her bravery.

And yet, even as I admired Allen's bold assertions about spirit beings and metaphysical realities, I was concerned by her sweeping claims and her gender-specific focus. (*Shades of Mary Daly!*) Look, for instance, at Allen's invitation to readers, her assertion that the stories in her book, "when used as ritual maps or guides, enable women to recover our path to the gynocosmos that is our spiritual home" (xv). As Allen explains in the preface, she has drawn from "the vast oral tradition of Native America" to select twenty-one stories that have been personally empowering for her; she believes that these stories can assist other women in "navigat[ing] the perilous journey along the path that marks the boundary between the mundane world and the world of spirit" (xiii). Outlining what she describes as the seven-fold path of "the medicine woman's way" (10), Allen suggests that the stories in her collection can teach readers how to follow this path in a sacred manner.

When I first read this description of the "medicine woman" and her "path," I became deeply troubled. I kept reading, but my respect for Allen was crumbling as my concerns grew. What's with this monolithic "medicine woman?" Doesn't Allen flatten out the many differences among Indigenous women, even as she reinforces some Disney-inspired, Pocahontas-like stereotype? And what could she possibly mean with this offer to use indigenous stories as "ritual maps" enabling women (*any women?!?*) to follow "the medicine woman's way"? (*One way? One monolithic singular path?*) Given the brutal history of interactions between Native and non-Native peoples in the Americas—a history Allen herself has explored in painful detail, a history of land theft, spirit murder, extermination, broken treaties, dehumanization, objectification, and extreme appropriation[5]—how could I possibly interpret this open invitation as anything other than an invitation to continue along a well-trod brutal historical path? What were the ethical implications of Allen's book? And what were my ethical obligations as a womanist scholar? Might I be violating my own standards, crossing some type of ethical line, by keeping this book alive through my analysis? (*Even worse, might I be breathing new life into it?*) Is Allen sharing sacred stories? Does she rely on sentimentalized Indian stereotypes pandering to non-Native readers who crave authenticity, certainty, and escape from their meaningless lives, as Gerald Vizenor might suggest? Has she succumbed to the "plastic shamanism" of Lynn Andrews and other (non)Indian women and men who make their fortunes through the "commercial exploitation of indigenous spiritual traditions" (Aldred)?[6] In other words, does *Grandmothers of the Light* represent yet another version of what Allen herself has previously condemned as the ongoing "New Age cooptation and recontextualization of Native thought" (*Off the Reservation* 97)—in this instance authorized, authenticated, and essentialized by Allen's family ties to the Laguna and Sioux? Has Allen, at this point in her career, become a sell-out? Is she using her family connections to pander to a non-Native audience? The twenty-first-century scholarly silence around Allen's work indicates that at least some recent scholars believe this interpretation to be plausible.

My ethical concerns further increased as I reflected on Allen's representations of gender. *Grandmothers of the Light* is filled with huge generalizations and essentialist, stereotyped references to women and men—references that reminded me of Mary Daly at her most egregious. Consider, for instance, Allen's discussion of the "disciplines of the medicine woman's way," which seems to contain stereotypical gendered roles and duties (*just the kind of stereotypically "feminine"/female duties that I, personally, find distasteful and have struggled against my entire life*). To make matters even worse, Allen seems to valorize women's suffering and self-sacrifice: "the way of the daughter, the way of the householder, the way of the mother, the way of the gatherer, the way of the ritualist, the way of the teacher, and the way of the wise woman" (10). What a reinforcement of status-quo thinking! Or look at these passages, where Allen describes the differences between men and women:

> The practice for women differs in many particulars from that for men, partly because of the historical differences between women's and men's life circumstances, but more because of the differences in male and female psychic structures. The psychic differences are reflected in hormonal and other physiological variances, though it is important to recognize that *the physical only reflects the essential.* (20, emphasis added)

> the masculine expression of multiversal energy/intelligence is movement of a dual, but not oppositional, nature. The duality that the masculine (which is a special case or subset of the feminine) embodies is complementary in essence, though that complementarity sometimes takes a form that appears adversarial or polar. (108)

Given my personal antipathy toward all forms of static essentialism and dichotomous thought, as well as my desire to transform (*not reinforce!*) status-quo thinking, how could I possibly make sense of Allen's views? What should I do?

By this point in my investigation of *Grandmothers of the Light*, I was so tempted to completely ignore the book, to pretend that I'd never read it or that someone else (*some other Paula Gunn Allen, perhaps*) had written it, and to keep my focus firmly on Allen's more conventional academic work. I wanted to erase *Grandmothers of the Light*, to dismiss it as an embarrassing deviation from Allen's important scholarly contributions to the fields of Native American studies, U.S. literature, and women's studies. After all, other scholars have adopted this approach. My thoughts grew even more extreme, and I wondered if I should take *Grandmothers of the Light* as a sign, a message, commanding me to move away from Allen and her quirky work, and to immerse myself in the writings of other, more accepted ("safer") scholars? I would not be alone in this departure. Just take a look at recent scholarship on Native American literary studies, and you'll see that Allen is often ignored or mentioned only briefly (*like that crazy family member who everyone tries to forget*).

And yet, despite these enormous concerns, I could not entirely reject *Grandmothers of the Light*. To do so would replicate the binary-oppositional energies I'm determined to transform. Moreover, I respected Paula Gunn

Allen and her contributions to Native American studies, literary studies, and feminist theory too much to dismiss her as a sell-out, a pandering feminist fool. (*Although, as you've probably realized, I was very tempted to do so.*) I could not let the book's limitations—though some of them seemed daunting—drive me entirely away from Allen and her work. I had to find a different way to make sense of this troubling text. After all, I told myself, Allen's other writings have so much value, such great insights. Surely *Grandmothers of the Light* does too—I just need to be more open, listen more closely. And so, I dived back into the text. Rather than automatically react to Allen's assertions, I entered into them, examined them from multiple angles. I tried to excavate the stereotypes and make (some kind of) sense out of Allen's curious book. As I hope you'll agree by the time you finish this chapter, this process of mindful, engaged reading—of attending to, and working through my ambivalent, sometimes-angry reactions to Allen and her *Grandmothers of the Light*—have been extremely productive, for it inspired me to develop a literary context, which I call "womanist self-recovery," that's large enough for Allen's work, and for the work of other nonconformist texts.

Womanist self-recovery, defined

As I use the term, *womanist self-recovery* represents a contemporary transcultural project and a holistic transformational process. This term is intentionally paradoxical and, I imagine, provocative because self-recovery/self-help movements are viewed with such skepticism by academics, as well as many others. But by juxtaposing the radical liberatory potential of womanism with the conservative tendencies in most mainstream self-help literature for women, I hope to complicate our understanding of these terms.[7] I borrow the word *womanist* from Alice Walker and use it to underscore the woman-loving, feminist-inflected, multicolored dimensions of this enterprise, as well as the personal agency and "outrageous, audacious, courageous, *willful* behavior" it generates (*Mother's Garden* xi, original emphasis), as well as its inclusionary potential. And I borrow the phrase *self-recovery* from women's self-help literature and use it to underscore both contemporary U.S. women's widespread desire and need for self-healing and the dangers of focusing exclusively on the individual that this "multi-billion-dollar publishing phenomenon" (Schrager 177) represents.

I have named this hybrid genre *womanist* rather than *feminist* for three intertwined reasons: I believe womanism (*as I define the term because* womanism, *like* feminism, *has multiple meanings*) to be more radical in its transformational promises, more able to embrace contradictions and ambivalence, and more inclusive in its vision. Unlike feminism, which seems almost always to make gender a (*if not "the"*) key focus, womanism does not. As Layli Phillips (Mapa-ryan) explains, "Unlike feminism, and despite its name, womanism does not emphasize or privilege gender or sexism; rather, it elevates all sites and forms of oppression, whether they are based on social-address categories like gender, race, or class, to a level of equal concern and action. Womanism's link to gender is the fact that the historically produced race/class-gender axis that is Black womanhood serves as the origin point for a speaking position that freely and autonomously addresses any topic or problem" ("Woman-ism" xvi–xviii).[8] To be sure, Paula Gunn Allen and many others who write what I've labeled "womanist self-recovery narratives" do not self-identify as womanist. But my point here is not to imply that they *should be* considered womanists. I use the term *womanist* not to describe the authors but rather to describe a transformational, inclusionary energy and vision infusing the texts they produce.

Womanist self-recovery creates communally based, multicultural transfor-mation narratives—stories of self-empowerment that begin, simultaneously, both with the author's personal experiences and with an outward movement designed to encourage and facilitate collective growth. Womanist self-recov-ery transformation stories do not focus exclusively (or even primarily) on the personal but instead synthesize self-love and self-reflection with a critical analysis of existing social conditions and a redemptive quest for social justice. Other womanist self-recovery narratives include Luisah Teish's *Jambalaya: The Natural Woman's Book of Personal Charms and Practical Rituals*, Marilou Awi-akta's *Selu: Seeking the Corn-Mother's Wisdom*, Elena Avila's *Woman Who Glows in the Dark: A Curandera Reveals Traditional Aztec Secrets of Physical and Spiritual Health*, Iyanla Vanzant's *Tapping the Power Within: A Path to Self-Empowerment for Women*, and Ana Castillo's *Massacre of the Dreamers: Essays on Xicanisma*.[9] Despite the many differences among them, these books share a number of significant traits, including their transgression of conventional literary genres; their authors' visionary beliefs in language's causal, performative power; their inclusion of autobiographical details; and their use of non-European cultural symbols, myths, and beliefs to develop inclusive communities.

In this chapter, though, I focus my attention on Allen's *Grandmothers of the Light* and use it to illustrate womanist self-recovery. I do so for several reasons. First, it was my attempt to make sense of this puzzling text that lead me to invent the term "womanist self-recovery" and to theorize it as a mode of literary and cultural intervention. Second, I hope that by reading *Grandmothers of the Light* in this fashion, I will encourage others to pay more attention to Allen and to take her work more seriously. Finally, my engagement with Allen's troubling text illustrates another form that threshold theorizing can take. And so, in what follows, I interweave a discussion of womanist self-recovery with an analysis of *Grandmothers of the Light*.

Six attributes of womanist self-recovery texts

Both popular self-help books for women and womanist self-recovery begin with the individual's quest for wholeness and adopt a twofold strategy designed to empower their readers who are often, but not always, women.[10] Emphasizing the importance of self-esteem, self-trust, and individual agency, these books offer readers tactics designed to enhance these qualities. There is, however, a crucial difference between the types of individualism they enact: Mainstream self-help books generally posit a restrictive self-enclosed individualism, and womanist self-recovery posits a relational self-hood. While mainstream self-help focuses primarily (and often exclusively) on the individual woman's problems, desires, and needs, womanist self-recovery does not. As a number of scholars have explained, popular self-help books for women attribute each woman's feelings of alienation and self-loss to the isolated individual self.[11] Often drawing on their own personal experiences, mainstream self-help authors employ what Maureen Ebben describes as a biblically inspired story of the Fall: "a descent into original sin through gluttony and loss of self-control, and an ascent accomplished through repentance and abstention" (116). In these stories (as in the Genesis account of Adam, Eve, the Serpent, and the Tree of Knowledge), the blame lies almost entirely with the individual herself. It is *her* lack of control and *her* inability to conform that lead to her unhappiness and the need for healing.[12]

As this extreme emphasis on the personal suggests, mainstream self-help books for women reinforce status-quo stories. Pathologizing the individual and ignoring the systemic nature of gender-, color-, and economic-based injustices, they do not challenge or try to alter the existing gender codes, social standards, or practices. Instead, they insist that the individual, not the larger culture, must change. She must adjust her self-perception and actions, in order to more successfully fulfill her role. As Elaine Rapping explains, "The terms of such discourse. ... lead to kinds of treatment in which women are subtly coerced into 'adjusting' to sexism by changing their own behavior, rather than changing sexist society" (123). Ebben makes a similar point: "By labeling women's unhappiness dysfunctional, and by locating these dysfunctions within the individual woman rather than in systemic social inequalities, self-help texts depoliticize women's discontentment and contribute little to fundamental structural reforms" (112). In short, conventional self-help books for women do not challenge the status-quo stories of self-enclosed individualism, but instead facilitate assimilation into existing social systems and thus create more "successful" individuals.

Unlike mainstream self-help, womanist self-recovery does not simply replicate status-quo stories but instead retells them, subtly changing the narrative and redefining the personal in broader, communal terms. Because womanist self-recovery often relies on the external markers of conventional self-help, these texts can engage those readers who have been socialized into the status-quo stories. Immersed in the texts, readers can more easily adopt womanist-self-recovery alterations.

Instead of focusing almost exclusively on the individual, womanist self-recovery incorporates political and collective dimensions, as well. As I explain in this chapter, these outward-directed movements and status-quo-story revisions take a number of forms, including these:

1. analyses of the underlying systemic causes contributing to women's alienation and self-loss;
2. revisionist mythmaking used both to affirm each woman's power and to critique negative stereotypes and beliefs about womanhood and the feminine;
3. an insistence on the communal dimensions of individual identity;
4. dynamic negotiations among diverse cultural traditions;
5. the creation of inclusive, multicultural communities; and
6. a metaphysics of interconnectedness that posits a fluid, cosmic spirit or force embodying itself within and as material and nonmaterial forms.

To begin with, Allen and other womanist self-recovery authors do not attribute an individual's difficulties solely to the individual herself or himself. Instead, they incorporate an analysis of how underlying systemic institutions and beliefs (linkages among hyper-capitalism, white-supremacism, sexism, and so on) contribute to individual experiences of alienation and self-loss. Thus, for example, Allen associates women's devalued positions in contemporary western cultures with the spiritual imbalance and the resulting over-emphasis on rational thought that occurred during European conquest of the Americas and continues today. According to Allen, many precontact tribal nations were "gynocratic," and gave both women and men important social, political, and spiritual roles (xiv). In such systems, women (like men) held recognized legislative and governing positions. For instance, the Women's Council of the Cherokee made decisions about war and public policy; the head of this council, referred to as "Beloved Woman," was viewed as the embodied representative of the "'Great Spirit.'" In gynecentric communities, the spiritual and the mundane were entirely interwoven, creating a balanced worldview that ensured each woman's vital role in maintaining the interconnectedness of all forms of life.

As she retraces the devastating impact of colonial conquest on indigenous North American peoples and beliefs, Allen charts the transition to male-dominated, hierarchical social and religious structures. These historical analyses are especially evident in *Grandmothers of the Light*'s final sections: the postscript, glossary, and bibliography. Here Allen uses conventional scholarly apparatus to educate and, potentially, politicize her readers.[13] While her overt purpose in the postscript seems to focus on a critique of anthropologists' overemphasis on the differences between various Indian nations (205–6), Allen also underscores the devastating impact that colonial conquest made in North America on specific tribal nations, ranging from the Aztec and Maya in the south to the Lummi/Nootsak in the northwest. Given the distorted versions of history taught in most western educational systems, these historical accounts are crucial.[14] By including them in *Grandmothers of the Light*, Allen subtly exposes and works to transform her readers' historical amnesia, thus making readers accountable for the ways they have benefitted from the conquest.

Second, womanist self-recovery often uses indigenous mythic figures both to affirm each woman's power and to critique the negative images of female identity circulating in contemporary cultures. Like Gloria Anzaldúa, Audre Lorde, and other revisionist mythmakers, Allen revises, retells, and in other ways employs mythological stories to develop alternate gender systems, epistemologies, and metaphysics. She does so, at least in part, to correct what she sees as the limitations in the mainstream U.S. women's movement and feminist theory. As she explains in a 1983 interview:

> [W]hat I'm really attempting to do is affect feminist thinking. Because my white sisters—and they have influenced the Black and Asian and Chicano sisters—have given the impression that women have always been held down, have always been weak, and have always been persecuted by men, but I know that's not true. I come from a people that that is not true of. (qtd. in Ballinger and Swann 10)

Allen uses revisionist mythmaking to recover (and re-create) alternatives to these mainstream views. In *Grandmothers of the Light*, her mythic women offer an important alternative to conventional binary-oppositional gender roles. Her women are not defined by their relationships with fathers, sons, husbands, or other men. Nor are they reduced to their biological reproductive functions. Instead, they are fully autonomous, nonstereotypical creative people. As in her more conventionally scholarly work, Allen claims that Native cosmologies offer contemporary women empowering models of female identity, models that counter the sexism and other forms of misogyny found in Judaeo-Christian socioreligious belief systems. Insisting that "relations between human women and supernaturals are as viable and powerful in the present time as in days gone by" (xvi), she uses indigenous stories to embolden and transform her readers.

Throughout *Grandmothers of the Light*, Allen retells a variety of culturally specific Native myths, exploring the central roles female creatrix figures such as Thought Woman (Keres Pueblo), Grandmother Spider (Keres Pueblo), Changing Woman (Navajo), Selu (Cherokee), and Xmucané/Grandmother of the Light (Mayan) play in tribal cultures. My personal favorite is Thought Woman. I absolutely love this creator. Whereas many female creatrix figures create the world through some type of supernatural birthing process that has clear connections with women's biological forms of childbirth, the Keres Pueblos' creator uses vibration, language, thought, sound, and song to create the entire cosmos, including nature, human and nonhuman beings, sociopolitical systems, literature, and the sciences. Everything! Thought Woman is a thinker who thinks and speaks the cosmos into existence:

> Grandmother Spider, Thought Woman, thought the earth, the sky, the galaxy, and all that is into being, and as she thinks, so we are. She sang the divine sisters . . . into being out of her medicine pouch or bundle, and they in turn sang

the firmament, the land, the seas, the people, the katsina, the gods, the plants, animals, minerals, language, writing, mathematics, architecture, the Pueblo social system, and every other thing you can imagine in this our world. (28)

This creation story redefines feminine creativity by associating Thought Woman with spiritual, intellectual, vibrational, and linguistic power. Positing a cosmic female-embodied intelligence, Allen displaces western cultures' traditional association of the body with the feminine, affirms women's intellectual and creative capacities, and challenges status-quo stories concerning women's subordinate status.[15]

I want to underscore the innovative nature of Allen's revisionist mythmaking, where creation occurs through language and thought. These remarkable narratives have little in common with standard phallocentric creation accounts that conflate "Woman" with "womb" and reduce the "feminine" to the highly sexualized yet passive bearer of (male) culture. Nor are they similar to those feminist origin myths that valorize women's previously undervalued maternal role by identifying goddess imagery and female power primarily with childbirth. By redefining the maternal as transformational thought, Allen re-appropriates and alters conventional gender categories. She destabilizes the hierarchical dichotomous worldview that equates the "masculine" with transcendence, culture, and the mind, and the "feminine" with immanence, nature, and the body.

Significantly, Allen does not simply replace one dualism with another by flipping the script and elevating immanence over transcendence. Her mythic creatrix represents a dynamic all-inclusive intellectual/creative power that generates both physical and nonphysical reality. Allen's cosmic Source is both *supernatural* (Allen equates it with Thought Woman) and *natural* ("Thought Woman's intelligence . . . permeates the land—the mountains and clouds, the rains and lightning, the corn and deer" [34]). Unlike Athene, the Greek goddess of (patriarchal) wisdom whose divine intelligence entails the sacrifice of the mother, Allen's mythic creator represents a maternalized embodied intelligence, or what Luce Irigaray might describe as "a spirituality of the body, the flesh" (135).[16]

As my emphasis on the embodied material dimensions of thought implies, Allen develops an epistemological system that avoids the Cartesian mind/ body dualism. Establishing a reciprocal relationship between intellectual, physical, and spiritual components of life, she destabilizes classical western definitions of reason and rationality (*those pseudo-universals I discussed in the previous chapter*) and invents what I call "embodied mythic thinking": a transformational, nondual epistemology where thoughts, ideas, and beliefs have physical, material forms and effects. In Allen's epistemology, language is transformational and thought gives us "magical" power: just as Old Spider Woman thought and sang the material world and everything in it into existence, so real-life women of all cultural backgrounds can, by directing their thought and using language in new ways, alter their physical surroundings as well as themselves and others.[17] As she asserts in the preface to *Grandmothers of the Light*, thought, "when exercised within the life circumstances common to women everywhere[,] can reshape (terraform) the earth" (xvi). By associating Thought Woman with a cosmic "feminine" intelligence that manifests itself in mutually interchangeable, unfolding physical and nonphysical forms, Allen affirms her readers' intellectual and creative capacities. In her epistemology, thinkers are not passive receptacles waiting to be filled by a divine source of guidance; they are, rather, co-creators in an unfixed, flexible reality: "Since all that exists is alive and must change as a basic law of existence, all existence can be manipulated under certain conditions and according to certain laws" (22). By focusing our thought and channeling its energy in specific ways, we can effect material change.

Third, womanist self-recovery emphasizes the communal dimensions of individual identity. Defining the "self" we recover as relational, womanist self-recovery authors seem to incorporate and yet go beyond the rhetoric of self-contained individualism deeply embedded in the United States and other Enlightenment-based cultures. As I explain in chapter 2, those of us raised or educated in western cultures are taught to define ourselves as unique, fully autonomous individuals with permanent, inflexible boundaries that separate each individual from all others. When taken to an extreme, as it so often is, this status-quo story of hyper-individualism makes it difficult, if not impossible, to recognize our interconnectedness with others. In fact, this solipsistic individualism dehumanizes and in other ways flattens the world, preventing us from recognizing the vitality, selfhood, and subjectivity of other human and nonhuman life. This extreme individualism leads to fragmentation and isolation. When we adopt status-quo individualism as our ethical system and identity formation, we distance ourselves from all that surrounds us. We assume that success depends only on each person's individual effort; those people who do not succeed have only themselves to blame, and their failure has absolutely no impact on our lives. We do not understand that what affects others—*all* others, no matter how separate we seem to be—ultimately affects us, as well. Not surprisingly, then, this highly personalized, self-enclosed individualism greatly increases self-blame and almost entirely inhibits social-justice work. After all: if each individual is fully responsible for his or her own life, there is no need for collective action and systemic social change.[18] (*Your problems, your fault. Fix your own situation. Pull yourself up by your own bootstraps.*)

In *Grandmothers of the Light* (as in her other writings), Allen associates this solipsistic individualism with male-centered, monotheistic religions like conservative versions of Christianity. She maintains that the belief in a single godhead is closely associated with the development of hierarchical worldviews that entirely separate the individual from the community (defined broadly to include the land, as well as human and nonhuman life). Thus in the preface to "Making Sacred, Making True" (her version of the Navajo story of Changing Woman and White Shell Woman), Allen contrasts non-indigenous cultures' monotheistic beliefs with indigenous cultures' beliefs in multiple gods: "In the native world, major gods come in trios, duos, and groups. *It is the habit of non-natives to discover the supreme being, the one and only head god, a habit lent to them by monotheism.* Because of this, Changing Woman is often spoken of alone in the literature of the bilagáana, the white people. But in the texts . . . singularity is sad and undesirable. Belonging to a people—a community, a clan—is a necessity for all beings, human, holy people, animals, everyone" (71, emphasis added). With this insistence on "multiplicity," Allen offers readers an important alternative to the self-contained, possessive individualism described above as well as a possible solution to the mono-thinking and fragmentation of contemporary cultures.[19] She models a relational individualism that meets each person's specific needs for self-affirmation without severing the individual from a larger whole. According to Allen, in gynecratic tribal systems "egalitarianism, personal autonomy, and communal harmony were highly valued, rendering the good of the individual and the good of the society mutually reinforcing, rather than divisive" (xiv). As Allen's emphasis on the value of "personal autonomy" and "the good of the individual" indicates, she does not reject individualism and deny each person's importance. However, by locating the individual within a larger social context, Allen replaces oppositional, self-enclosed types of individualism with a relational definition of selfhood that synthesizes the personal and collective dimensions of each individual's life.

Like other womanist self-recovery authors, Allen posits a relational individualism that balances the individual with(in) the community. She redefines individual identity, replacing oppositional dichotomies that juxtapose the individual *against* society with a complementary dualism with interlocking parts: Each individual's identity emerges from and is shaped by a larger, communal background. As she explains, "identity is formed by context and is a function of ritual purpose rather than of self-will or individuation" (109). Allen's description of the medicine woman's final stage, which she calls "*The Way of the Wise Woman*," illustrates one form this contextual, relational, ritualized identity can take: "The sphere of her work has broadened far beyond that of her personal, private self and of her familiar group; her community extends to the stars" (15). The community Allen posits here is remarkable in its complex expansion and radical inclusion; it goes beyond human beings to include noncorporeal life and cosmic consciousness—a type of planetary citizenship, as it were. No wonder so many scholars ignore *Grandmothers of the Light*! It's much easier to pretend that this book doesn't exist rather than try to insert it into any kind of larger worldview. Allen's bold assertions seem almost crazy in their huge threat to our Cartesian worldviews and our conventional academic standards.

By associating her broad cosmic vision with human life, Allen challenges status-quo stories of the typical human aging process, which is usually trapped in a trajectory of physical and intellectual decline. Her "Wise Woman" is a powerful human being with a strong sense of her identity both as a unique individual and as a member of the cosmos. She has reflected on and learned from her personal experiences; as Allen explains, she has "developed true wisdom through gathering information and experience and applying them in every area of her life" (15). She can recognize cosmic patterns, and she uses this knowledge to enhance others' lives.

Fourth, womanist self-recovery is transcultural. As I explain in chapter 2, *transcultural* indicates dynamic, nonhierarchical, potentially transformative negotiations among diverse traditions. Transculturalism does not ignore the differences among distinct cultures but instead uses these differences as pathways enabling us to generate highly complex commonalities. Although a womanist self-recovery writer generally "roots" herself in the indigenous-inflected beliefs of her particular geo-cultural location(s), she draws from additional indigenous and nonindigenous cultures, as well.[20] These negotiations among diverse traditions and beliefs serve useful epistemological and ontological functions, for they enable womanist self-recovery authors both to validate their words and to develop specific belief systems and practices designed to meet contemporary needs. Allen's work offers an especially useful illustration of this transcultural process.

Throughout *Grandmothers of the Light*, Allen carefully interweaves a variety of distinct Indian and non-Indian belief systems with each other and with her readers. In her introductory chapter, she insists that "[t]he ritual tradition is of ancient and worldwide standing" (8), defines "tribal people" globally, and maintains that all oral literature shares a supernatural, psychic trait: "The oral traditions of all tribal people—whether Native American, Hindu, Greek, Celtic, Norse, Samois, Roman, or Papuan—should be understood as psychic literature. It cannot adequately be comprehended except in terms of the universe of power, for it speaks to the relationships among humans, animals of all kingdoms, supernaturals, and deities in a landscape that is subject to influences of thought, intention, will, emotion, and choice under the kinds of conditions described above" (22). With these cross-cultural, cross-species connections, Allen redefines Enlightenment-based concepts of the universal in more generous terms and develops complex commonalities (*or transcultural universals*) that do not ignore the differences among people. As I suggest in the previous chapter, by definition, the "universal" should be all-inclusive and point to attributes shared by all people. However, all too often the universal has its source in narrow, eurocentric definitions of "people" that exclude far more people than they include. Rather than represent a shared category embracing *everyone*, these restrictive universals rely on difference-defined-as-deviation and thus dehumanize and in other ways delegitimize those who do not fit.

While some contemporary scholars have responded to universalism's potential dangers by rejecting the concept of the universal itself, Allen and other womanist self-recovery authors adopt a transcultural approach that enables them to reinvent the universal in open-ended ways. Look, for instance, at her introduction to the second section, "Cosmogyny: The Goddesses," where Allen nimbly moves between the cosmic (which she redefines as "the Great Goddess"), the intertribal (or what she calls "the gynocentric universe throughout the Americas"), the tribally specific (she discusses a variety of distinct tribal nations, including the Cherokee, the Hopi, and the Navajo), and the personal ("my tribe, the Laguna Pueblo") (27). Throughout this section, Allen talks in both general (universal) and particular (tribal) terms, associating a variety of cultural traditions with a cosmic worldview (or what she terms "cosmogyny"). By so doing, she draws connections among diverse North American cultural traditions in ways enabling her to redefine the universal in more expansive, open-ended terms. Similarly, in her discussion of the oral tradition, she underscores the parallels between a variety of spiritual practices—including "The Tao, the Sufi Path, the Way of the Madonna, the Quest for the Grail, the Good Red Road"—to support her assertion that "[s]piritual discipline is the hallmark of any ritual path" (9).

Fifth, as this emphasis on commonalities might imply, womanist self-recovery is inclusive and addresses itself to a wide multicultural audience. As I mentioned earlier, Allen provocatively suggests that the "path of the medicine woman" can be traveled by women of diverse cultural backgrounds. According to Allen, her stories illustrate "the great power women have possessed, and how that power, when exercised within the life circumstances *common to women everywhere* can reshape (terraform) the earth" (xvi, emphasis added). Allen is a fierce advocate of multiplicity, and her point here is not to imply that "All women are the same."[21] Her emphasis on commonalities (which must not be confused with sameness) plays a crucial role in her political intervention. More specifically, she attempts to create a broad-based movement for social change. She maintains that the sexism, racism, homophobia, and other forms of social injustice experienced today are directly related to the imbalance that occurred when masculinist, male-centered belief systems—with their hierarchical, dominant/subordinate worldviews—replaced "gynocratic" belief systems (xiv). Associating our commonalities with a sacred feminine power, she encourages readers to recognize and begin using an alternate, holistic mode of perception.

Sixth, and perhaps most importantly for my argument in this chapter, womanist self-recovery relies on a metaphysics of interconnectedness that posits a fluid cosmic spirit or force that manifests itself in—and as—material and nonmaterial forms. I would suggest that indigenous teachings from many cultures, recent developments in quantum physics and other branches of science, and even my own experiences confirm this relational, participatory worldview.[22] As Gregory Cajete explains, drawing on both Native science and quantum physics, "Our universe is still unfolding and human beings are active and creative participants. Creativity is both the universe's ordering principle and its process, part of the greater flow of creativity in nature. It flows from the 'implicate order' or inherent potential of the universe, and whatever it produces becomes a part of the 'explicate order' of material or energetic expressions. These expressions range from entire galaxies to the quarks and leptons of the subatomic world" ("Philosophy" 47). Leon Little Bear makes a similar point, noting that "[w]hat Native Americans refer to as spirit and energy waves are the same thing. All of creation is a spirit. Everything in creation consists of a unique combination of energy waves. In other words, what appears as material objects is simply the manifestation of a unique combination of energy waves. Conversely, all energy wave combinations do not necessarily manifest themselves in terms of material objects" (x–xi).

But my point here is not to argue that this spiritual-material spirit/energy/force/call-it-what-you-will "really" exists (*although I believe that it does*). Instead, I want to point out some of the pragmatic, performative functions this metaphysics of interconnectedness serves in womanist self-recovery texts. On the personal level, the belief in a dynamic cosmic energy offers those individuals who feel fragmented and self-divided a highly positive self-image that affirms their personal power. As Ana Castillo explains: "Espiritismo.... [the] acknowledgment of the energy that exists throughout the universe subatomically generating itself and interconnecting, fusing, and changing.... offer[s] a personal response to the divided state of the individual who desires wholeness. An individual who does not sense herself as helpless to circumstances is more apt to contribute positively to her environment than one who resigns with apathy to it because of her sense of individual insignificance" (159). Because she views herself as a vital part of a larger cosmic whole with the ability to impact other aspects of existence, the individual Castillo describes attains a sense of her own self-worth and power. This increased personal agency enables her to act and gives her the confidence that her actions will be meaningful, useful, relevant, and successful. On the collective level, the belief in a cosmic force generating all that exists offers a theoretical framework for social change, a relational approach connecting each individual with the entire cosmos. Those individuals who see themselves as integral parts of all that exists recognize their interdependence with others. This recognition fuels both the desire for social change and the assurance that individual actions—no matter how insignificant they may seem—can and do impact others.

Allen's metaphysics of interconnectedness takes a distinct mythic form. Whether she refers to it as "thought," as "female intelligences," as "language," or as "mind," Allen posits a cosmic mythic force creating, infusing, and uniting all that exists. In *Grandmothers of the Light* and elsewhere, Allen associates this force with the oral tradition shared by all tribal peoples.[23] Rejecting ethnocentric anthropological and literary descriptions of mythology as primitive belief systems, mystifying falsehoods, or nostalgic retreats into an irrecoverable past, she maintains that mythic stories offer an alternate, holistic worldview. Thus in *Grandmothers of the Light*'s opening pages, she describes the oral tradition as a type of guidebook: "An apprentice medicine person becomes familiar with a number of these stories because they act as general guides to that special universe. They enable practitioners of the sacred to recognize where they are and how to function, the entities they might encounter, their names, personalities, and likely disposition toward them, the kinds of instruction they might gain from them, and how to explore the universe of power to gain greater paranormal knowledge and ability" (3). Allen equates myth with the promise of transformation by defining it as a "ritual" mode of communication, "a language construct that wields the power to transform something (or someone) from one state or condition to another" (7). Focusing their thought and channeling thought's energy in specific ways, spiritual practitioners can align themselves with this spiritual force and bring about material "transformations"—ranging from "weather changes" to "physiological changes in both humans and animals" to "bodily changes" to "earth renewal [and] terraforming (making mountains, rivers, drainage plains, and other geological features), and other activities too numerous to mention" (16). According to Allen, the ability to effect these transformations has its source in a nondual mode of perception that recognizes and draws on thought's creative power. She explains that "practitioners function by thought, using language, movement, sound, painting, drawing, mimetics, gestures, dress, laughter, shock, herbs, minerals, and repetitive devices as foci for that thought. Most of all, they use their ability to deal adeptly in supernatural realms to achieve their objectives, depending on long training, familiarity with Great Mysterious and its (their) ways, and contacts among the supernaturals. The ability to dance, drum, chant dramatically, or alter consciousness so that one can see amazing things are of little use without the aid and protection of some helpers from the other side" (16–17). To be sure, these references to "supernatural realms" and "helpers from the other side" seem almost laughably naive when we read them relying only on the rational mind and empirically-based scientific knowledge systems. And indeed, Allen willingly acknowledges that this mythic worldview defies conventional linear thinking, yet she insists on its validity:

> In the ritual tradition, wholeness is the rule; in it chronology ceases to function, though both temporality and duration play a fundamental role. Ritual affirms an order of reality that secular materialists, logical positivists, and deconstructionist postmodernists believe to be false, imaginary, primitive, or impossible. Yet within the workings of ritual, the impossible becomes the very probable, the imaginary becomes the factual, the primitive becomes the sophisticated, and the false becomes the actuality. Within the ritual universe the entire matter of true/false is turned on its head, and the dancers bring down the rain. (8)

In *Grandmothers of the Light,* Allen invites readers to participate in—to embrace and adopt—this holistic, supernatural worldview. But in order to do so, people brought up under western knowledge systems must learn to perceive reality mythically. That is, they must forego their overreliance on empirical knowledge and rational, linear thinking by entering into a liminal space where alterations in perception can occur. Allen associates this liminal space, or what she calls "the universe of power" (3, 109), with mythic narratives. Locating these mythic narratives at the interface between the spiritual and mundane worlds invoked by the oral tradition, she suggests that the stories in her book (like other stories in an oral tradition) can facilitate a transformation in consciousness: "When these stories are entered as a room is entered, as wilderness is entered, as the surf (and self) is entered, one moves into mythic space and becomes a voyager in the universe of power" (109).

This puzzling metaphoric statement offers important clues to understanding Allen's project in *Grandmothers of the Light.* When we enter a room, we step into it; moving our bodies into the room's space, we locate ourselves within its walls. The room and all it contains become part of our reality; they define us, impacting and at least partially directing our sensory perceptions. Likewise, the transformational type of storytelling Allen describes requires entering into and existing within the story's world, accepting its reality—replete with supernatural beings, goddesses, and holy people—as our own, as "factual accounts" (7). This acceptance triggers a shift in perception, challenging readers to redefine what counts as facts, among other things. As Paula Toohey persuasively demonstrates in her important analysis of *Grandmothers of the Light,* Allen's multivoiced text functions ritually, challenging readers' westernized expectations and working on our consciousness, inviting us to change. The point, then, is not to convey factual, detailed information; it is, rather, about vision:

> Allen's discourse is not about close readings, anthropological accuracy, or reified social commentary from Western perspectives. It is not even about fulfilling the political and literary expectations of other tribal members. Rather, it is about the completion of a ceremonial healing that takes risks, contradicts itself as it grows, and ruptures prescriptive, boundaried language that, while brilliant in the canonical sun, misses the potential for transformation in the nuances of the shadows. (49–50)

Entering into Allen's ritual stories in *Grandmothers of the Light,* readers can recognize their interconnections with all existence.

Womanist self-recovery
and (as) visionary pragmatism

Transformation (as I define the term because of course *transformation* has many meanings) requires vision, motivation, and the desire for social justice. Allen and other womanist self-recovery writers attempt to embody this vision, this motivation, and this desire in their texts and—by extension (*or perhaps I should say by contagion?*)—in their readers. Womanist self-recovery authors insist on the affirmative.[24] Like the women-of-colors activist writers Cherríe Moraga describes in her preface to the 1983 edition of *This Bridge Called My Back*, womanist self-recovery authors are optimistic and have faith in human potential and the possibility of community building: "The political writer . . . is the ultimate optimist, believing people are capable of changing and using words as one way to try and penetrate the privatism of our lives. A privatism which keeps us back and away from each other, which renders us politically useless" ("Refugees"). Womanist self-recovery authors believe that people can and *must* change; they use their words to invite, evoke, and in other ways facilitate transformation—on personal, social, planetary, and sometimes even cosmic levels. Womanist self-recovery authors begin with both the personal—the individual trapped in the "privatism" of hir life—and the larger social and cosmic framework, demonstrating each individual's intimate interconnections with all that exists. They synthesize the personal with the communal, and use this synthesis to incite readers to work for social change. At times, womanist self-recovery authors seem merely to be repeating status-quo stories (as with some of Allen's references to an essentialized feminine), but this appearance is somewhat deceptive. Womanist self-recovery authors hook the reader, using multiple methods—including appeals to status-quo stories; but then, after carrying the reader along for a while, they slowly change those stories from within. These alterations increase as (to borrow Allen's analogy) we step into and make ourselves at home in new rooms.

Womanist self-recovery and the metaphysics of interconnectedness it posits resemble the "visionary pragmatism" and the "passionate rationality" Patricia Hill Collins associates with African American women's spirituality. As Collins explains, in the quest for social justice, many black women have developed ethical frameworks and spiritualized worldviews that combine utopian goals with pragmatic action; they merge "caring, theoretical vision with informed, practical struggle" (*Fighting Words* 188). The desire to achieve social justice is infused with deep feeling, or what Collins describes as "passionate rationality" that motivates us to work together for social change. As the term suggests, *passionate rationality* represents a nondualistic intervention synthesizing emotion with intellect. Collins makes a similar point: "[t]his type of passionate rationality flies in the face of Western epistemology that sees emotions and rationality as different and competing concerns. . . . [D]eep feelings that arouse people to action constitute a critical source of power" (243). Like the African American women Collins describes, Allen and other womanist self-recovery writers attempt to generate this passionate rationality in their readers. Their emphasis on the relational, interdependent nature of all existence inspires self-confidence, hope, and potentially radical social action.

Given U.S. culture's attraction to the personal (seen, of course, in the popularity of mainstream self-help books), Allen's womanist self-recovery, as well as that by other contemporary writers, can be useful for social actors in at least four interrelated ways. First, as I just explained, womanist self-recovery can trigger passionate rationality—the urgent desire to act, to join with others and work for concrete social change—in readers. Second, because it begins with the personal but redefines the individual as part of a much larger cosmic whole, womanist self-recovery provides a theoretical justification and motivation linking self-healing and self-affirmation with social transformation. Third, because it negotiates among culturally specific histories and traditions and uses these negotiations to generate relational commonalities, womanist self-recovery offers a nonoppositional alternative to contemporary critiques of the universal. More specifically, it demonstrates the possibility of inventing transcultural, particularized universals: new concepts of the universal that move between commonalities and particularities without sliding into monolithic sameness. And fourth, because it synthesizes personal, political, and spiritual concerns, womanist self-recovery gives us tools to achieve more inclusive activist communities. We can insist on underlying commonalities that allow us to forge "new connections" (155) and work together to transform our worlds.

CHAPTER SIX

Pedagogies of Invitation

From Status-Quo Stories
to Cosmic Connections

Womanists make change through
"harmonizing and coordinating."
Layli Maparyan, *The Womanist Idea*

Are we just little-brained creatures who wind up with
these limiting stories of reality because we can't
look and are afraid to listen? Really, what changes
the world is the power of a compelling story. But we
seem to carefully limit the stories that reach us to
those that won't push us to change.

Elana Dykewomon

When I was very young, maybe five or six years old, I became good friends
with a neighbor a few years older than me. We had a great summer, hanging
out together all the time—me at her house, she at mine. We were inseparable.
But when school started up in the fall, she suddenly terminated our friendship
. . . entirely ignoring me at school, refusing to play with me on the weekends.
The break was so sharp, the shift in her behavior so sudden, so inexplicable. I
could not make sense of the stark change in her actions, and I blamed myself.
It's my fault. I did something wrong. There's something wrong with me; I'm no good. I
was inconsolable. From my adult perspective, this brief childhood friendship, with its puzzling abrupt conclusion, is no big deal, but for the little-girl
version of myself, the abandonment still hurts.

To assist me in healing from my despair, my mother gave me a story about "fair-weather friends" designed to make sense of the event and shift my perspective from self-blame to an understanding of human beings. Most people are, by nature, "fair-weather friends," my mother explained. They will be your friend when it's convenient (*when the weather is good, the sun is shining, and everything is going well*). But as soon as the situation changes—a better offer comes along, or things get rough in any way (*the weather changes, and it rains*)— they won't stick around (*they move on, seeking sunnier conditions elsewhere*). She instructed me to be less trusting of people and warned me that I'd often encounter others like my fair-weather friend. These people might seem like friends, and to a certain degree they *are* friends, but they shouldn't be entirely trusted because at some point, they'll leave. If things get rough (or, in my childhood case, if they come across a better friendship, more popular people), they're gone. They don't have your back. They're off to their next friendship. My mother explained that it would have been difficult for my summer friend to be my friend at school, due to age and other differences in our situations. It might have been embarrassing for her to acknowledge our friendship in public, so—rather than address the potential challenges, it was easier for this young girl to just move on. "People are like that," said my mother. "They just don't stick around in challenging situations. It's human nature, so don't be sad." There was no point in blaming myself or being angry with my former friend. "This is just the way things are: fair-weather friends. People can only be trusted so far, and then no further. So, don't be too trusting."

I'm not criticizing my mother! That story was a lifeline, rescuing me from self-hatred and self-blame. The story of fair-weather friends was vital at the time; it assured me that I wasn't at fault. (*Don't blame yourself; don't even blame the other child. Blame human nature—this is just the way people are.*) I wasn't flawed and wrong. With this new story I could get on with my life, make new friends, but do so with more caution and reserve. I could move through childhood without losing my self-esteem; future rejections didn't hurt as much because I was prepared! The story impacted me so deeply that I've carried it with me throughout much of my life. For years—no, probably for *decades*—I used this story of fair-weather friends as a key ethical principle and guide: "Don't trust people too much. They'll just be fair-weather friends, leaving when something better comes along." I took this advice as Gospel truth: Human nature makes people unreliable. Trust yourself, not other people.

And so this story that saved me also limited my options. Because I believed that people were, by nature, fair-weather friends, I went through my adolescence and young adult life with a subtle wariness and a large degree of detachment and distrust. *Trust yourself, Keating!* was my mantra. *Other people will disappoint you. Keep your distance. Be detached. Every friendship is temporary.* And indeed, I encountered all sorts of fair-weather people and developed very few deep, sustaining friendships. I held myself, always, in reserve—in order to lessen the pain when people abandoned me because, hey! that's human nature. I had many fair-weather friends in my life. But can I attribute my series of fair-weather friendships to "human nature," or did my belief in this story, coupled with my actions-in-response-to-the-story, somehow help to construct this series of limited friendships? The story itself played a role in creating the reality it described. Because I was convinced that just about everyone I encountered was—by nature—flawed and only somewhat loyal, I approached everyone with a degree of distrust that kept me somewhat detached; I didn't even try to develop deep, sustaining friendships. No way! I had learned my lesson! Fortunately, through extensive self-reflection and several enduring friendships, I was able to recognize the ways this story was (mis)shaping my life and then modify it. By changing the story, I changed my perceptions and my actions; these slight alterations altered my life's trajectory in subtle but important ways.

My experience with fair-weather friends illustrates the power of status-quo stories. As I explained in chapter 1, status-quo stories describe worldviews, belief systems, and actions (ontologies, epistemologies, and ethics) that normalize and naturalize the existing social system, values, and standards so entirely that they stunt our imaginations and shape our lives. Status-quo stories contain core beliefs that can define our reality and thus greatly influence our lives, though we rarely (if ever) acknowledge their power—or even their existence. Because status-quo stories function as factual truths (or, for many people, as The Truth) about reality, they inhibit our ability to envision the possibility of change—on individual, collective, and social levels. So, for example, because I believed that people were, by nature, fair-weather friends, I viewed everyone with a degree of distrust and treated them with such detachment that I practically pushed them away!

Status-quo stories have a numbing effect. When we organize our lives around such stories or in other ways use them as ethical roadmaps or guides, they prevent us from extending our imaginations and exploring additional possibilities. To borrow Elana Dykewomon's words, status-quo stories do not "push us to change." It is, in fact, pretty much the reverse: status-quo stories block us from changing; they actively encourage us to remain the same:

"Don't waste your breath complaining; that's just the way things are!"
"It is what it is."
"People are always like that."
"People gonna do what people gonna do."
"Hey: I didn't make the rules; don't ask me to change them!"
"It's life. Get used to it."
"Oh, just live and let live."
"Don't rock the boat."
"It's always been this way!"
"You don't like it here? Then leave! Go back to your own country/your own
　　place. Just go somewhere else."
"It's God's will, my friend. Just pray for strength to endure."

Generally spoken with great certainty, these and similar comments (*commands, really*) reflect unthinking affirmation of the existing reality and a stubborn, equally unthinking resistance to change. Because we believe that our status-quo stories represent accurate factual statements about ourselves, other people, and the world, we view them as permanent, unchanging facts. This belief in the status-quo's permanence becomes self-fulfilling: We do not try to make change because change is impossible to make. "It's always been that way," we tell ourselves, "so why waste our energy trying to change things?" "People are just like that—it's human nature, so plan accordingly and alter your expectations! There's no point in trying to change human nature!" Status-quo stories trap us in our current circumstances and conditions; they limit our imaginations because they prevent us from envisioning alternate possibilities.

While it might be tempting to entirely reject each status-quo story we encounter, I believe that adopting a nonoppositional approach might be more effective. Rather than condemn these stories, we can redefine them. (*Kind of like how the womanist-self-recovery narratives I described in the previous chapter work with and then shift and transform status-quo stories.*) When we change our focus by defining these status-quo stories *as* status-quo stories—rather than as factual information about reality—we can reread them from additional perspectives. We can recognize their limitations and explore new options—which might range from revising the status-quo stories to entirely retelling them to moving beyond them and writing new stories.

My work as an educator is directly tied to my desire to expose, interrogate, and transform our status-quo stories and the divisive status-quo thinking which these stories normalize and reinforce. I am especially interested in exposing and transforming status-quo stories about "rugged individualism"—with their extreme faith in human agency, the subsequent pull-yourself-up-by-the-bootstraps theory of success these stories champion, and the dichotomous thinking on which they rely. My teaching experiences have convinced me that this Enlightenment-based story of the "self-made-man," with his hyper-individualism and radical independence, is one of the most damaging stories in U.S. culture. Even now, centuries after its emergence in seventeenth-century Europe, this story—this monolithic, one-size-fits-all explanation of our human reality—consumes and distorts us. This hyper-individualism is a reigning story of our time and in many ways invisibly shapes our expectations, our social circumstances, and our lives. In this chapter, I discuss some of the classroom tactics I've developed in order to challenge this status-quo story; these tactics include stories of interconnectivity, planetary citizenship, and pedagogies of invitation.

Self-enclosed individualism and the status quo

Please don't mistake my criticism of this status-quo story as a rejection of all forms of individualism. As I indicate in chapter 2, I respect and understand the value of personal agency, integrity, and relational forms of autonomy. I am, however, critical of the extreme versions of individualism that focus exclusively on the human and define this human self very narrowly, in *non*-relational, boundaried, terms. I describe this individualism (*or should I say "hyper-individualism"?*) as "self-enclosed" to emphasize its inflexible boundaries dividing self from other, its absolute isolation, and its intense focus on the particular individual human being. Self-enclosed individualism relies on a dichotomous framework that positions the individual in opposition to all other human and nonhuman beings. (*"It's me against the world."*) In this binary-oppositional structure, each individual is entirely separate from the external world. Self and society are mutually exclusive; to survive and thrive, each person must focus almost entirely on hirself, evaluating all actions in egocentric terms: *"What's in it for me?" "How can I succeed?" "How will this event, this situation, affect me?" "What can you do for me?" "What can I take from you?"* At perhaps its most superficial, self-enclosed individualism leads to the radical disconnection captured in the words of Facebook founder Mark Zuckerberg: "A squirrel dying in front of your house may be more relevant to your interests right now than people dying in Africa" (qtd. in Pariser, *Filter Bubble*).

Self-enclosed individualism has its roots in seventeenth-century European thought; it includes an extreme version of independence positing a total break between the individual human being and society; in this dichotomous framework, the degree of independence from society marks the degree of individualism (and full humanity) one possesses. The more independent one is, the more individualistic (and highly valuable) one is as well. Individualism becomes a type of self-ownership, where the "true" individual owns himself and is beholden to no one. As C. B. MacPherson notes, this "possessive individualism" defines the individual

> as essentially the proprietor of his own person or capacities, owing nothing to society for them. The individual was *seen* neither as a moral whole, nor as part of a larger social whole, but as an owner of himself. . . . The individual, it was thought, is free inasmuch as he is proprietor of his person and capacities. The human essence is freedom from dependence on the wills of others, and freedom is a function of possession. (3, original emphasis)

By definition, then, enslaved people and all women of whatever status could not be considered completely independent individuals because they did not own their own person or capacities. They were, to varying degrees, controlled and in other ways possessed by the property-owning men of European descent (*who were, therefore, the "true" individuals*).[1] Nor could these (nonindividual) people be considered members of society which, in this highly individualistic worldview, was defined as "a lot of free equal individuals related to each other as proprietors of their own capacities and of what they have acquired by their exercise" (3). Needless to say, this definition of society was biased from its inception, supporting only a very elite group. And yet, for most of us living in westernized cultures, possessive individualism has become a status-quo story; each individual has a rigidly circumscribed core self that must be nurtured, protected, and defended against other equally self-enclosed individuals; our individualism ensures our independence.

Possessive, self-enclosed individualism restricts our worldviews, fostering what I call "Me consciousness": an adversarial framework that valorizes and naturalizes competition and self-aggrandizement. I capitalize the word "me" to underscore the hierarchical nature of self-enclosed individualism's binary-oppositional consciousness, as well as the elevated claims for self-worth that accompany this perspective. It's "Every Man for Himself," to borrow an old sexist adage—and the sexism is quite appropriate here, given the very select group of human beings who met the requirements of this possessive individualism. With its restrictive definition of the individual—a definition that *ex*cludes far more people than it *in*cludes, Me consciousness is antagonistic and restrictive. Historically and even today, many women (of all colors) and other marginalized peoples have been found lacking when measured by this exclusionary standard. And, when we try to live our lives according to this standard, we damage ourselves.[2]

Possessive individualism is premised on a binary model of identity formation, or what Kelly Oliver describes as a "conceptual framework in which identity is . . . formed and solidified through an oppositional logic that uses dualisms to justify either opposition and strife or awkward or artificial bridging mechanisms" (*Witnessing* 51). This configuration sets up a hierarchical relationship between self and other, where the individual is entirely disconnected from all other human and nonhuman life. This hierarchy presumes and reinforces a model of domination, scarcity, and separation in which intense competition leads to aggressiveness and fear: *my* growth requires *your* diminishment. Interactions between self and other are conflict driven, and society is reduced to a collection of individuals motivated only by greedy, insatiable self-interest.

Me consciousness and the oppositional epistemology and ethics that it fosters prevent us from recognizing our connections with others and working together for compassionate social change. People who organize their lives according to this story of rugged individualism adopt a competitive, survival-of-the-fittest model of success. Distancing themselves from all that surrounds them, they become defensive, isolated, and alienated from the external world. They assume that success depends only on individual effort: Through hard work, personal dedication, and great commitment, *anyone* can achieve success. Those people who do not succeed have only themselves to blame, and their failure has absolutely no impact on anyone but themselves. This status-quo story of solipsistic individualism is deeply infused into mainstream U.S. culture and greatly inhibits social justice work. After all: if each individual is fully responsible for his or her own life, there is no need for collective action, systemic change, or any form of community support or government assistance. Just pull yourself up by your own bootstraps! And if you fail the first time, just try, try again! Kelly Oliver makes a related point: "The individualism behind notions of formal equality and a color- and gender-blind society reduces social problems to personal sins on the part of whites and men and mental instability or physical defects on the part of people of color and women" (*Witnessing* 163). As Oliver's statement implies, this status-quo story of self-enclosed individualism cannot acknowledge the possibility that color, economic status, gender, sexuality, and other human variables can shape people's lives in different ways.[3] Nor can this story acknowledge how powerful individuals have achieved their success at least partially with the assistance of others.

This denial of difference leads to an often-overlooked point: Although it sounds paradoxical, given hyper-individualism's apparent elevation of the uniqueness of each individual, this status-quo story is itself based on a hidden assumption of sameness. Self-enclosed individualism posits a monolithic (*and monochromatic!*) definition of the individual that leads to a type of group-think and a single standard of behavior. As john a. powell notes, "In a way individuality, even as it purports to take into account our distinctness, makes us all the same in fundamental ways. We are all rational, autonomous people and therefore we should all be treated the same" ("Disrupting Individualism" 9). In other words, all individuals are, at the core, essentially the same.

The majority of undergraduate students I've encountered have been seduced by these stories of rugged, self-enclosed individualism.[4] Defining themselves as unique, fully independent and autonomous human beings, they have adopted Me consciousness and are compelled to enact its competitive model of success. Perceiving themselves and their world through hyper-individualism's solipsistic lens, they value independence so entirely that they cannot recognize their interconnections with or accountability for others. Nor can they comprehend the continuing significance of gender, 'race,' sexuality, dis/ability, and other socially constructed categories. Instead, they firmly believe in the status-quo stories of meritocracy, equal opportunity, and fair treatment for all. These stories have persuaded them (and of course many others, as well) that the United States is a free democratic country where everyone is treated the same, everyone encounters the same obstacles, and everyone has the same opportunities to prosper. In the United States of America, anything is possible and all doors will open to those who work hard.[5] Hard work and great determination is the ticket to financial and personal success.

Given these status-quo stories of rugged individualism, is it any wonder that so many of my undergraduate students have expressed callous, judgmental, and/or dismissive attitudes about social-justice issues? Because they believe that each individual is the master of hir own fate, fully responsible and accountable only to hirself , they blame the individual for hir failure to succeed. Students have bought into this status-quo story, and it limits their lives in a variety of ways, restricting their social-justice perspectives, their empathy, and their ability to understand systemic issues. In addition to ignoring the systemic nature of social injustice, this dogma of meritocracy enables many 'white'-identified students to deny the ways color and other markers of difference materially impact people's lives.[6] As Harlan Dalton observes, "For a significant chunk [of 'white'-raced people], the inability to 'get' race, and to understand why it figures so prominently in the lives of most people of color, stems from a deep affliction—the curse of rugged individualism" (105). When students view the world through self-enclosed individualism's status-quo story, they cannot recognize that what affects others—*all* others, no matter how separate we seem to be—ultimately affects them, as well.

Status-quo stories of self-enclosed individualism have dominated our personal, professional, and socioeconomic lives for too long. These stories have not served us well, for they lead to an "increasingly privatized world" (Shapiro) and are too limited to bring about radical change. We need new stories . . . stories with transformational power . . . stories inviting our students to question and expose the status quo . . . stories enabling us to address social injustice and enact revolutionary change. We need stories of cosmic connection.

New stories for transformation: planetary citizenship

We need stories for transformation, stories that can shift students (and at times perhaps ourselves) from "Me" to "we" consciousness. And so, as the title to this section (*as well as the title to the entire chapter*) might suggest, I want to replace our status-quo stories of self-enclosed individualism with not-so-new, though very forgotten, stories of our radical interconnectedness—or what Gregory Cajete describes as the "ancient idea of relationship." Like Cajete, I believe that reclaiming (and, as necessary, revising) these old stories might be vital for us in the twenty-first century: "This ancient idea of relationship must be allowed to arise in our collective consciousness once again. In this perilous world of the twenty-first century, it may well be a matter of

our collective survival" (*Native Science* 105). According to this complex, holistic worldview—a worldview shared by many indigenous peoples, womanist
thinkers, systems theorists, and others—we are radically interconnected at
every level and in every way.

My point here is not to prove to my students (*or to you, dear reader*) that this
multidimensional interconnectivity "really" exists, defining "really" in some
scientistic fashion. Instead, I'm interested in using this "ancient idea of relationship" to develop new stories . . . innovative frameworks for teaching and
enacting social change. One of my primary goals as an educator is to invite
students to explore the limitations in our self-enclosed individualism and
to recognize our interconnectedness with all existence—to take up a sense
of planetary citizenship, as it were. As I explain in greater detail in the following section, planetary citizenship, as I define the term, includes but goes
beyond ethnic, racial, gender, and other human-identity categories; indeed,
planetary citizenship is not human-centered but embraces all forms of life.
And so, I offer interconnectivity and its relational worldviews, or what I call
"we consciousness," as alternatives to the highly celebrated belief in an entirely independent "American" self.

Seduced by their status-quo stories of self-enclosed individualism, the
majority of the undergraduate students I've encountered cannot recognize
their accountability to others; nor do they understand that their actions have
a profound effect on others, that "[w]hat affects one directly affects all indirectly" (Cone 200).[7] And so, I posit interconnectivity as my theoretical and
pedagogical framework and develop classroom strategies that invite students
to shift from Me to we consciousness. Positing interconnectivity serves three
closely related purposes: (1) It enables me to redefine individual and communal identities as mutually *inclusive*, rather than mutually *exclusive*; (2) it
offers alternatives to the binary-oppositional models of identity formation
fostered by self-enclosed individualism; and (3) it can fuel students' desire
to work for social change.

First, adopting this story of interconnectedness enables me to redefine
individual and communal identities as mutually *inclusive*, rather than mutually *exclusive*. I present students with nonoppositional alternatives to Me
consciousness and the solipsistic individualism on which it relies. These
alternatives do not deny individual identity but instead redefine it in broader
terms. Locating each individual within larger interlocking systems, I maintain that individual human beings are not self-enclosed. We have permeable

boundaries. I select texts and authors to illustrate some of the forms this relational individualism can take.[8] I don't deny the value of individualism and ask students to reject it; instead, I reframe the concept in relational terms. By so doing, I invite students to shift their perspectives and adopt a much broader—though inevitably partial—point of view. We are interconnected. As Gloria Anzaldúa explains, "[t]he self does not stop with just you, with your body. . . . [T]he self can penetrate other things and they penetrate you" (*Interviews/ Entrevistas* 160). This permeable self extends outward—meeting, touching, entering into exchange with other subjects (human and nonhuman alike). Significantly, this outward movement is not an imperialistic appropriation, where the self-contained subject grows larger by extending its boundaries to incorporate or annihilate every one, every thing in its path. It is, rather, a mutual, transformational encounter between subjects.[9] We are all changed through our interactions.

When I'm teaching, I offer this permeable concept of selfhood as an alternative to the stories of solipsistic individualism, an alternative that values both personal and collective integrity and self-respect. According to this relational model, self-definition and self-growth occur in the context of and in dialogue with other equally important individuals. (I define *individual* expansively to include both human and nonhuman life, as well as apparently inanimate things.) We are both distinct individuals and integral parts of a series of larger wholes. Living systems theorists' concept of the holon offers a useful analogy for this both/and approach. Coined by Arthur Koestler from the Greek word "holos" (whole), a holon is, simultaneously, an *autonomous* system and a vital part of a *larger* system. As Joanna Macy explains, "All living systems—be they organic like a cell or human body, or supra-organic like a society or ecosystem—are *holons*. That means they have a dual nature: They are both wholes in themselves and, simultaneously, integral parts of larger wholes."[10]

We—each and every individual—are both self-contained and collective, both open and closed. We do have boundaries, but these boundaries are porous, allowing exchange with our external environment. The divisions between self and other, between individual and world, still exist; however, these divisions are not nearly as rigid and inflexible as that old status-quo story of rugged individualism would lead us to believe. Social activist Fran Peavey offers a useful analogy to describe we consciousness and its fluid approach to individual identity:

Human beings are a lot like crabgrass. Each blade of crabgrass reaches up to the sun, appearing to be a plant all by itself. But when you try to pull it up, you discover that all the blades of crabgrass in a particular piece of lawn share the same roots and the same nourishment system. Those of us brought up in the Western tradition are taught to think of ourselves as separate and distinct creatures with distinct personalities and independent nourishment systems. But I think the crabgrass image is a more accurate description of our condition. Human beings may appear to be separate, but our connections are deep; we are inseparable. Pull on any part of our human family and we all feel the strain. (13)

Second, by positing our radical interconnectedness, I can offer my students alternatives to the binary-oppositional models of identity formation that self-enclosed individualism requires. I am especially interested in developing *inclusionary* identities that acknowledge yet transform status-quo stories of our human social identity categories, and I believe that interconnectivity itself offers a type of identity or a trigger for nonbinary identity formation at personal, communal, and perhaps planetary levels. Anzaldúa makes a similar point, stating that we share an interconnectedness that could serve as "an unvoiced category of identity, a common factor in all life forms" (*Interviews/Entrevistas* 164). As I interpret her statement, this category is "unvoiced" because it exceeds human language; it's too expansive for any human being to capture in words. This inexpressible "common factor" transcends—*but does not ignore*—social categories based on gender, 'race,' or other systems of difference; it is "wider than any social position or racial label" ("now let us shift" 558). Indeed, this shared identity is wider than *anything* in "human nature." As Anzaldúa explains, each person's identity "has roots you share with all people and other beings—spirit, feeling, and body comprise a greater identity category. The body is rooted in the earth, la tierra itself. You meet ensoulment in trees, in woods, in streams" (560). Anzaldúa is not alone in her insistence that we share a common trait with all people and, indeed, with all existence: "Source," "spirit," "God," "the Black mother," "Thought Woman," "Light" . . . this shared attribute had been variously named in many wisdom traditions. For the purpose of my pedagogies of invitation, however, the important point is not to label (and, dangerously, through this labeling to pin down) our shared trait. To offer a name could divert us, splinter a class, embroil us in useless/distracting debates. And so, I focus on the "unvoiced" relationality—not on the terms we use to define it. The point is our interconnectedness—not the label.

By positing interconnectedness as itself a shared identity trait, I shift from our status-quo binary systems of difference into a more expansive, relational approach to identity—a differential approach, as it were. Unlike hyper-individualism's hidden (*and* ironic) valorization of sameness, my approach does not ignore differences or in other ways deny the validity of each person's particular (and, to some extent, unique) experiences, beliefs, and desires. Instead, I can reposition these specific individualized differences within a larger, interwoven, holistic context—a context premised on the possibility of commonalities. Let me again emphasize: this repositioning does not negate individual differences, for "commonalities" and "sameness" are not synonymous. As I've tried to demonstrate throughout this book, I define commonalities as a rich matrix that contains—without erasing—synergistically interacting differences. I refer to this mix as *synergistic* to underscore its unpredictable, creative, alchemical dimensions. Offering pathways into complex, unexpected interactions with others, commonalities enable us to perceive differences in less divisive terms. We can retire our status-quo thinking (*at least occasionally*). We do not need to break the world into rigid categories and hide behind masks of sameness that demand we define ourselves in direct opposition to others. We can trust that, despite the many differences among us, we are all interconnected. This trust opens us up, frees our attention, enabling us to look at each other from additional, connectionist perspectives.

Third, I use the recognition of our interconnectedness to fuel students' desire to work for compassionate social change. I invite students to consider this possibility: Because self and other are irrevocably, utterly, *intimately* interrelated, our actions deeply impact each other. What affects you—no matter how distant, how separate, how different (from me) you seem to be—affects me as well. I select readings and develop assignments designed to foster perceptions of our radical interdependence. I want my students to consider their possible connections with others (both human and nonhuman) so that they might reflect more carefully on their actions.[11] We all rise or sink together. As Zen teacher and academic philosophy professor David Loy asserts in his application of Buddhist social theory to the September 9, 2011, attacks and other contemporary issues:

> This world is not a collection of objects but a community of subjects, a web of interacting processes. Our "interpermeation" means [that] we cannot avoid responsibility for each other. This is true not only for the residents of lower

Manhattan, many of whom worked together in response to the World Trade Center catastrophe, but for all people in the world, however hate-filled and deluded they may be . . . including even the terrorists who did these horrific acts, and all those who supported them. (108)

Like object-oriented ontologists and womanist thinkers, Loy posits a dynamic, vibrant world in which every action and object matters. This recognition of our radical interrelatedness can generate new forms of empathy and ethical action, fostering an emergent planetary (or perhaps cosmic?) citizenship.

Planetary citizenship, as I define the term, includes but goes beyond ethnic, racial, gender, and—indeed—human identity categories. I develop this concept in dialogue with Gloria Anzaldúa, whose own identity transitions offer a model for the type of radically inclusive planetary citizenship I envision. Throughout her career, Anzaldúa names her specific embodied identities: She labels herself "Chicana," "tejana," "campesino- to working- to middle-class," "short," "Spanish-speaking," "queer," "feminist," "mujer," "lesbian," "dyke," "woman of color," "person with diabetes," "spiritual activist," "Prieta," "Gloria Evangelina," "Anzaldúa," and so on.[12] And yet, even as she claims these specific identity locations, she also recognizes and acknowledges their limitations. As she asserts in "now let us shift," reflecting on her own experiences near (what would prove to be) the end of her life:

> Being Chicana (indigenous, Mexican, Basque, Spanish, Berber-Arab, Gypsy) is no longer enough, being female, woman of color, patlache (queer) no longer suffices. Your resistance to identity boxes leads you to a different tribe, a different story (of mestizaje) enabling you to rethink yourself in more global-spiritual terms instead of conventional categories of color, class, career. It calls you to retribalize your identity to a more inclusive one, redefining what it means to be una mexicana de este lado, an American in the U.S., a citizen of the world, classifications reflecting an emerging planetary culture. In this narrative national boundaries dividing us from the "others" (nos/otras) are porous and the cracks between worlds serve as gateways. ("now let us shift" 561)

Anzaldúa here replaces status-quo stories about identity—which define an individual in restrictive, categorized terms—with a new narrative—a relational selfhood, a mobile identity that does not reject these categories but instead repositions and rereads them within a larger framework. By so doing, she can reach out—through these identities—to make connections with differently situated, differently located, differently embodied others.

Anzaldúa does not ignore, deny, or in any way reject the specific sta-tus-quo social identities and the boundaries between them. Instead, she "retribalize[s]" them, creating new narratives with porous boundaries. Sig-nificantly, she does not gloss over the difficulties involved in this process:

> You examine the contentions accompanying the old cultural narratives: your ethnic tribe wants you to isolate, insisting that you remain within race and class boundaries. The dominant culture prefers that you abandon your roots and assimilate, insisting that you leave your Indianness behind and seek shelter under the Hispanic or Latino umbrella. The temptation to succumb to these assimilationist tactics and escape the stigma of being Mexican stalls you on the bridge between isolation and assimilation. But both are debilitating. How can you step outside ethnic and other labels while cleaving to your root identity? Your identity has roots you share with all people and other beings—spirit, feel-ing, and body comprise a greater identity category. The body is rooted in the earth, la tierra itself. You meet ensoulment in trees, in woods, in streams. The roots del árbol de la vida of all planetary beings are nature, soul, body. (560)

Once again, we see Anzaldúa critique and resist conventional social identity labels and restrictions without rejecting the identities themselves. Rather than reject them, she redefines them from a broader perspective. Look at the shifts in her interpretation of "root identity" in the above passage. In the "old cultural narratives"—narratives that Anzaldúa herself previously relied on—her "root identity" refers to a culturally specific ancestral tradition. But this version of rooted self-identity is too narrow. Asking herself, "How can you step outside ethnic and other labels while cleaving to your root identity?," she replies by replacing the singular root with a rhizome—multiple, intertwined, branching roots. She pluralizes her ancestral roots—shifting beyond the cul-turally specific, beyond the human, beyond the entire material world. She redefines identity in much more expansive, post-human terms by positing a new commonality: Each human being's radical interconnectedness with all existence. According to Anzaldúa, we (and this "we" goes far beyond human beings) are all rooted in "nature, soul, body."

Layli Maparyan's innovative reformulation of womanist thought illustrates another form that this planetary citizenship might take. As she explains in *The Womanist Idea,*

> Within this emerging global transculture comprised of people with planetary identities, the wealth of all cultures—historical and contemporaneous—be-comes a common human treasure trove. This only works when this cultural

wealth is approached from a place of genuine spiritual affinity—not co-op-tation and exploitation (the old modalities). As we move from historically based, socially ascribed group identities to planetary identity, Earth culture becomes all of ours. For this to work, we have to move away from acquisition and ownership "turf" models towards spiritually based "affinity" models that recognize our fundamental human connecting tendency and respect/revere both individual and collective expressions of divinity that manifest as cul-tures and subcultures. Although this may challenge a familiar way of life, it is time to accept that spiritual affinities may not match skin tone, language, or geographic origin—stated differently, "love (attraction, affinity, apprecia-tion) knows no boundaries." However, because we are in a transitional period cognitively and culturally, it is appropriate to remain vigilant with regard to processes of cultural cooptation and exploitation. (12)

Like Anzaldúa, Maparyan does not ignore contemporary understandings of social identities (based on color, language, ethnicity, region, and so on), but she expands identity to include a planetary dimension as well. For Maparyan, this planetary dimension occurs through lines of affinity that replace the pos-sessive individualism I describe above with relational models.

One of my primary goals as an educator is to offer this possibility to stu-dents. I invite them to recognize their cosmic connections and consider forg-ing a planetary citizenship.

Pedagogies of invitation . . . three premises

Like the threshold theories I explore throughout this book, invitational peda-gogies are nonoppositional and require intellectual humility, flexibility, and open-minded willingness to shift. I refer to these pedagogies in plural terms because my experience has taught me that pedagogies of invitation can (and must) take multiple forms. Pedagogies of invitation can structure an entire course (say, for instance, in the syllabus design, text selection, and reading clusters); or they can occur at a more temporally local level (a single class discussion, a specific assignment). Pedagogies of invitation can take place beyond the formal classroom—in workshops, articles, and books. No mat-ter what specific form a pedagogy of invitation might take, it will always be at least partially shaped by the specific context (defined broadly, to include audience, occasion, etc.) in which it occurs. Invitational pedagogies are ten-tative, performative, and visionary (but not naive).

Pedagogies of invitation are similar to but not identical with critical pedagogy. Critical pedagogy, like the oppositional critical discourse I describe earlier in this book, often relies on negative difference—an antagonistic, dichotomous worldview and an (*unintentionally*) essentializing epistemological framework. Invitational pedagogies facilitate movement through and beyond these oppositional modes, enabling us to replace critique with relational, connectionist thinking. Whereas critical pedagogy generally focuses on critique and often proceeds through various modes of binary-oppositional thought, pedagogies of invitation employ relational, connectionist thinking. I have found that by thus shifting my focus from critique to invitation, I can more effectively establish a classroom climate of generosity and respect.

Pedagogies of invitation are nonoppositional. They employ relational teaching tactics that invite and evoke but do not impose change on students. As such, pedagogies of invitation do not condemn students' perspectives—no matter how regressive these views might seem to be. Instead, pedagogies of invitation offer nonoppositional tactics to engage (*and, hopefully, transform*) these perspectives by inviting students to self-reflect and examine their perspectives from additional points of view.[13]

While pedagogies of invitation take a variety of forms, they are always based on three premises:

1. We are interrelated with all existence: All human and nonhuman life is interconnected and interdependent.
2. Transformation is optional and always—in some way or other—exceeds our conscious efforts, attempts, and expectations.
3. Transformation is more likely to occur when educators remain flexible, open-minded, and willing to be changed by what and who we teach.

PREMISE 1

Pedagogies of invitation begin with the premise that we are interrelated with all existence: All human and nonhuman life is interconnected and interdependent.[14] This radical interconnectivity affirms our current location (no matter where that location might be) and guarantees that we can immediately start exploring networks of relationality. We can make connections—because these connections already exist. This premise enables me to insist that there is no perspective—no worldview, no lifestyle, no belief system, no living system—that must remain entirely alien to my students.

No matter what courses I teach, I include stories of our interrelatedness. I introduce students to an array of perspectives on our radical interconnectedness, including Karen Barad's agential realist ontology and the theory of entanglement on which it is based; Layli Maparyan's discussions of spiritual constructionism and the womanist idea; Gregory Cajete's work on Native science; Joanna Macy's systems theory; David Bohm's theory of the implicate order; Christopher M. Bache's "field dynamics of mind"; and Rupert Sheldrake's theory of morphic resonance. Although the specific readings and perspectives are always context specific, one of my key goals remains pretty much the same: I want to provide students with alternatives to the status-quo stories of extreme individualism. I'm not marshaling evidence in order to "prove" to my students that this metaphysical interconnectedness "really" exists. Rather, I want to model connectionist thinking and invite them to consider some of interconnectivity's diverse manifestations. While students are well-versed in self-enclosed individualism, they're less familiar with relational perspectives. I begin with commonalities and frame differences in relational terms.[15]

My student and colleague Reanae McNeal beautifully illustrates one form this relational framing can take in her undergraduate women's studies course, U.S. Women of Colors, which she teaches at a public university to a racially diverse group of primarily first-generation women college students. When she teaches this course, she frames the classroom by giving herself and her students a common name: "Beloved Community." With this naming, she offers these students—from different racial, class, gender, religious, and regional backgrounds (to mention only the most obvious differences)—a shared identity category—a temporary, context-specific space, a "Beloved Community." She invites these diverse students to see themselves as interrelated and connected. Look, for instance, at the following statement from her syllabus: "I really hope that you will engage with the material and join me on this learning journey so that we can meet these goals. I am aware that as a teacher I can present these goals, but it is really up to us as a beloved community to collaboratively make them a reality. I welcome you to open your mind and heart on our collaborative learning journey together. *You are not expected to agree with all that you read, but I expect you to carefully read, engage with, and reflect deeply on what is presented*" (original emphasis). She shares her aspirations with the class—the "beloved community"—and invites each student to engage deeply with the material and, through this engagement, to build the community and generate insights. She underscores each student's important role as she invites them to interact open-mindedly with the material.[16] Similarly, she leads into the specific syllabus reading schedule by greeting each student as a member of this community: "Welcome Beloved Community to our Learning Journey!"

Throughout the semester—in email messages, class discussions, and assignments, McNeal refers to her students as "Beloved Community," thus reiterating her belief in their interconnectedness with each other and with her. While this (re)naming does not automatically create a blissful, problem-free classroom setting, it gives students a lodestone and a foundation—both a place to reconnect with when misunderstandings arise and a point of departure for healing conversations. (*Perhaps misunderstandings are inevitable, given the painful, complex, multilayered topics this course explores.*)

PREMISE 2

Second, pedagogies of invitation are premised on a fluid definition of transformation that always somewhat exceeds human intention, understanding, and will. In other words, we cannot entirely define or in other ways control the changes our students (and we ourselves) might undergo. Teaching can be a powerful tool for radical transformation on multiple levels, ranging from the individual student's psychic life (thoughts, beliefs, desires, perceptions, intentions) and outward actions, to larger social policies and systemic structures. However, these radical transformations cannot be entirely organized, dictated, commanded, imposed, predicted, or in any other way tightly controlled. Transformation is optional and always exceeds our conscious intentions and efforts. I can *invite* transformation into my own thinking, but I can't accurately pinpoint exactly what this transformation will look like or entail. I don't know precisely how I'll be pushed to change.

Transformation in the context of the classroom is even less within my control. I can neither predict nor direct it. I can't even guarantee that it will happen! All I can do is set the intention, carefully self-reflect, thoughtfully organize each activity, and remain open to my students' reactions. I can invite my students to open-mindedly consider an array of perspectives and worldviews. I can define open-mindedness, model this open-mindedness for them, and provide them with other examples. However, I cannot *make them* open their minds or change their existing beliefs. (*And really, when you think about it, how effective would such a forced and externally imposed transformation be?*) Transformation can't be known in advance, dictated, orchestrated, or in any way fully controlled, and there are absolutely no guarantees that transformation will occur.

Artivist and women's studies graduate student Erica Granados De La Rosa illustrates this open-ended invitational approach in her workshop, "Our Spoken Word: Performance Poetry for Self and Community." Relying on each person's creative potential and the collective power of the spoken word (or what, borrowing from Vanessa Sheared, she describes as language's "polyrhythmic reality") Granados De La Rosa invites participants to build additional forms of community. She offers structured yet open-ended activities that empower both the facilitator and each participant to draw on their personal experiences and their imaginal power as they learn from each other's experiences, making new connections. Through these activities, she aspires to create additional forms of individual and collective identity, as well as activist communities, based on complex commonalities. (See appendix 2.)

PREMISE 3

Although we cannot control transformation, we can (*and perhaps must!*) hope that it will occur, which brings us to the third premise: Pedagogies of invitation require educators' flexibility, open-mindedness, and willingness to be changed by what and who we teach. Note that I focus on the teacher, not the students. Because we're all interrelated, an educator's flexible open-mindedness will subtly impact hir students on several levels. At the most obvious level, when we model these qualities for our students, they have permission to enact these qualities as well. Say, for example, I open class discussion by informing my students that I'm eager to hear and learn from their perspectives. Then, at the end of our discussion, I summarize their key points and tell them that their insights have deepened my knowledge of the text, idea, and/or issue we're exploring. By openly charting the shifts in my own perspectives and emphasizing that I, too, grow as a thinker and scholar, I demonstrate that it's okay to change your views and to develop your ideas. Through my example, I assure students that they don't need to cling, defensively, to their interpretations and perspectives. At a less obvious, vibrational or psychic level, perhaps educators impact our students in other ways as well. Perhaps, through what Rupert Sheldrake calls "morphic resonance," educators' increasingly open attitudes and flexible thinking will facilitate their students' (and vice versa).[17] Or perhaps educators can tap into and subtly impact a class through what Christopher Bache describes as "the field dynamics of mind . . . influences that radiate invisibly around us as we teach" (1). As Bache explains, drawing on his three decades of teaching experiences:

the longer I have taught the more convinced I am that there is a form of collective consciousness operating in my classroom. For years I have watched a collective intelligence surface there, connecting individuals in semi-hidden projects and patterns. In the beginning I did not understand what I was seeing; my belief system simply could not accommodate such a thing. Gradually, however, I was forced to confront the impossible, to think the unthinkable. Groups have minds. They show signs of a true consciousness and intelligence. I watched as fields of influence grew around the courses I was teaching, the learning taking place in one semester influencing the learning taking place in subsequent semesters. But this is impossible, I objected. These are different students with separate minds and this is a new semester. We should be starting from scratch every term. But we weren't. There seemed to be a punctuated rhythm of learning that pulsed beneath the cycle of semesters, a connectivity that linked one class to another in subtle but discernible ways. (1)

I have noticed a similar type of progression in some of the courses that I've taught repeatedly over the years, as students more quickly embrace concepts like connecting through difference, listening with raw openness, and dynamic, complex commonalities.

Our knowledge will always be partial and incomplete. If we can remind ourselves and our students of this inevitable partiality, we can invite them (and ourselves) to be less oppositional and more generous in our thinking. It's likely that we'll make mistakes—that we'll get it (whatever "it" might be) partially wrong. In such instances, the point should not be to condemn ourselves or each other for our errors but rather to use these desconocimientos as learning experiences and opportunities for new growth. Indeed, it was through a very challenging semester of teaching a graduate course on U.S. women of colors—when I made many mistakes—that, in conjunction with my work on *this bridge we call home* (described in chapter 1) I received/created the seed for my theory and practice of listening with raw openness.[18]

Open invitation to readers

Throughout these chapters, I call for and try to develop accessible, useful theory that does not replicate conventional academic oppositional discourse—which generally relies on bold assertions, nuanced yet direct oppositionality, and critical assessments of the limitations in other scholars' perspectives. I take a different approach in this book. And so, I conclude not with definitive statements nor with a critique of the critiques, but rather with an open-ended invitation: Let's expand our thinking and break out of the status quo. Let's take new risks and create planetary identities.[19] Let's develop robust conversations among apparently divergent theoretical perspectives and groups—like contemporary western thinking, Indigenous thought, and women-of-colors' theories . . . and let's do so with the courage, the imagination, the intellectual humility, and the intentional vulnerability that Gloria Anzaldúa, Paula Gunn Allen, and the other authors we've explored model in their work. Transformation now!

Abridged Syllabus for a U.S. Women of Colors Course

REANAE McNEAL

Everything is sacred. . . . And at the seed of everything is relations. That anyone is really separate from anyone else or anything that is happening in the world is an illusion. . . . This is true for all the kingdoms of nature, as well as for humanity. Every time a tree is felled in the Amazon, a tree in Africa responds.

The International Council of Thirteen Indigenous Grandmothers

When we engage in transcultural dialogues, we do not ignore differences among distinct groups but instead use these differences to generate complex commonalities. Through this process of translation and movement across a variety of borders—including but not limited to those established by ability/health, class, ethnicity, gender, 'race,' region, religion, and sexuality—we engage in a series of convers(at)ions that destabilize the rigid boundaries between apparently separate individuals, traditions, and cultural groups.

AnaLouise Keating

Racism is a gaze that insists upon the power to make others conform, to perform endlessly in the prison of prior expectation, circling repetitively back upon the expired utility of the entirely known. Our rescue, our deliverance perhaps, lies in the possibility of listening across that great divide, of being surprised by the Unknown, by the unknowable. Old habits of being give way, let us hope, to a gentler genealogy of Grace.

Patricia J. Williams

Course Description

This class is multidisciplinary and adopts a relational approach to explore U.S. women-of-colors' histories, theories, cultures, consciousness, and lives from a variety of perspectives. Readings, discussions, and writing assignments will focus especially on womanist/indigenous/feminist issues related to conflict, racism, agency, survival, resistance, intervention, and transformation. Our topics will be explored through diverse texts, including novels, letters, essays, poetry, and documentary films.

STUDENT LEARNING OUTCOMES

1. Upon successful completion of this course, students will be able to: Critically analyze the intersectionality and interrelationality of identities, especially as they impact U.S. women of colors.
2. Accurately identify some of the historical and contemporary roles class, color, gender, sexuality, and other social differences play in shaping identity.
3. Reflect insightfully on women-of-colors' histories, contemporary issues, and interventions into so-called "mainstream" feminist theory.
4. Critically analyze the history and contemporary status and dynamics of 'race' and racism in U.S. culture, including women's movements.
5. Reflect insightfully on some of the cultural and spiritual ways that women-of-colors use to resist and survive.
6. Accurately recognize key connections that U.S. women of colors' liberation struggles have with women-of-colors internationally.
7. Reflect insightfully on how commonalities, similarities, and differences work together.

Each of the above student learning outcomes must be performed at an appropriate level as stated in each course assignment, requirements, grading scale, or rubric.

MY ASPIRATIONS FOR THIS COURSE ARE

1. To build community in a way that allows us to recognize our commonalities while acknowledging our differences.
2. To create a space for cross-cultural dialogue to take place while building bridges of understanding.
3. To have students recognize social inequalities and injustices while being empowered to enact social transformation.
4. To recognize the beauty of diversity in the world and our interrelatedness to one another.
5. To have students demonstrate an increased ability to think relationally, improved writing skills, and enhanced holistic-critical thinking skills.

I really hope that you will engage with the material and join me on this learning journey so that we can meet these goals. I am aware that as a teacher I can present these goals, but it is really up to us as a beloved community to collaboratively make them a reality. I welcome you to open your mind and heart on our collaborative learning journey together. *You are not expected to agree with all that you read, but I expect you to carefully read, engage with, and reflect deeply on what is presented.*

CENTRAL COURSE QUESTIONS

1. How do the frameworks provided by U.S. women of colors enable us to ask important questions about power, agency, survival, intervention, resistance, and transformation?
2. How do U.S. women of colors' theories, stories, and texts raise our awareness of the marginalization of U.S. women of colors and their communities?
3. How have U.S. women of colors' theorizing and social transformation complicated the rigid categorization embedded in a Eurocentric knowledge system?
4. How are U.S. women of colors' liberation struggles connected to the liberation struggles of women of colors internationally?
5. How have womanist/indigenous/feminist worldviews impacted social transformations nationally and internationally?

REQUIRED TEXTS

this bridge we call home: radical visions for transformation, ed. Anzaldúa and Keating
Kindred by Octavia Butler
A People's History of the United States: 1492–Present (P.S.) by Howard Zinn
Grandmothers Counsel the World: Women Elders Offer Their Vision for Our Planet by Carol Schaefer
Sisters in Spirit: Haudenosaunee (Iroquois) Influences on Early American Feminists by Sally Roesch Wagner
Elements of Style by William Strunk and E. B. White
Teatro Chicana: A Collective Memoir and Selected Plays, ed. Laura E. García et al.

READINGS

Beth Roy, "For White People, on How to Listen When Race Is the Subject"
Cherríe Moraga and Gloria Anzaldúa, ed., *This Bridge Called My Back: Writings by Radical Women of Color*, 2nd ed. (1983)
"Slave Narratives" [compilation]
Keating, "Background information on the second half of *This Bridge*" and "Sample Essay on Listening"
Harriet Jacobs, *Incidents in the Life of a Slave Girl*

Keating, "This Bridge Background"
Keating, "Octavia Butler Background Information"
Kenan, "An Interview with Octavia Butler"
Smith, "Octavia Butler Retrospective"
"Indigenous Peoples and Boarding Schools"
"Native History and Background"
"Grandmothers' Blessing for Two Spirit People"
Incite! Women of Color Against Violence and Critical Resistance, "Statement on Gender Violence and the Prison Industrial Complex"

FILMS

Rabbit Proof Fence
Turning Prayer into Action
Unchained Memories: Readings from the Slave Narratives
Bajo Juarez
This Black Soil: A Story of Resistance and Rebirth
Arte Sana Victim Advocacy SIN Fronteras
Incite! Women of Color Against Violence

GRADES

1. Attendance

Because much of our learning will take place through in class, it is crucial that you attend all classes.

2. Participation

Participation entails both discussion and engaged listening. *We'll explore a variety of issues, some of them quite controversial. Thus, it's important that we all listen and speak respectfully. We do not need to agree with each other.* As June Jordan states, "Agreement is not the point. Mutual respect that can accommodate genuine disagreement is the civilized point of intellectual exchange, particularly in a political context." Personal opinions and anecdotes play a role in class dialogues but do not substitute for discussions of the assigned readings. *Because of the controversial issues we explore it is important that everybody is fully engaged in participating. This includes being engaged listeners. . . . As part of our presuppositions of Listening with Raw Openness it is particularly important that we honor each other in our beloved community by being engaged listeners in our conversations.*

3. Response Cards

Index cards with at least one question concerning *each* of the assigned readings, as indicated in the syllabus. . . . *I encourage you to take these cards seriously: They'll play the major role in shaping class discussion. (In other words, boring questions/comments = boring class time.) Each set of response cards is worth up to 10 points. (I reserve the right to give additional points for exceptionally insightful questions.) Please put asterisks by questions that you really want to have discussed.* Cards are due by the first five minutes of class. I do not accept late response cards.

Response Card Question Format Instructions: If you ask a question about a specific passage, please provide the quotation and page number(s); if you ask a question about an issue found on specific pages, please include the page numbers. (There is no need to provide full bibliographical information for these questions.) Do not ask definition-based or other easily researched questions (For instance: "What does the word hegemonic mean?" or "What is the difference between feminism and womanism?" or "When did the Trail of Tears occur, and how many people did it affect?" Please proofread your questions! Here are three sample DQs: 1) "I'm curious about my classmates' interpretations of the last lines of Nellie Wong's poem: How would you describe the speaker's view of herself?" 2) "In 'La Prieta,' how would you describe Anzaldúa's relationship with her mother?" 3) "How did you interpret the bridge in Rushin's poem?"

As You Read: Please read carefully, and take notes! Here are some questions you might ask yourself as you read: Do you like the material? Why or why not? What don't you understand? What questions do you have? Does it remind you of any other readings? How?

In order to create as much dialogue as possible, I will interact with your questions as they guide our classroom discussion. *Please do not take my interactions as judgments, attempts to force you to change your views, or even my personal views.* Instead, I expect you to view my comments as attempts to expand the dialogue and open our conversation up to multiple perspectives. Sometimes, I might play devil's advocate or trickster.

4. Race Worksheet

This worksheet will consist of a number of questions that will allow us, as a beloved community, to explore the connections between racial categories and the ways they intersect with other identities in our lives such as gender, class, nationality, sexuality, etc. By doing this worksheet we will gain a deeper understanding of the contemporary status and dynamics of 'race' and racism in U.S. culture as well as the influence that racialization has had on us. This worksheet will give us an opportunity to self-reflect and analyze race in our own lives and others.

5. Grandmother Summary

Students select one of The International Council of Thirteen Indigenous Grandmothers to critically reflect on their cultural and spiritual ways and how they utilize them for survival, resistance, and transformation. Each student will write a 300-word summary on their selected Grandmother, explaining the lesson that they learned from her.

6. Ubuntu Journals

See definitions and instructions at the end of the syllabus. Ubuntu will guide our reflection when we do our journals as we seek to acknowledge commonalities while recognizing our differences. Through the Ubuntu Journals we will reflect insightfully on how commonalities, similarities, and differences work together. The journal is a place for you to put your thoughts into words, experiment with your writing, and make connections between our class texts and your academic, activist, and intellectual interests. The journals must be a minimum of 300 words. They should not be a mere summary of the material, but rather your reflections, opinions, questions, observations, and insights about how commonalities, similarities, and differences work together; they should be directly related to the course materials and Ubuntu commentary.

7. Final Project: Class Presentations

Working in groups of two or three, you'll select a reading from *this bridge we call home* and lead a 15-minute class discussion.

Support and Guidance for Students

[In my syllabus I include information that guides students to the campus counseling service, to the disability support office, and to university information on academic integrity, honor code, and policy on plagiarism. RM]

Course Ground Rules

Our class community will be guided by these presuppositions which can create a space where we honor our diversity and humanity.

Dialogue: Some of My Presuppositions, by Dr. AnaLouise Keating

Here are some of the presuppositions for our class discussions.

1. Social injustice exists

People are not treated equitably. We live in an unjust society and an unfair world; the remarkable promises of democracy have yet to be fulfilled. Oppression (racism, classism, sexism, ableism, homophobia, etc.) exists on multiple seen and unseen levels.

2. Our educations have been biased

The eurocentric educational systems, media outlets, and other institutions omit and distort information about our own groups and others. These hidden mechanisms sustain oppression, including an often invisible and normative 'white' supremacy. This 'white' supremacist thinking has affected all of us in various ways; we all have "blank spots," desconocimientos (Anzaldúa), and so forth.

3. Blame is not useful, but accountability is

It is nonproductive to blame ourselves and/or others for the misinformation we have learned in the past or for ways we have benefitted and continue benefitting from these unjust social systems. However, once we have been exposed to more accurate information, we are accountable! We should work to do something with this information—perhaps by working towards a more just future.

4. "We are related to all that lives"

We are interconnected and interdependent in multiple ways, including economically, ecologically, linguistically, socially, spiritually.

5. Categories and labels shape our perception

Categories and labels, although often necessary and sometimes useful, can prevent us from recognizing our interconnectedness with others. Categories can (a) distort our perceptions; (b) create arbitrary divisions among us; (c) support an oppositional "us-against-them" mentality that prevents us from recognizing potential commonalities; and (d) reinforce the unjust status quo. Relatedly, identity categories based on inflexible labels establish and police boundaries—boundaries that shut us in with those we've deemed "like" "us" and boundaries that shut us out from those whom we assume to be different.

6. People have a basic goodness

People (both the groups we study and class members) generally endeavor to do the best they can. We will all make mistakes, despite our best intentions. The point is to learn from our errors. In order to learn from our errors, we must be willing to listen and to speak (preferably, in this order!).

Listening with Raw Openness, by Dr. AnaLouise Keating

Listening is a crucial yet too often overlooked element in effective class discussions and other forms of dialogue. Below are some suggestions which, if we all practice, will enhance class discussions. I describe this process as deep listening, or "listening with raw openness."

Deep listening entails respect for each speaker's
"complex personhood" (Cervenak et al.)

As we listen, we remind ourselves that each individual we encounter has a specific, highly intricate history, an upbringing and life experiences which we cannot fully know. We don't know the forces that shaped her and, at best, we can only partially ascertain her intentions and desires. Our understanding is always partial and incomplete.

Deep listening entails vulnerability and flexibility
When we're vulnerable, we can be open to others' perspectives and willing to acknowledge the possibility of error. Vulnerability can facilitate transformation. As Paula Gunn Allen suggests, such vulnerability can be an important part of growth: "And what is vulnerability? Just this: the ability to be wrong, to be foolish, to be weak and silly, to be an idiot. It is the ability to accept one's unworthiness, to accept one's vanity for what it is. It's the ability to be whatever and whoever you are recognizing that you, like the world, like the earth, are fragile, and that in your fragility lies all possibility of growth and of death, and that the two are one and the same" (65).

Deep listening entails asking for clarification
Before we respond, we should clarify the speaker's message, to make sure that we've understood as fully as possible what s/he's saying.

Deep listening entails frequent pauses and the ability to remain silent
Sometimes it's best simply to listen, and not respond verbally (especially if those responses would involve offering solutions, drawing analogies with our own experiences or those of others, or speaking without first self-reflecting).

Deep listening enables us to challenge the ideas, not the speakers
We can respectfully, but forthrightly, challenge desconocimientos, misunderstandings, and expressions of falsehoods and stereotypes about our own groups and other groups. When doing so, it is vital that we challenge the stereotypes/racism/ideologies/etc. not the speaker herself.

Sources

Allen, Paula Gunn. *Off the Reservation: Reflections on Boundary-Busting, Border-Crossing Loose Canons.* Boston: Beacon Press, 1998.

Anzaldúa, Gloria E. "now let us shift . . . the path of conocimiento . . . inner work, public acts." *this bridge we call home: radical visions for transformation.* Eds. Gloria E. Anzaldúa and AnaLouise Keating. New York: Routledge, 2002. 540–78.

Cervenak, Sarah J., Karina L. Cespedes, Caridad Souza, and Andrea Straub. "Imagining Differently: The Politics of Listening in a Feminist Classroom." *this bridge we call home: radical visions for transformation.* Eds. Gloria E. Anzaldúa and AnaLouise Keating. New York: Routledge, 2002. 341–56.

Hogue, Cynthia, Kim Parker, and Meredith Miller. "Talking the Talk and Walking the Walk: Ethical Pedagogy in the Multicultural Classroom." *Feminist Teacher* 12 (1998): 89–106.

Keating, AnaLouise. "Women of Color and Feminism: Twenty Years after *This Bridge Called My Back.*" Paper presented at New York University. WS/SOCI 5463. Fall 2002.

Instructions for Ubuntu Journal One

The Ubuntu paper is an opportunity for you to express yourself while drawing connections to your lived experiences, others' lived experiences, the world around you, and the material that we have been exploring on women of colors. Additionally you will do this exploration in the framework of the Ubuntu concept where we see our connections to each other while not ignoring our differences.

Reflect on the following two passages carefully.

Reverend Desmond Tutu, the former Archbishop of Cape Town and Nobel Peace Prize Laureate, describes Ubuntu in the following way:

> Africans have this thing called "UBUNTU." It is part of the gift that Africa will give the world. It speaks to the very essence of being human. When we want to give high praise to someone we say "Yu, u nobuntu": he or she has Ubuntu. This means that they are generous, hospitable, friendly, caring, and compassionate. They share what they have and are able to go that extra mile for the sake of others. I am human because I belong, I participate, I share. A person with Ubuntu is open and available to others, affirming of others, does not feel threatened that others are able and good; for he or she has proper self-assurance that comes with knowing he or she belongs in a greater whole. We believe that a person is a person through other persons, that my humanity is caught up, bound up, inextricably, with yours. The solitary human being is a contradiction in terms and therefore when I dehumanize you, I inexorably dehumanize myself. (qtd. in Sayers 8)

Ms. Barbara Nussbaum, an author from South Africa, describes a greeting from Zimbabwe that is spoken in the Shona language and is symbolic of Ubuntu:

> Morning greetings: "Mangwani. Marara sei?" (Good morning.
>   Did you sleep well?)
> Reply: "Ndarara, kana mararawo." (I slept well, if you slept well.)
> Mid-day greetings: "Maswera sei?" (How has your day been?)
> Reply: "Ndaswera, kana maswerawo." (My day has been good if
>   your day has been good.)

> This exchange means that we are so connected with each other that if you did not sleep well, or if you were not having a good day, how could I sleep well or have a good day? (qtd. in Sayers 12)

After reflecting on these passages on Ubuntu, please do the following in your journal.

1. Attach an image to your paper that you feel symbolizes Ubuntu. Use your imagination!

2. Develop a well-written, one-page paper explaining why this image is symbolic of Ubuntu to you.

3. Reflect on the material that we have engaged in so far while drawing connections to your life, others' lives, and the world that we live in while engaging in the Ubuntu concept.

4. Explore your feelings about the material and the issues that we covered while revealing what it means for our wellness to be connected to others' wellness in the world. When I say "wellness," I mean the physical, mental, emotional, and spiritual well-being of others especially as it pertains to every living being having a place of respect and honor in the world. For example, what does it mean when there are people in the world who do not have access to good water so that they can live healthy lives? In the concept of Ubuntu, where we are all connected, how does this interconnectedness influence our wellness? What does it mean for some groups to be persecuted based on spiritual and religious beliefs? How does this persecution influence our wellness when we think of Ubuntu? These are just a few examples that we can consider when we think about the suffering of others and how we are impacted by it as well. Use this paper as an opportunity to reflect deeply on the ways that our wellness is connected to others' wellness across our diversity

Instruction for Ubuntu Journal Two

To prepare for your assignment I would like you to reflect on the following proverbs and words of wisdom. As you read these proverbs and words of wisdom, you will notice that they are given in diverse ways. This is to illustrate how proverbs and words of wisdom are spoken, revealed, and passed down in diverse communities.

Here is a list of proverbs and words of wisdom from around the world:

Generosity is not giving me that which I need more than you do, but it is giving me that which you need more than I do. (qtd. in Sayers 23)
—Kahlil Gibran, Lebanon

I am doing my prayers around the world to create a world without war and tension; I want to see this world full with natural beauty, where everybody will have equal rights and opportunity to share nature's womb. (qtd. in Schaefer 84)   —Grandmother Aama Bambo, Nepal

Our technology has exceeded our humanity. (qtd. in Sayers 23)
—Albert Einstein, Germany

You are here to shine your light from every pore of your being. Glorify your own nature, taking your power back and standing in your own spiritual light, a quantum consciousness of awareness. How are you using your gifts? How will you serve the planet? Are you walking your talk? (Grandmother Agnes, "Quotes from Grandmother Agnes")   —Grandmother Agnes, USA

Having two ears and one tongue, we should listen twice as much as we speak. (qtd. in Sayers 23)   —Turkey

What I do today does not surprise me. I saw it all a long time ago. I didn't deduct anything from all I saw, and I haven't added anything. The temple that we build is from all that is inside us. This little voice within that each one of us has is our own advisor. (qtd. in Schaefer 25)
—Grandmother Bernedette, Africa

Takipar bich che melolinge ma: It is easy to defeat those who do not kindle the fire (a community is strong that gathers together—round the fire—to discuss and resolve conflicts). (qtd. in Sayers 23)   —Tugen, Kenya

Humanity is at a crossroads: we can only go one way, as one can't go in two directions at the same time. We do not know what we need to do as a human species; there is only one place to go and that is into the light, as one tribe. (Grandmother Flordemayo, "Quotes from Grandmother Flordemayo")
—Grandmother Flordemayo, Honduras

As we continue on our journey exploring Ubuntu, here are two significant quotations that I would like you to reflect on.

As long as you recognize that what binds humanity together is stronger than what divides us, you can help. By reaching out to people from different backgrounds you can become a global citizen. In this way, person to person, community to community, country to country, we can build a better world. (qtd. in Sayers 15)   —Ban Ki-moon, Secretary General United Nations

We are at the beginning of a new age of discovery, an era that sees us connecting openly and rediscovering ourselves and our neighbors. (qtd. in Sayers 26).   —Her Majesty Queen Rania of Jordan

After reflecting on these passages on Ubuntu please do the following in your journal. (It is important that you follow my instructions very carefully.)

1. Attach an image of a girl/woman or group of girls/women who are engaged in enacting Ubuntu in the world. Use your imagination as you select your image. The women could be family members and/or friends, or they could be well-known activists or other well-known women. I also

want to remind you to reflect on the diverse women that we have explored in this course as well as the readings in *Teatro Chicana*, the poems in *this bridge we call home*, and the videos in our weekly unit. You have the opportunity as a class community to share with us some of the many beautiful diverse women in the world who are practicing Ubuntu.

2. Write briefly why you chose this image and why you feel this girl/woman or girls/women are practicing Ubuntu.

3. Give your reflections on the material that we have engaged in so far while drawing connections to your life, others' lives, and the world that we live in while engaging in the Ubuntu concept. Use at least two quotations from readings and/or videos that you find interesting.

4. Drawing from the class readings and videos, as well as your own life experiences, create a proverb or words of wisdom that reflect the spirit of Ubuntu and put it at the end of your journal.

Works Cited

Grandmother Agnes Baker-Pilgrim. *Quotes by Grandmother Agnes Baker-Pilgrim.* Native Village. Web. 5 Oct. 2011.

Grandmother Flordemayo. Quotes from Grandmother Flordemayo. Native Village. Web. 5 Oct. 2011.

Sayers, Helen. *Introducing Ubuntu! Re-ignite the Spirit of Humanity!: Rediscover the Art of Living Together in Harmony.* Self-published, 2010. Print.

Schaefer, Carol. *The Grandmothers Counsel the World: Women Elders Offer Their Vision for Our Planet.* Boston: Trumpeter, 2006. Print.

Final Project

The final project focuses on *this bridge we call home* and requires students to lead a class discussion on one of the essays in the book. We will assign groups of 2 to 3 students. Working with your group, you'll design a set of discussion questions. It's crucial that all members participate equally in designing the questions. If one of your group members does not participate, please let the instructor know.

Class Presentation: During the fifteen-minute presentation, you'll lead a discussion, asking your classmates (who will have read the essay ahead of time) questions about your text. Consider using PowerPoint or other audiovisuals for your discussion. *Every member of your group will be expected to talk in your presentation in order for you to receive your full points.*

You will have class time to work with your group. Please make every effort to attend during these days. I also strongly recommend that you research your author.

The final project includes:

1. A list of *at least ten questions* that you'll be discussing with the class.
2. 1½ to 2 page essay (not including Works Cited page) explaining the lessons that you learned in the course and from preparing your final project.

Scores will be based on the following criteria:

- How much research, thought, and other forms of effort went into this project?
- Are you extremely familiar with your selected text and author? (Some of the authors have written other books, others are important literary figures, etc. It's important that you be aware of this information.)
- How well-organized and thought-provoking are your questions?
- Do some of your questions draw connections with other course readings and/or issues?
- Do your questions engage your classmates?
- Have you learned much from your project?

SPECIAL THANKS

I would like to extend a warm thanks to Dr. AnaLouise Keating for the use of her material in this syllabus and course as well as her mentoring and guidance for the U.S. Women of Colors Course.

Guidelines for a Workshop on Our Spoken Word

Poetry for Self and Community

ERICA GRANADOS DE LA ROSA

Art continues to be a powerful tool as we tackle strategies to negotiate multidimensional identities and diverse experiences. There is a need to find courage to embrace individual and collective narratives within a both/and reality rather than what AnaLouise Keating refers to as an oppositional binary in the introduction to her book *Teaching Transformation: Transcultural Classroom Dialogues*. Stepping out of this oppositional binary and into the poetic narration of storytelling allows us to dialogue with each other in ways that common political/identity rhetoric does not allow.

The ethos of spoken word embodies historical principles contained in the foundations of Womanist practices and theory. In particular, spoken word enables individuals to find voice for what Vanessa Sheared describes in "Giving Voice: An Inclusive Model of Instruction—A Womanist Perspective" as a polyrhythmic reality. This performance practice enables individuals to connect to the collective in a way that gives room for their personal stories, emotions, bodies, and realities to exist powerfully within a space of what I refer to as collective vulnerability.

The understanding of an "open mic" or "cipher" gives way to a community agreement that implies a dialogue will occur in which participants (both performers and audience) will engage with an individual narrative that must be understood as both the performer's story and a story connected to each individual audience member, or receiver. Consequently, formations of solidarity, empathy, anger, sadness, happiness, excitement, inspiration, etc. belong to the community as inspired by each individual. Like many womanist practitioners, I believe this form of communal discourse to be an essential pedagogical practice that must be introduced in the way that we listen and speak to each other in every space but particularly as communities move forward in working for social justice.

This teaching activity is grounded by the question: "What is spoken word and what power does it have within community?" This question serves at least two purposes: 1) It engages others in acknowledging a potential power found in spoken word spaces as it has been experienced by others; 2) it engages participants in the creation of community, so that they might imagine its possibilities in their own diverse communities and context.

Learning Objectives and Environment

This interactive workshop is designed to engage participants of all levels in the artistic production and power of Spoken Word. Through this engagement participants will explore questions that touch on three major objectives:

- Understand the creative practice of Spoken Word
- Develop skills to engage in performance poetry
- Collectively and individually understand some of the ways that Spoken Word can be a cultural and political tool within community

This workshop includes opportunities to engage in writing and performing poetry as well as dialogue on how poetry can and has been used in community building.

The target audience is fluid and can vary from youth in community, to classroom university setting, to formal educators, and beyond. The intent is to highlight/teach a particular medium in which diverse stories can both be told and heard, and safe spaces can be created through language both written and spoken.

KEY CONCEPTS

Poetic Narrative and story telling, collective vulnerability, community empowerment, diversity, safe space.

Activity

Introduction: Key Concepts and learning objectives should be written out and introduced to the community.

LEARNING IS DOING: WHAT DOES SPOKEN WORD IN COMMUNITY LOOK LIKE?

Step 1
Facilitator performs an original piece of spoken word. (5 minutes)

Step 2
Facilitator asks group to write down the first four words that come to mind. (15 minutes)

Step 3
The facilitator asks each participant to use their four words and write a brief poem that presents who they are in some form or way to an audience that does not know them.

Step 4
Group Introductions: Facilitator opens the floor and asks each participant to introduce/read their poem, state their name (or, if they prefer, their poetic name), explain why they are here, and share a question they may have that led them to the workshop. (20 minutes)

Facilitator writes these questions on the board and suggests possible answers throughout or at the end of the workshop.

Note: For a larger group, the facilitator asks a few people to introduce themselves, share their poems, and ask questions.

Step 5
Open Discussion: Facilitator should ask the group about their reactions to writing their poem. Questions to begin dialogue may include the following:

- How was the writing process difficult? How was it fun?
- How was it empowering? (Particularly ask those who shared their poems.)
- Was the translation of emotion particularly impacted by the physical presentation of an original poem?
- How was the space changed? How are we different to each other?

Facilitator should write common themes on the board.

Step 6
Making Connections: Systematize. (15 minutes)

Facilitator gathers responses and introduces the following questions to allow for ideas and experiences to serve as models for the contextualizing of the spoken word experience:

- What is the power of spoken word?
- How can spoken word poetry cross borders between experiences, politics, etc?
- How do you think it can be used in your own community?

Step 7

Concluding: Additional Q&A. Facilitator should be sure to answer all the questions that were presented by the group at the beginning of the workshop. (10–15 min)

Conclusion: Facilitator can present another poem, if appropriate. (3–5 min)

Total time: 90 minutes

SUPPLIES NEEDED

- Paper and pens for participants
- Classroom-style board to write on
- (Optional)—Spoken Word Performance Tips Handout

References

Keating, AnaLouise. "Introduction." *Teaching Transformation: Transcultural Classroom Dialogues.* New York: Palgrave Macmillan, 2010. Print.

Sheared, Vanessa. "Giving Voice: An Inclusive Model of Instruction—A Womanist Perspective." Ed. Layli Phillips. *The Womanist Reader.* New York: Routledge, 2006. 269–79. Print.

Notes

Introduction. Post-Oppositional Resistance?
Threshold Theories Defined and Enacted

1. I define *my people* very broadly, to include all human and nonhuman life, and I define *life* very broadly as well.

2. For an extensive discussion of oppositional consciousness, see Chela Sandoval, *Methodology of the Oppressed*. Unlike Sandoval, though, I do not describe differential consciousness as a form of oppositional consciousness. I discuss the differences between my view and Sandoval's in chapter 3 of this book.

3. The "science wars" represent a variety of intellectual debates between scientific realists and post-structural scholars. Latour refers specifically to the debates between career scientists and sociologists of science. For his views, see his *Pandora's Hope*.

4. See also Mark Laurence McPhail's observation that "When critics participate in argumentative critical discourse they are grounded in the very epistemological sensibility that they hope to transcend. They are privileged by the theory of knowledge that, ostensibly, they are calling into question" ("Complicity" 11).

5. I borrow the phrase *women of colors* from Indigo Violet and use it, rather than the more commonly used phrase *women of color*, to underscore the diversity among us and to destabilize readers' thinking.

6. I intentionally write the word *western* in lowercase letters in order to destabilize the concept itself.

7. For examples of how oppositional movements fragment from within, see Chela Sandoval's discussion of the twentieth-century U.S. women's movement in "Feminism and Racism: A Report on the 1981 National Women's Studies Association Conference" and *Methodology of the Oppressed*; Jacqui Alexander's analysis of progressive anticolonial and liberation movements in "Remembering *This Bridge*, Remembering Ourselves"; Timothy B. Powell's discussion of progressive academics in "All Colors Flow into Rainbows and Nooses: The Struggle to Define Academic Multiculturalism"; and Vicki Kirby's "Natural Convers(at)ions: Or, What If Culture Was Really Nature All Along?"

8. According to many supporters of the "hardwired" theory, oppositional thought is part of our evolutionary heritage. However, as theoretical physicist Basarab Nicolescu reminds us, the human brain has developed to parse the world into binary opposites; the problem is that we have carried this approach too far; it has seeped into everything: "The brain constructs in such a way, during the evolutionary process, a binary representation of the world, very useful for survival in a hostile environment. However, culture extended this binary representation, in terms of exclusive contradictories, to ethical, mythological and metaphysical representations, like good and evil, the space-time background of such representations being erased. The binary operator describes, in fact, the neurological operations of the inferior parietal lobe. The classical logic is a product of the inferior parietal lobe."

9. My discussion in this section was inspired by Gloria Anzaldúa's description of our epistemological condition as a time of nepantla and transformation: "We stand at a major threshold in the extension of consciousness, caught in the remolinos (vortices) of systemic change across all fields of knowledge.... Many are witnessing a major cultural shift in their understanding of what knowledge consists of and how we come to know, a shift from the kinds of knowledge valued now to the kinds that will be desired in the 21st Century" ("now let us shift" 541).

10. See my discussion of Gloria Anzaldúa's mestiza consciousness in *Women Reading Women Writing*, chapter 2. As I explain there, this passage from *Borderlands/ La Frontera* illustrates one possible constellation of both/and/neither/nor thinking: "As a mestiza I have no country, my homeland cast me out; yet all countries are mine because I am every woman's sister or potential lover. (As a lesbian I have no race, my own people disclaim me; but I am all races because there is the queer of me in all races.) I am cultureless because, as a feminist, I challenge the collective cultural/religious male-derived beliefs of Indo-Hispanics and Anglos; yet I am cultured because I am participating in the creation of yet another culture" (102–3).

11. For extensive discussions of the many ways we are interconnected with all existence, see Gregory Cajete's work and the first chapter of my *Teaching Transformation*. Layli Maparyan offers the most succinct yet inclusive explanation of

this metaphysics of interconnectedness I've yet encountered in her discussion of "spiritual constructionism." As she explains in *The Womanist Idea*,

Unlike philosophical essentialism, which assumes that all phenomenal (material) things possess a noumenal (ideal) essence, spiritual constructionism maintains that there is a structure to the *process* of creation as well as to the vibrational spectrum that organizes spirit/energy. This third position articulates that all outward manifestations of form, from identity to society to materiality, are expressions of inner states of consciousness in both individuals and various collectivities. Furthermore, they may be influenced by non-human entities. The cosmos is lawful but dynamic; its fundamental substance is mind, and like the Creator, humans and other volitional entities are always already creators. This position is not earth-bound like social constructionism, nor is it removed from quotidian reality like philosophical essentialism or idealism; rather, it is always directly linked with and embodied within humanness, understood in its full spiritual multidimensionality. (41, original emphasis)

12. I view relational oppositionality, nonbinary oppositionality, and post-oppositionality as closely related and perhaps inseparable. They all draw from but (attempt to) move beyond conventional forms of dichotomous oppositional thought.

13. Anzaldúa's nepantlera represents an extension of her earlier theory of the new mestiza as described in her well-known book, *Borderlands/La Frontera*. See, for instance, her 1991 interview with me, where she explains that "With the nepantla paradigm I try to theorize unarticulated dimensions of the experience of mestizas living in between overlapping and layered spaces of different cultures and social and geographic locations, of events and realities—psychological, sociological, political, spiritual, historical, creative, imagined" (*Interviews/Entrevistas* 176).

14. Throughout *Transformation Now!*, I mark *race* with scare quotes in order to call attention to the term and thus (I hope) to denaturalize it. I discuss this unnatural status of 'race' in more detail in chapter 2.

15. Autohistoria is Anzaldúa's term for a type of autobiographical genre that focuses on but sometimes fictionalizes one's life story.

16. In brief, status-quo stories are conservative worldviews that normalize and naturalize the existing social system, values, and standards so entirely that they prevent us from imagining the possibility of change. See chapter 1 for more on status-quo stories.

17. Thanks to Reanae McNeal for reminding me about this Hester and Cheney article.

18. See especially the last two sections of Anzaldúa's "now let us shift": section 6, "the blow-up . . . a clash of realities," and section 7, "*shifting realities . . . acting out the vision or spiritual activism.*"

19. I discuss Anzaldúa's health-related challenges in "'Working towards wholeness': Gloria Anzaldúa's Struggles to Live with Diabetes and Chronic Illness."

20. For another example of threshold theorizing, see Chela Sandoval's analysis of the 1981 NWSA conference in her essay, "Feminism and Racism." Sandoval compassionately explores the "blistering divisions" (69) between women of colors and white-raced women, critiques the binary oppositional strategies that reinforce these divisions, and offers possible solutions.

21. For a discussion of language's agentic force, see Keating, "Speculative Realism, Visionary Pragmatism."

22. My doctoral training focused on canonical American literature: The Puritans, the transcendentalists, and the James family; and my dissertation, which functioned as what Four Arrows might call a personal sacred quest (18), explores Ralph Waldo Emerson's epistemology, with a special emphasis on epistemological conversions. Almost immediately after finishing my doctoral work, I jumped to contemporary writings by U.S. women of colors.

23. There are, of course, important exceptions to this avoidance of Anzaldúa's and Lorde's revisionist mythmaking. See, for instance, work by George Hartley, Irene Lara, and Cheryl Clarke.

24. In the 1970s, Anzaldúa obtained a master's degree in education and completed all course work for a doctoral degree in comparative literature at the University of Texas, Austin. In the 1990s, she entered the doctoral program in American literature at the University of California, Santa Cruz. At the time of her death in 2004, she was within months of receiving her doctoral degree. For a more detailed timeline that includes her educational experiences, see *The Gloria Anzaldúa Reader*.

25. Thanks to Suzanne Bost for pointing out the "declarations of feeling" aspect of my writing to me.

26. I'm playing off of Maparyan's assertion at the opening of her bold book, *The Womanist Idea*: "As a scholar, I am aware that I am going out on a limb, but if that limb forms a bridge across a river we must cross, then my choice is to proceed intrepidly" (3).

Chapter One. Beyond Intersectionality: Theorizing Interconnectivity with/in *This Bridge Called My Back: Writings by Radical Women of Color*

I dedicate this chapter to everyone who worked to create *This Bridge Called My Back: Writings by Radical Women of Color*, with special thanks to Gloria Anzaldúa for her nepantlera vision. *Mil gracias* to the students in my fall 2007 U.S. Women of Colors graduate course for reading and commenting on an earlier draft of this chapter. The first version of this chapter appeared in Michele Tracy Berger and Kathleen Guidroz's edited collection, *The Intersectional Approach: Transforming Women's and Gender Studies through Race, Class, and Gender*; the second version I presented at an "Intersectional Approach" session at the 2010 NWSA annual conference. I'm grateful to Michele for pointing out to me that my attempts to move beyond intersectionality were rather bold. I had not considered the riskiness, but by reflecting on her comment (*diving into this boldness, as it were*), I was able to take my insights further.

1. For a twenty-first-century example of *This Bridge*'s iconic status, see the 2007 National Women's Studies Association (NWSA) annual conference, which featured a tribute panel to *This Bridge* as part of the main events; or see the titles of recent projects, like *This Bridge Called My Baby: Legacies of Radical Mothering* (http://thisbridgecalledmybaby.wordpress.com/) and This Bridge Called Cyberspace (http://www.thisbridgecalledcyberspace.net/).

2. I borrow the phrase *women of colors* from Indigo Violet and use it, rather than the more commonly used phrase *women of color*, to underscore the diversity within this collection.

3. Significantly, *This Bridge* contributors theorized intersectionality seven years before Kimberlé Crenshaw showcased the term. The fact that scholars so rarely connect *This Bridge* with early theories of intersectionality underscores the fact that we often overlook *This Bridge*'s theoretical innovations.

4. For statements of *Bridge*'s importance, see *this bridge we call home*, especially the first section. *Bridge* has also impacted diverse women in other countries, but due to its publication history it is best known among U.S. women.

5. For additional critiques of mainstream scholars' superficial treatment of *This Bridge*, see Cynthia Franklin and Rebecca Aanerud. More recent work in queer of color studies acknowledges *This Bridge*'s importance.

6. Valerio's work *This Bridge Called My Back* was published under his previous name, Anita Valerio. For a discussion of his transition, see his autobiographical essay, "'Now That You're a White Man.'"

7. I want to underscore the intentionality of *This Bridge Called My Back*'s exclusive focus on women of color. Although Cherríe Moraga suggests in "The Salt that Cures" that Anzaldúa disliked this exclusive focus, evidence from Anzaldúa's papers, as well as her comments in interviews and in her 2002 foreword to *This Bridge*, does not support this interpretation. In the late 1970s, when Anzaldúa conceived the idea of creating a collection of writings by women of color, she was very clear that all the contributors would be women who identify as nonwhite. This exclusive focus was central to *This Bridge* at all stages of its development and represents its historical moment. For additional historical background, see

Anzaldúa's early interviews in her *Interviews/Entrevistas* and her archival materials, located in the Nettie Lee Benson Latin American Collection at the University of Texas, Austin.

8. For examples of these quick, unexamined references to *This Bridge*, see Joe Parker and Ranu Samantrai ("Similar positions on intersectionality are found in publications from the late 1970s and early 1980s, including the important 1981 anthology of the writings of women of color, *This Bridge Called My Back: Writings by Radical Women of Color*, edited by Cherríe Moraga and Gloria Anzaldúa" [12]); and Teresa de Lauretis ("the shift in feminist consciousness that has been taking place during this decade may be said to have begun (if a convenient date is needed) with 1981, the year of publication of *This Bridge Called My Back*" [10]). There are, however, important exceptions to this lack of serious scholarly attention, seen especially in the work of some women-of-colors scholars and the growing field sometimes called queer of color critique (Hong and Ferguson). See also Aimee Carrillo Rowe's *Power Lines*, Grace Kyungwon Hong's *The Ruptures of American Capital*; Hong and Roderick A. Ferguson's introduction to their edited collection, *Strange Affinities*; and Michael Hames-Garcia and Ernesto Javier Martinez's "Introduction."

9. For a really great analysis of core beliefs, see Robinson's "Human Agency, Negated Subjectivity, and White Structural Oppression."

10. See Keating, *Teaching Transformation*, especially chapter 1, for additional discussion of status-quo stories.

11. For an exploration of the ways we co-create our racial reality, see Robinson's "Race Consciousness," and for an extensive discussion of the problems with racialized status-quo stories, see Keating, *Teaching Transformation*.

12. For critiques of self-enclosed individualism, see Leela Fernandes's *Transforming Feminist Practice* and chapter 3 in *Transformation Now!*

13. Similarly, Malini Joshar Schueller argues that 'white'-raced feminists incorporate 'race' through analogies that subordinate racial issues to gender-specific issues like sexism, sexuality, and sexual oppression. These analogies, while giving superficial acknowledgment to differences among women create a false sameness, for they "function to suppress the specific differences introduced by race" (71). This practice inadvertently reinstates 'whiteness' as an invisible norm: "When the (universalist) theorist of gender or sexuality argues that modalities of race function similarly, the theorist's primary object of analysis is not simply gender or sexuality but white gender and white sexuality, particularly when gender and sexuality are not marked as such" (71). See also Leela Fernandes's discussion in "Unsettling 'Third Wave Feminism'": "In its institutionalized forms within women's studies curricula and intellectual agendas in the academy, intersection-

ality is increasingly becoming a marker of multicultural inclusion in many of the same ways that previous narratives of identity politics were. Intersectionality in this context has been transformed into a heuristic device that is used to signify a politics of inclusion." For additional arguments, see also Vivian May's "Intersectionality" and Sally L. Kitch and Mary Margaret Fonow's "Analyzing Women's Studies Dissertations." Kitch and Fonow examine WGS doctoral dissertations produced between 2001 and 2008 and find that "despite programs' emphasis on race, class, sexuality, and the importance of intersectional scholarship to the field—and despite numerous references to the importance of intersectionality in the dissertations themselves—[there were] few examples of truly intersectional analyses (i.e., discussing the mutual constitutiveness of social identities or their inseparability from one another)" (107).

14. As Anzaldúa explains, this connectionist faculty facilitates coalition building and the development of new affinities: "Where before we saw only separateness, differences, and polarities, our connectionist sense of spirit recognizes nurturance and reciprocity and encourages alliances among groups working to transform communities" ("now let us shift" 568).

15. In my desire to not replicate the oppositional criticism I describe in the introduction, I don't want to spend much time analyzing these contributors' status-quo stories. However, to briefly explain: In each instance, the contributor uses homogenizing stereotypes that reinforce the dominating culture's social divisions, reinscribe stark breaks between different groups, and thus prevent us from considering possible interconnections among them. nellie wong's speaker valorizes, without resolving, a 'white'-raced beauty standard that triggers self-hatred: "I felt / dirty. I thought that god / made white people clean / and no matter how much I bathed, / I could not change" (8); doris davenport offers outrageous, parodied stereotypes of 'white'raced women that arguably function to turn the tables on these white women, heaping onto them the egregious stereotypes historically placed on black women; Jo Carrillo brilliantly depicts a certain type of upper-class woman who unthinkingly consumes "Authentic Navajo Hopi Zuni Indian made" culture (66). These status-quo stories were vital to the authors; I'm not criticizing their use in these twentieth-century writings. I'm just suggesting that I do not find them effective for transformative coalitional work.

16. See also this assertion by Morales: "*Color and class don't define people or politics. I get angry with those in the women's movement and out of it who deal with class & color as if they defined politics and people*" (91, original emphasis).

17. See also Audre Lorde's "Open Letter to Mary Daly," where Lorde posits a series of commonalities with Daly while, simultaneously, challenging Daly to recognize profound differences among women.

18. In the last decade or so of her life, Anzaldúa associates this theory of El Mundo Zurdo with her theory of the new tribalism. See her "Preface" and *The Gloria Anzaldúa Reader* for examples.

19. For examples of Anzaldúa's later versions of El Mundo Zurdo, see her *Interviews/Entrevistas*, "now let us shift," and "Foreword, 2001."

20. Note the change in spelling from "El Mundo *Surdo*" to "El Mundo *Zurdo*." The shift from *s* to *z* in the word *Zurdo* occurred when *This Bridge Called My Back* was in press. Although Anzaldúa was not pleased with this alteration, eventually she accepted and adopted it. For more on this issue, see her archives at the Nettie Lee Benson Latin American Collection.

21. I explore Anzaldúa's relational worldview in more detail in "Shifting Perspectives."

22. See, for instance, Anzaldúa's discussions of interconnectivity in *Interviews/Entrevistas*, especially in her interviews from the early 1980s and late 1990s.

23. These manuscripts are in Anzaldúa's archives at the Nettie Lee Benson Latin American Collection.

24. Indeed, the implications are so enormous that I'll spend my entire life learning to more fully comprehend and embody our profound interrelatedness.

25. Although I generally refer to Gloria Anzaldúa as Anzaldúa, rather than Gloria, in order to grant her the respect her work merits by treating her according to standard scholarly practices, when I refer specifically to our interactions during certain points of co-editing *this bridge*, I shift to her first name.

26. Even now, years later, I still don't understand how these contributors overlooked the fact that the collection went beyond "women-of-color" categories. Our call for proposals was very specific in that we invited people of all colors/backgrounds/genders to submit abstracts for possible inclusion. Gloria and I surmised that the iconic status of *This Bridge*—its automatic connection with "women of color" overrode (*overwrote!*) the actual words in our call for proposals.

27. I discuss my interrelational pedagogy in more detail in chapter 6.

28. "Coming to voice" is a common phrase in the mainstream women's movement; "talking back" is a phrase used by bell hooks in her book of that title; and "transforming silence into language and action" is a phrase made "famous" by Audre Lorde in her essay of the same title, in *Sister Outsider*.

29. For important accounts of the diverse ways U.S. feminist women of colors were devalued in women's studies and various portions of the mainstream women's movement during the 1970s and into the 1980s, see Chela Sandoval's "Feminism and Racism," Barbara Smith's "Racism and Women's Studies," and Maxine Baca Zinn et al.'s "Costs of Exclusionary Practices in Women's Studies."

30. I emphasize the diversity of this collective effort. While *This Bridge* chal-

lenges 'white'-raced women feminists to recognize their racism, the book owes its genesis partially to inspiration and energy provided by a handful of 'white' women. As the editors explain in their introduction, Anzaldúa's conversation with Merlin Stone, a 'white'-raced woman, was instrumental in the book's origin. See also Anzaldúa's discussion of the book's multicultural roots in "Foreword, 2001." I underscore this diversity not to champion any particular group of women but rather to intervene in binary-oppositional interpretations of *This Bridge* that associate it entirely with women of colors.

31. For discussions of these difficult classroom/conference politics, see Fernandes, *Transforming Feminist Practice*; Cervenak et al., "Imagining Differently"; and Anzaldúa, "Haciendo caras, una entrada" and "En rapport, In Opposition."

32. I borrow the idea of complex personhood from Cervenak et al., who borrow it from Avery Gordon.

33. See, for instance, Moraga's observation in her 1983 preface that the book lacks international perspectives. As Anzaldúa pointed out in conversations with me, the book also lacks adequate attention to environmental issues.

34. Recently, some scholars have been very critical of the term *holistic*, dismissing it as an oversimplified monolith. I define *holistic* differently, as a complex, complicated, extremely messy relationality. As Jane Bennett explains, "not all theories of relationality are holistic on the model of a smooth organism. There are harmonious holisms but also fractious models of systematicity that allow for heterogeneity and even emergent novelty within. These ontopictures are formally monistic but substantively plural. The whole can be imaged as fractious and self-diversifying process of territorializations and deterritorializations (Deleuze and Guattari) or as creative process (Bergson, Whitehead) or as some combination thereof (the various new materialisms)" ("Systems and Things" 227). I use the word *holistic* in the "fractitious and self-diversifying" manner Bennet describes. See also Bennett, *Vibrant Matter*.

35. Even to this day, Anzaldúa is primarily known as Chicana, lesbian, and feminist . . . labels that she adopted during earlier portions of her career. For an overview of these identity shifts, see the timeline in the *Anzaldúa Reader*.

36. Throughout section 2 of "now let us shift," Anzaldúa questions the existing forms of racialization in the United States: "You begin to see race as an experience of reality from a particular perspective and a specific time and place (history), not as a fixed feature of personality or identity" (549).

37. Anzaldúa builds this acknowledgment of the risks that can accompany our desires to create inclusionary communities into her theory of nepantleras, which she develops most thoroughly in her essay for *this bridge we call home*. She describes the nepantleras' threshold-crossing work as dangerous and, potentially, damag-

ing, although ultimately worthwhile: "Las nepantleras must alter their mode of interaction—make it more inclusive, open. In a to-and-fro motion they shift from their customary position to the reality of first one group then the other. Though tempted to retreat behind racial lines and hide behind simplistic walls of identity, las nepantleras know their work lies in positioning themselves—exposed and raw—in the crack between these worlds, and in revealing current categories as unworkable. Saben que las heridas (wounds) that separate and those that bond arise from the same source" ("now let us shift" 567).

Chapter Two. "American" Individualism, Variations on a Theme; or, Self-Reliance, Transformed!

1. Toni Morrison describes Sula as "a classic type of evil force" (Morrison and Stepto 475).

2. I call Anzaldúa a "sometimes-self-described 'Chicana, tejana, working-class, dyke-feminist poet, writer-theorist'" because Anzaldúa's self-descriptions varied considerably throughout her life; moreover, she did not describe herself in such specific terms in her later years. For more on this topic, see the piece included in the final section of her *Gloria Anzaldúa Reader*.

3. This section was inspired by Trinh T. Minh-ha's bold explorations of multiculturalism. Rather than abandon the language of multiculturalism, Trinh seriously wrestles with and revises it. Like Trinh, I believe that it's more useful to struggle with multiculturalisms (*plural*) than simply to reject them: "To make a claim for multi-culturalism is not, therefore, to suggest the juxtaposition of several cultures whose frontiers remain intact, nor is it to subscribe to a bland 'melting-pot' type of attitude that would level all differences. It lies instead, in the intercultural acceptance of risks, unexpected detours, and complexities of relation between break and closure. Every artistic excursion and theoretical venture requires that boundaries be ceaselessly called to question, undermined, modified, and reinscribed" (*Moon* 232).

4. In this section, I refer specifically to scholars who focused on the literature of the United States. Generally, these twentieth-century scholars conflated "American literature" with literature produced in (and about) the United States, rather than in other parts of the Americas. My use of the term "American" in this section is designed to capture their perspective, which conflated "American" with "U.S."

5. Lawrence W. Levine offers a useful summary of American literature's belated appearance in U.S. colleges and universities in chapter 4 of *The Opening of the American Mind*. As Levine notes, "In 1928 Ferner Nuhn found that in American colleges and universities Scandinavian literature was taught as often as American

literature, Italian literature twice as often, Spanish and German literature three times as often, French literature four times as often, Latin and Greek literature five times as often, and English literature ten times as often. More undergraduate courses were devoted to two English poets, Chaucer and Milton, than were offered in all of American literature. Thirteen years later, Floyd Stovall surveyed seventy English departments and found that American literature constituted no more than 20 percent of the offerings" (84). On Adamic innocence, see Joanna Brooks's insightful analysis of R. W. B. Lewis's influential book, *The American Adam: Innocence, Tragedy, and Tradition in the Nineteenth Century*. On American exceptionalism, see Peter Carafiol, "'Who I Was'"; Sacvan Bercovitch, "Afterword"; Gregory Jay, "The End of 'American' Literature"; and David Shumway, *Creating American Civilization*. On the canon-forming role played by New England writers and scholars, see Luis Leal, "The Rewriting of American Literary History."

6. If we add other social identity categories—like sexuality, dis/ability and health, region, and economic status, there's probably more diversity among these canonized authors. However, in the status-quo literary story I'm summarizing here, these more nuanced social differences are generally ignored.

7. Thus, for example, Bonnie TuSmith maintains that, "[g]iven the long overdue inclusion of ethnic and women's writings into the curriculum, our understanding of American literary tradition—at least the version promoted in the 1950s and 1960s—must be revised.... At a minimum, we must distinguish ... Eurocentric culture or literary tradition from ethnic traditions in this country. Since many of us agree that cultural diversity is an undeniable characteristic of American society, we must beware of applying monolithic terms to non-WASPS. Many times these terms simply do not fit" (21). John Maitino and David Peck make a similar call in their introduction to *Teaching Ethnic American Literature*, where they explain that "traditional academic literary criticism has not worked as well with ethnic writers. Older criticism functions best with literary works that are finished, completed. Ethnic American literature is itself a process—in its stories of assimilation and resistance, of immigration and oppression—and demands a criticism that is equally flexible and fluid" (4).

8. I discuss separatist multiculturalism in more detail in *Teaching Transformation*.

9. See Gene Andrew Jarrett and Christopher Douglas for critiques of narrow definitions of ethnic-specific literary traditions.

10. As Jarrett notes in "Judging a Book by Its Writer's Color," many leading African American authors wrote what he calls "anomalous literature"—works that focus not on overtly racialized characters or themes but on "our common humanity, regardless of racial differences." Scholars pay almost no attention to these anomalous texts. Jarrett's 2004 search of the MLA bibliography revealed

"that anomalous stories constituted the main subject matter of less than 2 percent of all the dissertations, articles, chapters in edited collections, and books published on African-American writers since 1963."

11. Jack Salzman, director of the Columbia University Center for American Culture Studies, makes a similar point:

What first astounded me here was the lack of interest that people in various ethnic communities have in other ethnic communities. If I do a panel, whether fairly low-keyed or high-powered, let us say on the African American community, the audience will be, for the most part, African Americans. There will be very few Hispanics, very few Asians. If I do a panel on Asian Americans, almost no one who is not Asian American will show up. We use terms such as *discourse* and *dialogue* all the time, but, in fact, there seems to be relatively little interest in dialogue between and among various communities. (qtd. in Kroeber 56, original emphasis)

As Salzman's observation indicates, these literary boundaries translate into everyday life, when people assume that the differences between themselves and the various others they encounter are too different—too *other*, as it were—to have anything of importance in common.

12. I was introduced to Morejón's work and this concept of the transcultural in Françoise Lionnet, *Autobiographical Voices*.

13. Even the sketchiest biographical information indicates some of the many differences among the writers examined in this chapter: Ralph Waldo Emerson (1803–1882), born in Boston to a long line of ministers who immigrated from England in the 1630s; Henry David Thoreau (1817–1862), another New Englander, born in Concord, Massachusetts, to a second-generation French American father and a mother of Scottish descent; June Jordan (1936–2002), daughter of Jamaican immigrants, born in Harlem, New York; Paula Gunn Allen (1939–2008), born on the Cubero Spanish-Mexican land grant in New Mexico to a Laguna-Sioux-Scottish mother and a Lebanese American father; and Gloria Anzaldúa (1942–2004), born in the Rio Grande Valley of south Texas in 1942 to sixth-generation *mexicanos*.

14. See also Charlene Avallone's analysis of the racist, masculinist ideology inherent in constructions of the American Renaissance as a literary period.

15. See, for example, Juan Bruce-Novoa's discussion of Chicano canon formation.

16. For another fascinating parallel between Emerson and Jordan, consider Emerson's description of leadership in his journal:

I have been writing & speaking what were once called novelties, for twenty-five or thirty years, & have not now one disciple. Why? Not that what I said was not true; not that it has not found intelligent receivers but because it did not go from any wish in me to bring men to me, but to themselves. I delight in driving them from me. What could I do, if they came to me? They would inter-rupt & encumber me. This is my boast that I have no school & no follower. I should account it a measure of the impurity of insight, if it did not create in-dependence. (*Emerson* 434)

17. My language is intentional in my reference to "a distinctive, highly complex social dimension that *readers rarely associate with Emerson or Thoreau*." I've carefully expressed this contrast as one of interpretation because, as some recent schol-arship hints at, these authors were more aware of systemic social issues than standard interpretations of their work generally indicates. (See, for instance, Len Gougeon's work.) Moreover, both Thoreau and Emerson had extensive so-cial networks.

18. David Lyttle makes a related point in "Emerson's Transcendental Indi-vidualism." According to Lyttle, in Emerson's theory of transcendental identity, "persons, defined (from the low perspective of the Understanding) as separate entities, can also be in reality each other[;]. . . . one person can be, at the same time, all persons[;] . . . one can be many" (92).

19. Emerson does not always use the term "Reason" to describe this univer-sal, intuitive faculty. Throughout his career he uses a variety of terms, including "Imagination," "Genius," "Intuition," and "Intellect."

20. While it is not surprising that *Nature* readers assume Emerson advocated an abandonment of the personal, this assumption does not correspond to Em-erson's life. As Robert Richardson notes, "*Nature* has been read as a gospel of selfishness, illogic, optimism, and parochialism. Emerson's life and his reading while he worked on *Nature* show the book to be rooted in family life, formal logic, Greek tragedy, and Asian classic" (233). As Richardson demonstrates, Emerson himself did not reject personal connections; throughout his life he maintained intimate ties with family and friends, offering them all sorts of support.

21. I intentionally capitalize "Author" to underscore the fact that Anzaldúa aspired to become a canonical, highly regarded and frequently read author—"up there" with Hawthorne, Whitman, and others.

22. For Emerson's description of the personal paralysis that occurs when we attempt to follow society's dictates see, for example, "Self-Reliance." For Tho-reau's rejection of social standards, see the first chapter of *Walden*.

23. Anzaldúa discusses the new mestiza throughout *Borderlands/La Frontera*, but see especially chapter 7, "*La conciencia de la mestiza*: Towards a New Consciousness." She offers a revised definition in her later work; see, for instance, "now let us shift."

24. By feminizing the term "mestizo," Anzaldúa's "mestiza" implicitly critiques twentieth-century Chicano literary and theoretical movements, which were dom-

inated by male-centered issues. For discussions of this male bias, see Ramón Saldívar, *Chicano Narrative*; Lee Bebout, *Mythohistorical Interventions*; Anzaldúa, "To(o) Queer the Writer," and Moraga, *Last Generation*.

25. See, for example, Christopher Douglas, *A Genealogy of Literary Multiculturalism*.

26. As I explain in *Women Reading Women Writing*, Allen does occasionally draw on her personal experiences; however, in her academic work, she does not include the types of intimate details found in Jordan's and Anzaldúa's writings. We can attribute these differences at least partially to the fact that for much of her life, Allen followed a more conventional academic trajectory in her career than Jordan and Anzaldúa. But as I suggest in chapter 5, the academic breaks down pretty thoroughly in Allen's *Grandmothers of the Light*.

27. Possessive individualism—a theory developed by C. B. MacPherson in *The Political Theory of Possessive Individualism Hobbes to Locke*—originated in the seventeenth century and defines the individual by his (my use of this pronoun is intentional) autonomy and radical independence from society. I discuss this theory in more detail in chapter 6.

28. For discussions of language's performative effects, see Richard Bauman, *Verbal Art as Performance*; and Manulani Aluli Meyer, "Acultural Assumptions of Empiricism."

29. On rebirth in Thoreau, see, for example, the final chapter in *Walden*.

30. Emerson did not eschew politics, and in much of his work he aspired to intervene in existing social and political issues, including the Cherokee Trail of Tears, slavery, and women's rights. However, he did not focus as closely on these issues as Allen, and his political speeches and writing have been underexamined. For more on Emerson's politics, see the essays in Gregory Garvey's *The Emerson Dilemma*, as well as Len Gougeon's work.

Chapter Three. "I am your other I": Transformational Identity Politics

1. This author could be "marginal" for any number of reasons: because she's female and/or queer and/or a person of color, and the list goes on.

2. I use the term *self-identified* to indicate the volitional dimension of contemporary feminist identity politics.

3. Suleri's essay, "Woman Skin Deep," includes a biting critique of bell hooks's and other "postcolonial" feminists' (mis)use of the rhetoric of the margin/center discourse. Finke makes a related point, asserting, "There are no oppressed groups pure and simple, only shifting relations between oppressors and oppressed. Yet, the relational nature of marginality frequently remains unacknowledged, even by feminists" (253). For an additional analysis of the epistemic privilege claimed by some self-identified women of color, see Bat On, "Marginality and Epistemic

Privilege." While I disagree with her interpretation of Anzaldúa, I appreciate her analysis of the limitations in margin-center language. See also Cresside Heyes's discussion of identity politics.

4. Chela Sandoval makes a similar argument in *Methodology of the Oppressed*.

5. For additional critiques of U.S. feminists' identity politics, see Jenny Bourne; Judith Butler, *Gender Trouble*; Kathy Ferguson; and June Jordan.

6. I say "quadrupally" because Anzaldúa and Lorde also could be classified as "disabled"—Anzaldúa because of her lifelong health battles and diabetes, and Lorde because of her childhood vision difficulties and her adult cancer.

7. Spivak discusses strategic essentialism in *In Other Worlds* (197–221) and *Outside in the Teaching Machine* (3–8). For a useful explanation of the differences between strategies and tactics, see de Certeau, *The Practice of Everyday Life*.

8. For discussions of the importance of place to Native peoples, see Cajete's *Native Science* and *Look to the Mountain*; Four Arrows's edited collection, *The Authentic Dissertation*; and Thomas Norton-Smith's *The Dance of Person and Place*.

9. I acknowledge the riskiness of Allen's invitation and examine it in more detail in chapter 5.

10. As Allen notes, shadows are neither light nor dark but rather involve the interplay of both light and dark (*Sacred Hoop* 224).

11. I return to the questionable, potentially objectionable, aspects of Allen's work in chapter 5.

12. See especially Anzaldúa's discussion in the preface and chapter 7 of *Borderlands/La Frontera*.

13. For explorations of Anzaldúa's new tribalism, see her *Interviews/Entrevistas* and Keating, "Shifting Worlds, Una Entrada."

14. In an article I'm working on, I describe this relational identity (trans)formation as "self-dis-identification." Based on the belief that each human being is multilayered and interconnected with all existence, self-dis-identification represents a contradictory movement in which one shifts away from personal identity and individual selfhood while, simultaneously, shifting toward a larger, more inclusionary type of belonging and identification with the cosmos (or perhaps with some type of cosmic Self). I borrow from and build on Leela Fernandes's important theory of disidentification, which she develops in *Transforming Feminist Practice*.

Chapter Four. "There is no arcane place for return": Revisionist Mythmaking with a Difference

The quotation in the main title of this chapter is from Trinh T. Minh-ha, *When the Moon Waxes Red* (20).

1. As I define it, revisionist mythmaking is a transformational practice that rewrites status-quo versions of mythic stories. These revisions can take a number of

forms, including, but not limited to, the following: (1) We can retell a well-known mythic story from a different point of view. (2) We can rewrite the story—alter the plot and thus revise the story itself. (3) We can recover alternative, previously lost or forgotten versions of commonly accepted myths. (4) We can go entirely outside of our mythic traditions, bringing in new stories, which we then revise. For discussions of feminists' revisionist mythmaking, see Rachel Blau DuPlessis, *Writing Beyond the Ending*. For discussions of gender- and cultural-revisionist mythmaking, see Lee Bebout, *Mythohistorical Interventions*, and chapter 2 of Keating, *Women Reading Women Writing*.

2. For a discussion of some of the positive and negative ways that cultural myths can impact our beliefs about human nature (among other things), see Drucilla Cornell, *Beyond Accommodation*.

3. Butler summarizes this view in *Gender Trouble* 3–6.

4. Thanks to Lindsay Robertson for introducing me to Puar's essay, "'I would rather be a cyborg than a goddess.'"

5. I use the phrase "twentieth-century theorists" here, even though I'm discussing people who have survived into the twenty-first century. I do so to underscore the historical moment and to acknowledge that, quite possibly, some of these theorists have taken their work in new directions that might not be quite so critical of issues touching on the revisionist mythmaking debates I explore in this chapter.

6. Karlyn Crowley makes a similar point in "Secularity."

7. Throughout this chapter I capitalize "Woman" when indicating the term's metaphoric character, including both the oppressive and potentially liberatory aspects of the term. Also, in this chapter, I put "feminine" in quotation marks in order to emphasize the provisional, speculative, and potentially transformative dimensions of the term.

8. See, for instance, Elinor W. Gadon, *The Once and Future Goddess*.

9. This section's comparison between Anzaldúa's and Daly's theories and uses of metaphoric language was inspired by the following two quotations: "I say mujer magica, empty yourself. Shock yourself into new ways of perceiving the world. Shock your readers into the same. Stop the chatter inside their heads" (Anzaldúa, "Speaking in Tongues" 34). "Only confirmation of one's own Reality awakens that Reality in another" (Daly, "Be-Friending" 201).

10. For examples of these critiques of the "linguistic turn" see, for instance, Stacy Alaimo and Susan Hekman, "Introduction"; and Karen Barad, *Meeting the Universe Halfway*. For a brief summary of the history of this critique, see Rey Chow, "European Theory in America."

11. For discussions of the performative, language-based dimensions of indigenous metaphysics and ontologies, see Gregory Cajete, *Native Science*; Kirstin

Squint, "Choctawan Aesthetics, Spirituality, and Gender Relations"; and Thomas Norton-Smith, *The Dance of Person and Place*.

12. While in *Borderlands*, Anzaldúa does refer to a culturally specific shaman, in "Metaphors in the Tradition of the Shaman," her use of the term is somewhat transcultural, for she associates the word "shaman" with its Sanskrit roots.

13. Indeed, revisionist mythmaking functions as a type of roadmap or guidebook throughout Anzaldúa's career, from her early poetry to *Borderlands* to her post-*Borderlands* theories of the Coyolxauhqui imperative and conocimiento. For additional discussion of Anzaldúa's revisionary myths, see Irene Lara, "Daughter of Coatlicue" and "Goddess of the Américas in the Decolonial Imaginary."

14. I describe Coatlicue as *god/dess* to underscore this divine figure's ambivalently gendered status; Coatlicue contains but goes beyond the typical gender duality. See Irene Lara's discussion of Coatlicue in "Goddess of the Américas."

15. For discussions of Anzaldúa's theory of conocimiento, see Kelli Zaytoun's "New Pathways towards Understanding Self-in-Relation" and "Theorizing at the Borders" and Nathalia E. Jaramillo's *Immigration and the Challenge of Education*.

16. Throughout "now let us shift," Anzaldúa uses second person, in part to create a bridge between her experiences and her readers. The events she describes in this essay develop from her autobiographical experiences.

17. I define, explore, and apply Anzaldúa's poet-shaman aesthetics in "Speculative Realism, Visionary Pragmatism, and Poet-Shamanic Aesthetics in Gloria Anzaldúa—and Beyond."

18. For discussions of stereotype threats, see the work of social psychologist Claude Steele; Richard T. Ford's analysis in *Racial Culture* of Steele's work; and Loriann Roberson and Carol T. Kulik, "Stereotype Threat at Work."

19. Similarly, in *Borderlands/La Frontera*, Anzaldúa describes the writing process as a conversation between her "Self" and the world: "I am in dialogue between my Self and el espíritu mundo. I change myself, I change the world" (70).

20. Daly uses the metaphor of shape-shifting in *Gyn/Ecology*, where she describes her writing process as "a Stunning experience of *Shape-shifting*" (xviii–xix, original emphasis). Unlike Anzaldúa, however, Daly does not associate this shape-shifting with any culturally specific traditions.

21. For Daly's comments on goddess terminology, see *Gyn/Ecology* lxv–lxvi and *Beyond God the Father* xviii–xix.

22. Anzaldúa discusses her theory of "putting Coyolxauhqui together" in "now let us shift" and in her essay of the same name. See also her discussions of "the Coyolxauhqui Imperative" in *Interviews/Entrevistas* and *The Gloria Anzaldúa Reader*.

23. As William Doty explains, because mythical symbols contain "units of information that are bound up by the immediate contours of what presently is

being experienced, . . . [they] provide concrete conveyances for (abstract) thought. Alive in a world of metaphoric and symbolic meanings, they allow experimentation and play with images, ideas, and concepts that otherwise would remain too incorporeal to be engaged" (20).

24. For one example of Anzaldúa's more radical inclusivity, consider that she, unlike Daly, invites men and transpeople to participate in her culture-building activities, and does so throughout her career, from the late 1970s until 2004. For more on this inclusiveness see Keating, *Women Reading Women Writing*.

25. My interest in putting Audre Lorde in dialogue with Mary Daly was inspired by the authors' own words. More specifically, it's these two statements that called out to me, challenging me to investigate possible points of connection:

> The function of much of what I read about Africa and about Black women, that is meaningful to me, is frequently to keep me from feeling crazy. That's one of the horrors of being locked into the mouth of the dragon: not only do you not have any role models, but there no resonance for your experience. That's what made me begin to think about writing what I've been writing. We (Black lesbian feminists) have been around a long time. . . . Yes, we do need role models. I wish I'd had some. It would have saved a lot of time. (Lorde, qtd. in Hammond 28)

> Having been a Pirate for many years, I have Righteously Plundered treasures of knowledge that have been stolen and hidden from women, and I've struggled to Smuggle these back in such a way that they can be seen as distinct from their mindbinding trappings. (Daly, *Gyn/Ecology* xxiv)

26. I use "pragmatically" in the philosophical sense, to signal my belief that we could read Audre Lorde's work as an innovative contribution to the philosophical school of pragmatism initiated by William James (or possibly Ralph Waldo Emerson). But exploring this lineage is the topic of another project!

27. For discussions of this erasure, see Lorde, "Open Letter to Mary Daly"; Sabrina Sojourner, "From the House of Yemanja"; and Diedre L. Bádéjó, "The Goddess Osun as a Paradigm for African Feminist Criticism."

28. For an extensive discussion of these stereotypes, see Melissa Harris-Perry, *Sister Citizen: Shame, Stereotypes, and Black Women in America*.

29. For a discussion of vibrational metaphysics, see Layli Maparyan, *The Womanist Idea*, especially chapter 1. As Maparyan explains,

> This spiritual universe is energetic and vibrational. That means spirit is energy, energy is spirit. Spirit is an efflux of the Creative Presence, whether called God or Mind or Allah or Source or YHVH or Olodumare or Divine Intelligence or the Unified Field or Brahma or Self. In its infinite dynamism reflecting the unbounded expressivity of this Creative Presence, spirit exists at different levels

and rates of vibration, making it possible to talk in terms of a transcendent spiritual reality alongside the immanent one (a both/and relationship). All things, including humans, mirror this Creative Presence—a reality encapsulated in the Hermetic aphorism, "As within, so without; as above, so below," as well as by quantum scientists in notions such as the implicate order and the holographic universe. All things manifest in a way that reflects their rate of vibration, and vibration is manipulable by humans and others. Humans are not assumed to be the only kinds of volitional beings in the universe, and all things exist in energetic interrelation. (35)

30. See, for example, Rosi Braidotti's discussions of Gilles Deleuze. See also the Melissa Gregg and Gregory J. Seigworth edited collection, *The Affect Theory Reader*.

31. I describe Lorde's mythic stories as "new-yet-old" to underscore their inventiveness.

32. I use the term *transgendered* to emphasize that Lorde's and Anzaldúa's transcultural communities are not always gender-specific and often include more than the typical two genders. As I explain in *Women Reading Women Writing*, they use nonwestern myth to break down dichotomous male-female gendered identities. This deconstructive gesture is, perhaps, one of the greatest differences between their writings and Daly's, for Daly's work focuses almost entirely on women and female identity. Perhaps the fact that Daly focuses so intentionally only on women limits her work in other ways. Maybe this exclusionary mechanism, this not-for-men gesture, has other side effects, as well.

33. Anzaldúa's revisionist mythmaking has been criticized for other reasons, as I explain in "Speculative Realism, Visionary Pragmatism, and Poet-Shamanic Aesthetics in Gloria Anzaldúa—and Beyond."

34. For a classic discussion of reason's nonuniversal dimensions, Genevieve Lloyd, *The Man of Reason*.

35. For more on this issue, see Cornell, *Beyond Accommodation*; Paula Moya, "Cultural Particularity versus Universal Humanity"; and David Palumbo-Liu, "Introduction."

36. See, for example, *Gyn/Ecology*, where Daly points to Libyan, Irish, pre-Hellenic, and Hellenic versions of "the Triple Goddess" (75—76). Similarly, in *Pure Lust* she finds "Egyptian/African sources" for Mexican and European black Madonnas and associates these culturally specific images of female divinity" both with a cosmic commonality and with nature: "[T]hese glimmerings of our Archaic Elemental heritage . . . stir deep Memory, enabling Hags to ride the Metaphors of the Black Madonnas to spheres of imagination that transcend insipid caucasian cookie-cutter depictions of the Arch-Image. Having glimpsed the Arch-image as black earth, we are prepared to see her associations with other elements" (117).

37. For a concrete example of the ways Daly's universalism inhibits dialogue among women, see Meaghan Morris, *The Pirate's Fiancée*.

38. I would also argue that Anzaldúa's and Lorde's transcultural universals rely on and are energized by "LUXOCRACY," which, as I explain in chapter 2, is a foundational component of the womanist idea. As such, their revisionist mythmaking participates in what Layli Maparyan describes as "the luminous revolution." According to Maparyan, this

> is that which will establish a new universal understanding around Innate Divinity, or the inherently luminous nature of humans and all creation. Thus, the most important work any of us can do right now is to bring awareness of Innate Divinity, of the Inner Light, and make it stick. There are so many ways to do this, so many paths, so many voices in which this message must be spoken to reach all humanity. Thus, we are in a necessary and underappreciated period of intense polyvocality, through which Spirit—SOURCE—speaks to and through multiple populations simultaneously, sometimes in mutually unintelligible tongues. (14)

39. For an extensive exploration of how Anzaldúa and Lorde redefine ethnicity, gender, and sexuality, see Keating, *Women Reading Women Writing*.

40. Ernesto Laclau and Chantal Mouffe describe this process of articulation in *Hegemony and Socialist Strategy*.

41. I borrow the term *metaphoric transference* from Cornell; she explains that "[t]he metaphors of Woman, in and through which she is performed, are enacted signifiers which, as such, act on us as genderized subjects. But this performance keeps us from 'getting to the Other' of the rediscursive 'reality' of gender or of sex. Metaphoric transference, in other words, recognizes the constitutive powers of metaphor, but only as metaphor" (*Beyond Accommodation* 100).

42. As both Cornell and Mark Bracher point out, these shifts in self-image play a vital role in transforming social systems. Bracher, for example, insists that "any real social change must involve not just changes in laws and public but alterations in the ideals, desires, and jouissances of a significant number of individual subjects" (73).

43. By lowercasing "mexicanize" and "africanize," I underscore the inventive, nonproper, as it were, forms that their identity creation (*and identity invitation*) can take.

44. Cornell further asserts that "[w]e re-collect the mythic figures of the past, but as we do so we reimagine them. It is the potential variability of myth that allows us to work within myth, and the significance it offers, so as to reimagine our world and by so doing, to begin to dream of a new one. In myth we do find Woman with a capital letter. These myths, as Lacan indicates, may be rooted in

male fantasy, but they cannot, as he would sometimes suggest, be reduced to it" (*Beyond Accommodation* 178).

Chapter Five. From Self-Help to Womanist Self-Recovery; or, How Paula Gunn Allen Changed My Mind

1. According to Allen, "The long poem text that runs through the center [of *Ceremony*]. . . . is a clan story, and is not to be told outside of the clan" ("Special Problems"). Allen first made these claims in a paper presented at the 1988 Modern Languages Association annual conference. This paper was published two years later in *American Indian Quarterly*.

2. The term "New Age" has been much abused and is often used in dismissive ways, especially by academics. (See, for instance, Jennifer Rindfleisch, "Consuming the Self"; Esther de Bruijn, "Coming to Terms with New Ageist Contamination"; and Douglas McCabe, "'Higher Realities.'" While a great deal of New Age thought has a distinct consumerist, liberal-but-apolitical strand, other aspects of New Age thinking are highly political and combine personal development with social change. For examples of these more complex versions of New Age thought that have significant parallels with some Indigenous worldviews, see the writings of David Spangler and Dorothy MacLean. For definitions and discussions of New Age thought, see Paul Heelas, *The New Age Movement*; and Martin Green, *Prophets of a New Age*.

3. As Maparyan explains, "luxocracy" means "rule by Light." "Light in this instance refers to the Inner Light, the Higher Self, the Soul, the God Within—what I hereafter refer to as Innate Divinity—as described by mystics and others across cultures, across faiths, and across the centuries, if not millennia" (*Womanist Idea* 3). I discuss luxocracy in more detail in chapter 2.

4. I discuss my time as a closeted womanist spiritual activist in "'Making Face, Making Soul.'"

5. See Allen's explorations of Native history in *The Sacred Hoop* and *Off the Reservation*.

6. I describe these plastic shaman as "(non)Indian" to indicate that while some have no family ties to indigenous peoples, others can trace their lineage to Native Americans.

7. For a discussion of mainstream self-help literature for women and its elision of feminism, see writings by Marilyn Ebben, Cynthia D. Schrager, Elaine Rapping, and Micki McGee.

8. For further discussion of womanism and its connections with feminist thought, see Layli Maparyan, *The Womanist Idea*. Because womanism can include feminism, my decision to name this genre "womanist self-recovery" does not

ignore those womanist self-recovery authors (like Allen) who personally identify as feminists. Nor do I assume (or expect) all of the authors would self-identify as womanist. "Womanist self-recovery" describes a genre and an energy, not an identity category for writers and/or readers.

9. For Vanzant's *Tapping the Power Within*, I'm thinking especially of the first edition.

10. While popular self-help books for women target women readers (*as the genre's name implies!*), womanist self-recovery books do not always focus exclusively on women.

11. See, for instance, Elayne Rapping, *The Culture of Recovery*; and Cynthia D Schrager, "Questioning the Promise of Self-Help."

12. See also Micki McGee's discussion in *Self-Help, Inc.* of how self-help literature generally attributes an individual's lack of success to personal inadequacies.

13. To be more precise, in *Grandmothers of the Light* Allen uses but also modifies scholarly apparatus, as we see in the creative but rather unconventional title of her postscript: "Postscript: Cultural Dimensions, Ge-ological Locations, and Herstorical Circumstances of the Goddesses, the People, and the Ritual Tradition."

14. For discussions of historical distortions, see Howard Zinn, *A People's History of the United States*; and James W. Loewen, *Lies My Teacher Told Me*.

15. For an extensive discussion of how Allen's creatrix figures and other mythic images challenge patriarchal beliefs and representations of women see Keating, *Women Reading Women Writing*.

16. According to Greek mythology, Athene represents the goddess of wisdom who was born, fully grown, from Zeus's head. Significantly, Zeus did not create Athene on his own; he had swallowed her mother, Metis (also a divine figure representing wisdom), in an attempt to prevent Metis from giving birth.

17. Regarding "magical" power, according to Allen, "The basic nature of the universe of power is magic," and she associates this "magic" with language: "the name given to the practice of a mage *Ma* (the *m*-syllable again) comes in variants. . . . All are versions of the same morpheme . . . and refer in one way or another to the Great Mother of Great Goddess or the Indo-Germanic tradition" (*Grandmothers* 15).

18. For additional critiques of this solipsistic individualism, see Gerdien Blom, "Divine Individuals, Cultural Identities"; Harlon Dalton, *Racial Healing*; and Kelly Oliver, "The Look of Love."

19. For a related critique of monotheism, see Jan Assmann, *The Price of Monotheism*. Assmann associates monotheism and what he calls "the Mosaic distinction" with a negative oppositional energy and perspective that leads to a dichotomous sacred/profane worldview, a sharp distinction between truth and falsehood, and a method of exclusion.

20. I describe these beliefs as indigenous-inflected, rather than indigenous, to underscore the inventive (re)claiming process that womanist self-recovery authors use in their revisionist mythmaking.

21. Allen emphasizes multiplicity throughout *Grandmothers of the Light*. She maintains that "The essential nature of the cosmos is female intelligences, that is, goddesses. There are several rather than one, indicating that multiplicity is a fundamental characteristic of all that is" (107). See also Paula Toohey's excellent discussion of Allen's radical multiplicity.

22. For indigenous teachings, see Lee Hester and Jim Cheney, "Truth and Native American Epistemology"; Manulani Aluli Meyer, "Acultural Assumptions of Empiricism" and "Indigenous and Authentic"; editors Ladislaus M. Semali and Joe L. Kincheloe, *What Is Indigenous Knowledge?* and their introduction to that volume. For recent developments in quantum physics, see Albert-Lázló Barabási, *Linked*; David Bohm, *Wholeness and the Implicate Order*; Joanna Macy, *Mutual Causality in Buddhism and General Systems Theory*; Rupert Sheldrake, *Morphic Resonance*, and *The Sense of Being Stared at and Other Aspects of the Extended Mind*; and Duncan J. Watts, *Six Degrees*. For connections between indigenous worldviews and quantum physics, see Gregory Cajete, *Native Science*; and F. David Peat, *Blackfoot Physics*. For my own experiences, see Keating, "Forging El Mundo Zurdo."

23. See especially Allen, *The Sacred Hoop* and *Off the Reservation*.

24. I borrow the term "the affirmative" from Ralph Waldo Emerson (*and here's another possible point of transculturalism's unexpected connections!*). Emerson uses this term both in his journals and in his final lectures on the Natural History of the Intellect.

Chapter Six. Pedagogies of Invitation: From Status-Quo Stories to Cosmic Connections

1. john a. powell makes a similar point. As he explains in "Disrupting Individualism," "The ideology of individuality had its origins in the Enlightenment, which came concurrently with the emergence of Colonialism. During this germinative period, the essence of individualism was that Europeans were individuals as opposed to other people who were a 'collective.' The collectivity of the other served as a rationale and justification for the exploitation of the collective other. . . . In that sense, individuality was already racialized" (3–4). See also Grace Kyungwon Hong, *The Ruptures of American Capital*; Joyce Warren, *The American Narcissus*; and David Goldberg, *Racist Culture*.

2. For an excellent example of how we can internalize this status-quo story in unintentionally destructive ways, see Melissa Harris-Perry's discussion of the "strong black woman" self-image developed by African American women.

3. See also john powell's assertion: "How does individualism operate on race and gender today? The answer from the individualist camp is that race and gender do not exist. We are all just individuals. . . . [A]ny marker of gender, race, or sexuality around which meaning is constructed socially is largely irrelevant" ("Disrupting Individualism" 9).

4. The majority of my *graduate* students in women's studies have not been so naive. Their awareness of self-enclosed individualism's limitations is not surprising, given their decision to pursue graduate work in women's studies (which generally underscores the importance of social change) in our department (which strongly emphasizes social-justice and radical multiculturalism). See also M. Rich and A. C. Cargile, "Beyond the Breach."

5. For an important critique of meritocracy, equal opportunity, and fair treatment, see Derald Wing Sue, "Whiteness and Ethnocentric Monoculturalism." As Sue notes,

> The myth of meritocracy operates from the dictum that there is a strong relationship between ability, effort, and success. Those who are successful in life are more competent, capable, intelligent, and motivated. Those who fail to achieve in society are less capable, intelligent, and motivated. The myth of equal opportunity assumes that everyone encounters the same obstacles in life and that the playing field is a level one. Thus, everyone has an equal chance to succeed or enjoy the fruits of their labor. The myth of fair treatment equates equal treatment with fairness, whereas differential treatment is considered discriminatory or preferential. All three often act in unison to mask disparities and inequities and to allow actions that oppress groups that are not in the mainstream. (767)

6. By 'white'-identified I mean people who look, act, or think in 'white' ways. Generally, but not always, these people would be classified as 'white.'

7. As James Cone asserts, "Martin Luther King was right: We are bound together as one humanity. What affects one directly affects all indirectly. The sooner we realize the interconnectedness of our social existence, the sooner we will end our isolation from each other and begin to develop ways that we can work together toward the liberation of the poor throughout the world" (200).

8. Among the texts I've used are *This Bridge Called My Back* and *Grandmothers Counsel the World*; among the authors are Jacqui Alexander, Gloria Anzaldúa, Ralph Waldo Emerson, Leela Fernandes, Joy Harjo, June Jordan, Irene Lara, Layli Maparyan, Walt Whitman. The list of possible texts is expansive.

9. For an illustration of a mutual subject-to-subject transformational encounter, see Anzaldúa's discussion of nepantleras in the final two sections of her "now let us shift."

10. See Joanna Macy's website, *Understanding Our interconnections*, for additional discussion.

11. For examples of assignments about our interdependence, see the appendices in Keating, *Teaching Transformation*.

12. See, for instance, Anzaldúa's various self-positionings in the interviews collected in *Interviews/Entrevistas*. After *Borderlands/La Frontera*'s publication, Anzaldúa's economic status slowly shifted into the middle class. Her self-labeling in the interviews (which span almost two decades) tracks this movement.

13. I'm not advocating an "anything-goes" approach, where students can say whatever they want in a classroom. Rather, I suggest that when we take an invitational approach, we can more effectively engage with students' ideas and beliefs. As I explain in *Teaching Transformation*, we can use nonoppositional methods to challenge racist, sexist, and other -ism comments. Specifically, I suggest that an educator offer students a set of premises (or what I call "Dialogue Presuppositions") on which a course is based.

14. See the introduction for my discussion of our radical interconnectivity.

15. For a discussion of this approach, see chapter 5 in Keating, *Teaching Transformation*.

16. For McNeal's full syllabus, as well as two invitational assignments, see appendix 1.

17. Sheldrake discusses morphic resonance in *Morphic Resonance*.

18. For a discussion of "listening with raw openness," see chapter 1.

19. Like Layli Maparyan, I believe that "[a]s we move from historically based, socially ascribed group identities to planetary identity, Earth culture becomes all of ours. For this to work, we have to move away from acquisition and ownership 'turf' models towards spiritually based 'affinity' models that recognize our fundamental human connecting tendency and respect/revere both individual and collective expressions of divinity that manifest as cultures and subcultures" (*Womanist Idea* 12).

Works Cited
and Consulted

Aanerud, Rebecca. "Thinking Again: *This Bridge Called My Back* and the Challenge to Whiteness." Anzaldúa and Keating 69–77.

Alaimo, Stacy, and Susan Heckman. "Introduction: Emerging Models of Materiality in Feminist Theory." *Material Feminisms*. Ed. Stacy Alaimo and Susan Heckman. Bloomington: Indiana University Press, 2008. 1–19. Print.

Alarcón, Norma. "The Theoretical Subject(s) of *This Bridge Called My Back* and Anglo-American Feminism." Anzaldúa 356–69.

Aldred, Lisa. "Plastic Shamans and Astroturf Sun Dances: New Age Commercialization of Native American Spirituality." *American Indian Quarterly* 24 (2000): 329–52. JSTOR.

Alexander, M. Jacqui. *Pedagogies of Crossing: Meditations on Feminism, Sexual Politics, Memory, and the Sacred*. Durham, N.C.: Duke University Press, 2005. Print.

———. "Remembering *This Bridge*, Remembering Ourselves: Yearning, Memory, and Desire." Anzaldúa and Keating 81–103.

Allen, Paula Gunn. "The Autobiography of a Confluence." *I Tell You Now: Autobiographical Essays by Native American Writers*. Ed. Brian Swann and Arnold Krupat. Lincoln: University of Nebraska Press, 1987. 143–54. Print.

———. *Grandmothers of the Light: A Medicine Woman's Sourcebook*. Boston: Beacon, 1991. Print.

———. *Off the Reservation: Reflections on Boundary-Busting, Border-Crossing Loose Canons*. Boston: Beacon Press, 1998. Print.

234 · Works Cited and Consulted

———. Rev. of *This Bridge Called My Back. Conditions* 5 (1982): 121–27. Print.

———. *The Sacred Hoop: Recovering the Feminine in American Indian Traditions.* Boston: Beacon Press, 1986. Print.

———. "Special Problems in Teaching Leslie Marmon Silko's *Ceremony.*" *American Indian Quarterly* 14 (fall 1990): 379–86. JSTOR.

———. *The Woman Who Owned the Shadows.* San Francisco, Calif.: Spinsters/Aunt Lute, 1983. Print.

Anzaldúa, Gloria. *Borderlands/La Frontera: The New Mestiza.* 1987. San Francisco, Calif.: Spinsters/Aunt Lute, 1999. Print.

———. "The coming of el mundo surdo." 1977. *Gloria Anzaldúa Reader* 36–37.

———. "Correspondence." Box 43, folder 12. Gloria Evangelina Anzaldúa Papers. Nettie Lee Benson Latin American Collection, University of Texas, Austin.

———. "El Mundo Zurdo: The Vision." 1981. Moraga and Anzaldúa 193–96.

———. "En rapport, In Opposition: Cobrando cuentas a las nuestras." *Making Face, Making Soul/Haciendo Caras: Creative and Critical Perspectives by Women of Color.* Ed. Gloria Anzaldúa. San Francisco, Calif.: Aunt Lute Foundation, 1990. 142–48. Print.

———. "Foreword, 2001: counsels from the firing . . . past, present, future." *This Bridge Called My Back: Writings by Radical Women of Color.* 3rd edition. Ed. Cherríe Moraga and Gloria Anzaldúa. Berkeley: Third Woman Press, 2002, xxxiv–xxxix.

———. "Foreword to the Second Edition." Moraga and Anzaldúa n.p.

———. *The Gloria Anzaldúa Reader.* Ed. AnaLouise Keating. Durham, N.C.: Duke University Press, 2009. Print.

———. "Haciendo caras, una entrada." *Making Face, Making Soul/Haciendo Caras: Creative and Critical Perspectives by Women of Color.* Ed. Gloria Anzaldúa. San Francisco, Calif.: Aunt Lute Foundation. xv–xxviii, 1990. Print.

———. *Interviews/Entrevistas.* Ed. AnaLouise Keating. New York: Routledge, 2000. Print.

———. "La Prieta." 1981. *Gloria Anzaldúa Reader* 38–50.

———. "Let us be the healing of the wound: the Coyolxauhqui imperative—la sombra y el sueño." 2005. *Gloria Anzaldúa Reader* 303–17.

———. "Metaphors in the Tradition of the Shaman." 1990. *Gloria Anzaldúa Reader* 121–23.

———. "now let us shift . . . the path of conocimiento . . . inner work, public acts." Anzaldúa and Keating 540–78.

———. "O.K. Momma, Who the Hell Am I?: an Interview with Luisah Teish." Moraga and Anzaldúa 221–31.

———. "Preface: (Un)natural bridges, (Un)safe spaces." Anzaldúa and Keating 1–5.

———. "Second Edition, Foreword, 1983." Box 45, folder 4. Gloria Evangelina

Anzaldúa Papers. Nettie Lee Benson Latin American Collection, University of Texas, Austin.

——. "Speaking across the Divide." *Gloria Anzaldúa Reader* 282–94.

——. "Speaking in Tongues: A Letter to Third World Women Writers." 1981. *Gloria Anzaldúa Reader* 26–35.

——. "To(o) Queer the Writer—Loca, escritora y chicana." *Inversions: Writing by Dykes, Queers, and Lesbians.* Ed. Betsy Warland. Vancouver, B.C.: Press Gang, 1991. 249–64. Reprinted in Gloria Anzaldúa Reader. Print. 163–75.

——, ed. *Making Face, Making Soul/Haciendo Caras: Creative and Critical Perspectives by Women of Color.* San Francisco, Calif.: Aunt Lute Foundation, 1990. Print.

Anzaldúa, Gloria, and AnaLouise Keating, ed. *this bridge we call home: radical visions for transformation.* New York: Routledge, 2002. Print.

Arnold, Ellen. "Listening to the Spirits: An Interview with Leslie Marmon Silko." *Studies in American Indian Literatures* 10.3 (1998):1–33. Print.

Assmann, Jan. *The Price of Monotheism.* 2003. Trans. Robert Savage. Stanford, Calif.: Stanford University Press, 2010. Kindle file.

Avallone, Charlene. "What American Renaissance? The Gendered Genealogy of a Critical Discourse." *PMLA* 112 (1997): 1102–20. JSTOR.

Avila, Elena. *Woman Who Glows in the Dark: A Curandera Reveals Traditional Aztec Secrets of Physical and Spiritual Health.* New York: Tarcher/Putnam, 2000. Print.

Awiakta, Marilou. *Selu: Seeking the Corn-Mother's Wisdom.* Golden, Colo.: Fulcrum, 1993. Print.

Bache, Christopher M. *The Living Classroom: Teaching and Collective Consciousness.* Albany: State University of New York Press, 2010. Kindle file.

Bádéjó, Diedre L. "The Goddess Osun as a Paradigm for African Feminist Criticism." *Sage: A Scholarly Journal on Black Women* 6 (1989): 27–32. Print.

Baldwin, James. *The Price of the Ticket: Collected Nonfiction 1948–1985.* New York: St. Martin's, 1985. Print.

Balibar, Etienne. "Ambiguous Universality." *differences: A Journal of Feminist Cultural Studies* 7 (1995): 48–74. Print.

Ballinger, Franchot, and Brian Swann. "A MELUS Interview: Paula Gunn Allen." *MELUS* 10 (1983): 3–25. Print.

Bambara, Toni Cade. "Foreword." Moraga and Anzaldúa vi–viii.

Barabási, Albert-Lázló. *Linked: The New Science of Networks.* Cambridge, Mass.: Perseus, 2002. Print.

Barad, Karen. *Meeting the Universe Halfway: Quantum Physics and the Entanglement of Matter and Meaning.* Durham, N.C.: Duke University Press, 2007. Kindle file.

Bar On, Bat-Ami. "Marginality and Epistemic Privilege." *Feminist Epistemologies.* Ed. Linda Alcoff and Elizabeth Potter. New York: Routledge, 1993. 83–100. Print.

Bauman, Richard. *Verbal Art as Performance*. Prospect Heights, Ill.: Waveland Press, 1984. Print.

Baym, Nina. "Melodramas of Beset Manhood: How Theories of American Fiction Exclude Women Authors." 33.2 *American Quarterly* (1981): 123–39. JSTOR.

Bebout, Lee. *Mythohistorical Interventions: The Chicano Movement and Its Legacies*. Minneapolis: University of Minnesota Press, 2011. Kindle file.

Bennett, Jane. "Systems and Things: A Response to Graham Harman and Timothy Morton." *New Literary History* 43 (2012): 225–33. Project Muse.

———. *Vibrant Matter: A Political Ecology of Things*. Durham, N.C.: Duke University Press, 2009.

Bercovitch, Sacvan. "Afterword." *Ideology and Classic American Literature*. Ed. Sacvan Bercovitch and Myra Jehlen. Cambridge: Cambridge University Press, 1986. 418–42. Print.

Berger, Tracy Michele, and Kathleen Guidroz, ed. *The Intersectional Approach: Transforming Women's and Gender Studies through Race, Class, and Gender*. Durham, N.C.: University of North Carolina Press, 2009. Print.

Blom, Gerdien. "Divine Individuals, Cultural Identities: Post-Identitarian Representations and Two Chicana/o Texts." *Thamyris: Mythmaking from Past to Present* 4 (1997): 295–324. Print.

Bohm, David. *Wholeness and the Implicate Order*. 1980. London and New York: Routledge, 1996. Print.

Bourne, Jenny. "Homelands of the Mind: Jewish Feminism and Identity Politics." *Race and Class* 29 (1987): 1–24. Print.

Bracher, Mark. *Lacan, Discourse, and Social Change: A Psychoanalytic Cultural Criticism*. Ithaca, N.Y.: Cornell University Press, 1993. Print.

Braidotti, Rosi. *Nomadic Subjects: Embodiment and Sexual Difference in Contemporary Feminist Theory*. New York: Columbia University Press, 1994. Print.

———. *Patterns of Dissonance: A Study of Women in Contemporary Philosophy*. Trans. Elizabeth Guild. New York: Routledge, 1991. Print.

Bredin, Renae. "So Far from the Bridge." Anzaldúa and Keating 325–30.

Bridges, Flora Wilson. *Resurrection Song: African-American Spirituality*. Maryknoll, N.Y.: Orbis Books, 2001. Print.

Brooks, Joanna. *American Lazarus: Religion and the Rise of African-American and Native American Literatures*. New York: Oxford University Press, 2003. Kindle file.

Bruce-Novoa, Juan. "Canonical and Noncanonical Texts: A Chicano Case Study." *Redefining American Literary History*. Ed. A. LaVonne Ruoff and Jerry Washington Ward. New York: Modern Languages Association, 1990. Print.

Bruchac, Joseph. *Survival This Way: Interviews with American Indian Poets*. Tucson: University of Arizona Press, 1987. Print.

Bruijn, Esther de. "Coming to Terms with New Ageist Contamination: Cosmo-politanism in Ben Okri's *The Famished Road.*" *Research in African Literatures* 38.4 (2007): 170–86. Print.

Butler, Judith. *Gender Trouble: Feminism and the Subversion of Identity.* New York: Routledge, 1990. Print.

Cajete, Gregory. *Look to the Mountain: An Ecology of Indigenous Education.* Skyland, N.C.: Kivaki Press, 1994. Print.

——. *Native Science: Natural Laws of Interdependence.* Santa Fe, N.M.: Clear Light Publishers, 2000. Print.

——. "Philosophy of Native Science." *American Indian Thought: Philosophical Essays.* Ed. Ann Waters. Malden, Mass.: Blackwell Publishers, 2004. 45–57. Print.

Canaan, Andrea. "Brownness." Moraga and Anzaldúa 232–37.

Caputi, Jane. "Interview with Paula Gunn Allen." *Trivia* 16 (1990): 50–67. Print.

Carafiol, Peter. "'Who I Was': Ethnic Identity and American Literary Ethnocentrism." *Criticism and the Color Line: Essays on Race and the Discourse of Revisionism in American Literary Studies.* Ed. Henry Wonham. New Brunswick, N.J.: Rutgers University Press, 1996. Print.

Carrillo, Jo. "And When You Leave, Take Your Pictures with You." Moraga and Anzaldúa 63–64.

Carrillo Rowe, Aimee. *Power Lines: On the Subject of Feminist Alliances.* Durham, N.C.: Duke University Press, 2008. Kindle file.

Castillo, Ana. *Massacre of the Dreamers: Essays on Xicanisma.* Albuquerque: University of New Mexico Press, 1994. Print.

Certeau, Michel de. *The Practice of Everyday Life.* Trans. Steven Rendall. Berkeley: University of California Press, 1984. Print.

Cervenak, Sarah J., Karina L. Cespedes, Caridad Souza, and Andrea Straub. "Imagining Differently: The Politics of Listening in a Feminist Classroom." Anzaldúa and Keating 341–56.

Chopin, Kate. *The Awakening.* 1890. New York: Oxford University Press, 2008. Print.

Chow, Rey. "European Theory in America." Introduction to *The Age of the World Target: Self-Referentiality in War, Theory, and Comparative Work.* Durham, N.C.: Duke University Press, 2006. Kindle file.

Clarke, Cheryl. *After Mecca: Women Poets and the Black Arts Movement.* New Brunswick, N.J.: Rutgers University Press, 2005. Kindle file.

Cocker, Emma. "R.S.V.P.: Choreographing Collectivity through Invitation and Response." *rhizomes* 21 (winter 2010): 1–30. Web.

Collins, Patricia Hill. 1990. *Black Feminist Thought: Knowledge, Consciousness, and the Politics of Empowerment.* 2nd edition. New York: Routledge, 2008. Print.

———. *Fighting Words: Black Women and the Search for Justice.* Minneapolis: University of Minnesota Press, 1998. Print.

Combahee River Collective. "A Black Feminist Statement." 1977. Moraga and Anzaldúa 210–18.

Cone, James. "Afterword." *A Black Theology of Liberation.* New York: Orbis Books, 1970. 197–201. Print.

Cornell, Drucilla. *Beyond Accommodation: Ethical Feminism, Deconstruction, and the Law.* New York: Routledge, 1991. Print.

———. *The Imaginary Domain: Abortion, Pornography, and Sexual Harassment.* New York: Routledge, 1995. Print.

———. *Transformations: Recollective Imagination and Sexual Difference.* New York: Routledge, 1993. Print.

Crenshaw, Kimberle. "Demarginalizing the Intersection of Race and Sex: A Black Feminist Critique of Antidiscrimination Doctrine, Feminist Theory and Antiracist Politics." *University of Chicago Legal Forum* (1989): 139–67. LexisNexis.

Crowley, Karlyn. "Secularity." *Rethinking Women's and Gender Studies.* Ed. Catherine M. Orr, Ann Braithwaite, and Diane Lichentstein. New York: Routledge, 2012. 240–57. Kindle file.

Dalton, Harlon L. *Racial Healing: Confronting the Fear Between Blacks and Whites.* New York: Doubleday, 1995. Print.

Daly, Mary. "Be-Friending: Weaving Contexts, Creating Atmospheres." Ed. Judith Plaskow and Carol P. Christ. *Weaving the Visions: New Patterns in Feminist Spirituality.* San Francisco, Calif.: Harper & Row, 1989. 199–207. Print.

———. *Beyond God the Father: Toward a Philosophy of Women's Liberation.* 1973. Boston: Beacon, 1985. Print.

———. *Gyn/Ecology: The Metaethics of Radical Feminism.* 1987. Boston: Beacon, 1990. Print.

———. *Pure Lust: Elemental Feminist Philosophy.* Boston: Beacon Press, 1984. Print.

de Lauretis, Theresa. *Technologies of Gender: Essays on Theory, Film, and Fiction.* Bloomington: Indiana University Press, 1987. Print.

Doniger, Wendy. 1998. *The Implied Spider: Politics and Theology in Myth.* Rev. ed. New York: Columbia University Press, 2011. Kindle file.

Doty, William G. *Mythography: The Study of Myths and Rituals.* Tuscaloosa: University of Alabama Press, 1986. Print.

Douglas, Christopher. *A Genealogy of Literary Multiculturalism.* Ithaca, N.Y.: Cornell University Press, 2011. Kindle file.

DuPlessis, Rachel Blau. *Writing Beyond the Ending: Narrative Strategies of Twentieth-Century Women Writers.* Bloomington: Indiana University Press, 1985. Print.

Dykewomon, Elana. "The Body Politic—Mediations on Identity." Anzaldúa and Keating 599–612.

Ebben, Maureen. "Off the Shelf Salvation: A Feminist Critique of Self-Help." *Women's Studies in Communication* 18 (1995): 111–22. Print.

Elia, Nada. "The 'White" Sheep of the Family: But *Bleaching* Is Like Starvation." Anzaldúa and Keating 223–31.

Ellison, Ralph. *Invisible Man.* 1947. New York: Vintage, 1990.

Emerson, Ralph Waldo. *Emerson in His Journals.* Ed. Joel Porte. Cambridge, Mass.: Harvard University Press, 1984.

———. *The Journals and Miscellaneous Notebooks of Ralph Waldo Emerson,* vol. 11, *1848–1851.* Ed. A. W. Plumstead, William H. Gilman, and Ruth H. Bennett. Cambridge, Mass.: Belknap Press, 1975.

———. *Natural History of the Intellect: The Last Lectures of Ralph Waldo Emerson.* 1871. Ed. Maurice York and Rick Spaulding. Chicago: Wrightwood Press, 2008.

———. *Nature.* 1836. *Selections from Ralph Waldo Emerson.* Ed. Stephen E. Whicher, 21–58, Boston: Houghton Mifflin, 1960. 21–58. Print.

———. "The Poet." *Essays: Second Series.* 1844. Web.

———. "Self-Reliance." *Essays: First Series.* 1841. Web.

Erickson, Peter. "The Love Poetry of June Jordan." *Callaloo* 9.1 (1986): 221–34.

Eysturoy, Annie O. "Paula Gunn Allen." *This Is about Vision: Interviews with Southwestern Writers.* Ed. John F. Crawford, William Balassi, and Annie O. Eysturoy. Albuquerque: University of New Mexico Press, 1990. 95–107. Print.

Feidelson, Charles. *Symbolism and American Literature.* Chicago: University of Chicago Press, 1983. Print.

Ferguson, Kathy E. *The Man Question: Visions of Subjectivity in Feminist Theory.* Berkeley: University of California Press, 1993. Print.

Fernandes, Leela. *Transforming Feminist Practice: Non-Violence, Social Justice and the Possibilities of a Spiritualized Feminism.* San Francisco, Calif.: Aunt Lute Books, 2003. Print.

———. "Unsettling 'Third Wave Feminism' Feminist Waves, Intersectionality, and Identity Politics in Retrospect." *No Permanent Waves: Recasting Histories of U.S. Feminism.* Ed. Nancy Hewitt. New Brunswick, N.J.: Rutgers University Press, 2010. Kindle file.

Finke, Laurie A. "Rhetoric of Marginality: Why I Do Feminist Theory." *Tulsa Studies in Women's Literature* 5 (1986): 251–72. Print.

Ford, Richard T. *Racial Culture: A Critique.* Princeton, N.J., and Oxford: Princeton University Press, 2005. Print.

Foss, Sonja K., and Cindy Griffin. "Beyond Persuasion: A Proposal for an Invitational Rhetoric." *Communication Monographs* 62 (1995): 1–18. Communication & Mass Media Complete.

Four Arrows (Donald Trent Jacobs). *The Authentic Dissertation: Alternative Ways of Knowing, Research, and Representation.* New York: Routledge, 2008. Kindle file.

Fuss, Diana. *Essentially Speaking: Feminism, Nature, and Difference.* New York: Routledge, 1989. Print.

Gadon, Elinor W. *The Once and Future Goddess: A Symbol for Our Time.* San Francisco, Calif.: Harper & Row, 1989. Print.

Gallegos Nava, Ramón. *Holistic Education: Pedagogy of Universal Love.* Brandon, Vt.: Foundation for Educational Renewal, 2001. Print.

Garvey, T. Gregory, ed. *The Emerson Dilemma: Essays on Emerson and Social Reform.* Athens: University of Georgia Press, 2001. Print.

Gatens, Moira. "Towards a Feminist Philosophy of the Body." *Crossing Boundaries: Feminism and the Critique of Knowledges.* Ed. Barbara Caine, E. A. Grosz, and Marie de Lepervanche. Sydney: Allen & Unwin, 1989. 59–70. Print.

Gates, Henry Louis, Jr. "'Ethnic and Minority' Studies." *Introduction to Scholarship in Modern Languages and Literatures.* Ed. Joseph Gibaldi. New York: Modern Language Association, 1992. 288–302. Print.

Giroux, Henry. *Living Dangerously: Multiculturalism and the Politics of Difference.* New York: Peter Lang, 1993. Print.

Goldberg, David T. *Racist Culture: Philosophy and the Politics of Meaning.* Cambridge, Mass.: Blackwell, 1993. Print.

Gordon, Avery. *Ghostly Matters: Haunting and the Sociological Imagination.* 2nd ed. Minneapolis: University of Minnesota Press, 2008. Kindle file.

Gougeon, Len. *Emerson and Eros: The Making of a Cultural Hero.* Albany, N.Y.: State University of New York Press, 2007. Print.

——. "Emerson and the Woman Question: The Evolution of His Thought." *New England Quarterly* 71 (1998): 570–92. JSTOR.

——. "Emerson's Abolition Conversion." *The Emerson Dilemma: Essays on Emerson and Social Reform.* Ed. T. Gregory Garvey. Athens: University of Georgia Press, 2001. Print.

——. "Emerson, Whitman, and Eros." *Walt Whitman Quarterly Review* 23 (2006): 127–47. Web.

——. "Fortune of the Republic: Emerson, Lincoln, and Transcendental Warfare." *ESQ: A Journal of the American Renaissance* 6.5 (1999): 259–324. Print.

——. "Looking Backwards: Emerson at 2003." *Nineteenth-Century Prose* 39 (2003): 50–73. Literature Resource Center.

——. *Virtue's Hero: Emerson, Anti-Slavery, and Reform.* Athens: University of Georgia Press, 2010. Print.

Green, Martin. *Prophets of a New Age: Counter Culture and the Politics of Hope.* Mount Jackson, Va.: Axios Press, 2011. Kindle file.

Gregg, Melissa, and Gregory J. Seigworth, ed. *The Affect Theory Reader.* Durham, N.C.: Duke University Press, 2010. Kindle file.

Grosz, Elizabeth. "Bodies and Knowledges: Feminism and the Crisis of Reason." *Feminist Epistemologies.* Ed. Linda Alcoff and Elizabeth Potter. New York: Routledge, 1993. 187–215. Print.

Hames-Garcia, Michael, and Ernesto Javier Martinez. "Introduction: Re-membering Gay Latino Studies." *Gay Latino Studies: A Critical Reader.* Ed. Michael Hames-Garcia and Ernesto Javier Martinez. Durham, N.C.: Duke University Press, 2011. Kindle file.

Hammond, Karla M. "Audre Lorde: Interview." 1978. *Conversations with Audre Lorde.* Ed. Joan Wylie Hall. Jackson: University Press of Mississippi, 2004. 26–44. Print.

Hanson, Elizabeth I. *Paula Gunn Allen.* Boise State University Western Writer Series. Boise, Idaho: Boise State University Press, 1990. Print.

Haraway, Donna. "A Manifesto for Cyborgs: Science, Technology, and Socialist Feminism in the 1980s." *Feminism/Postmodernism.* Ed. Linda J. Nicholson. New York: Routledge, 1990. 190–23. Print.

Harjo, Joy. *How We Became Human: New and Selected Poems.* New York: W. W. Norton & Company, 2004. Kindle file.

———. "Introduction." *Reinventing the Enemy's Language: Contemporary Native Women's Writings of North America.* Ed. Joy Harjo and Gloria Bird. New York: W. W. Norton & Company, 1997. 19–31. Print.

———. *She Had Some Horses.* 1983. New York: W. W. Norton, 2008. Print.

———. *The Spiral of Memory: Interviews.* Ed. Laura Coltelli. Ann Arbor: University of Michigan Press, 1996. Print.

Harris-Perry, Melissa. *Sister Citizen: Shame, Stereotypes, and Black Women in America.* New Haven: Yale University Press, 2011. Kindle file.

Hartley, George. "'Matriz sin tumba': The Trash Goddess and the Healing Matrix of Gloria Anzaldúa's Reclaimed Womb." *MELUS* 35.1 (fall 2010): 41–61. Project Muse.

Heelas, Paul. *The New Age Movement: The Celebration of the Self and the Sacralization of Modernity.* Cambridge, Mass.: Blackwell, 1996. Print.

Hernández-Ávila, Inés. "In the Presence of Spirit(s): A Meditation on the Politics of Solidarity and Transformation." Anzaldúa and Keating 530–38.

Hester, Lee, and Jim Cheney. "Truth and Native American Epistemology." *Social Epistemology* 15.4 (2001): 319–34. Academic Search Complete.

Heyes, Cressida. "Identity Politics." *The Stanford Encyclopedia of Philosophy* (spring 2009 ed.). Ed. Edward N. Zalta. Web.

Hodge, Joanna. 1988. "Subject, Body, and the Exclusion of Women from Philosophy." *Feminist Perspectives in Philosophy.* Ed. Morwenna Griffiths and Margaret Whitford. Bloomington: Indiana University Press, 1988. 152–68. Print.

Hogue, Cynthia, Kim Parker, and Meredith Miller. "Talking the Talk and Walking the Walk: Ethical Pedagogy in the Multicultural Classroom." *Feminist Teacher* 12.2 (1998): 89–106.

Holloway, Karla F. C. *Moorings and Metaphors: Figures of Culture and Gender in Black Women's Literature.* New Brunswick, N.J.: Rutgers University Press, 1992. Print.

Holmes, Barbara A. *Race and the Cosmos: An Invitation to View the World Differently.* Harrisburg, Pa.: Trinity Press International, 2002. Print.

Hong, Grace Kyungwon. *The Ruptures of American Capital: Women of Color Feminism and The Culture Of Immigrant Labor.* Minneapolis: University of Minnesota Press, 2006. Kindle file.

———, and Roderick A. Ferguson, ed. *Strange Affinities: The Gender and Sexual Politics of Comparative Racialization.* Durham, N.C.: Duke University Press, 2011. Kindle file.

hooks, bell. *Yearning: Race, Gender, and Cultural Politics.* Boston: South End Press, 1990. Print.

Hull, Gloria. "Living on the Line: Audre Lorde and *Our Dead Behind Us.*" *Changing Our Own Words: Essays on Criticism, Theory, and Writing by Black Women.* Ed. Cheryl A. Wall. New Brunswick, N.J.: Rutgers University Press, 1989. 150–72. Print.

Hurston, Zora Neale. *Seraph on the Suwanee.* 1948. New York: Harper, 1991. Print.

Irigaray, Luce. *Sexes and Genealogies.* Trans. Gillian C. Gill. New York: Columbia University Press, 1993. Print.

Jaramillo, Nathalia E. *Immigration and the Challenge of Education: A Social Drama Analysis in South Central Los Angeles.* New York: Palgrave, 2011. Print.

Jarrett, Gene Andrew. "Judging a Book by Its Writer's Color." *Chronicle of Higher Education* 52.47 (28 July 2006): B12.

———. "Not Necessarily Race Matter." *African American Literature Beyond Race; A Reader.* Ed. Gene Andrew Jarrett. New York: New York University Press, 2006. 1–22. Kindle file.

Jay, Gregory. "The End of 'American' Literature: Toward a Multicultural Practice." *College English* 53 (1991): 264–81. JSTOR.

Jordan, June. *Civil Wars.* Boston: Beacon Press, 1981.

———. *Naming Our Destiny: New and Selected Poems.* New York: Thunder's Mouth Press, 1989. Print.

———. *On Call: Political Essays.* Boston: South End Press, 1987. Print.

———. *Some of Us Did Not Die: New and Selected Essays.* 2002. New York: Basic Books, 2003.

———. *Technical Difficulties: African-American Notions and the State of the Union.* New York: Pantheon, 1993. Print.

Keating, AnaLouise. "Forging El Mundo Zurdo: Changing Ourselves, Changing the World." Anzaldúa and Keating 518–30.

———. "'Making Face, Making Soul': Spiritual Activism as Social Transformation." *Feminist Solidarity at the Crossroads: Intersectional Women's Studies for Transracial Alliance.* Ed. Kim Vaz and Gary Lemons. New York: Routledge, 2011. Print.

———. "Shifting Perspectives: Spiritual Activism, Social Transformation, and the Politics of Spirit." Keating 241–54.

———. "Shifting Worlds, Una Entrada." Keating 1–12.

———. "Speculative Realism, Visionary Pragmatism, and Poet-Shamanic Aesthetics in Gloria Anzaldúa—and Beyond." *Women's Studies Quarterly* 40.3–4 (December 2012): 51–69. Print.

———. *Teaching Transformation: Transcultural Classroom Dialogues.* New York: Palgrave Macmillan, 2007. Print.

———. *Women Reading Women Writing: Self-Invention in Paula Gunn Allen, Gloria Anzaldúa, and Audre Lorde.* Philadelphia, Pa.: Temple University Press, 1996. Print.

———. "'Working towards wholeness': Gloria Anzaldúa's Struggles to Live with Diabetes and Chronic Illness." *The Cultural Mediations of Latina Health.* Ed. Angie Chabram-Dernersesian and Adela de la Torres. Tucson: University of Arizona Press, 2008. Print.

———, ed. *EntreMundos/AmongWorlds: New Perspectives on Gloria Anzaldúa.* New York: Palgrave Macmillan, 2005. Print.

Kingston, Maxine Hong. *Tripmaster Monkey.* 1987. New York: Vintage, 1990. Print.

———. *The Woman Warrior: Memoir of a Girlhood among Ghosts.* 1976. New York: Vintage Books, 1989. Print.

Kirby, Vicki. "Natural Convers(at)ions: Or, What If Culture Was Really Nature All Along?" *Material Feminisms.* Ed. Stacy Alaimo and Susan Heckman. Bloomington: Indiana University Press, 2008. 214–36. Print.

Kitch, Sally L., and Mary Margaret Fonow. "Analyzing Women's Studies Dissertations: Methodologies, Epistemologies, and Field Formation." *Signs: Journal of Women in Culture and Society* 38.1 (2012): 99–26. JSTOR.

Kroeber, Karl, "An Interview with Jack Salzman, Director of the Columbia University Center for American Culture Studies." *American Indian Persistence and Resurgence.* Ed. Karl Kroeber. Durham, N.C.: Duke University Press, 1994. 50–57. Print.

Laclau, Ernesto. "Subject of Politics, Politics of the Subject." *differences: A Journal of Feminist Cultural Studies* 7 (1995): 146–64. Print.

———, and Chantal Mouffe. *Hegemony and Socialist Strategy: Towards a Radical Democratic Politics.* London: Verso, 1985. Print.

Lara, Irene. "Daughter of Coatlicue: An Interview with Gloria Anzaldúa." Keating 41–55.

———. "Goddess of the Américas in the Decolonial Imaginary: Beyond the Virtuous Virgen/Pagan Puta Dichotomy." *Feminist Studies* 34.1–2 (spring 2008): 99–130. Print.

———. "Healing Sueños for Academia." Anzaldúa and Keating 433–38.

Latour, Bruno. *Pandora's Hope: Essays on the Reality of Science Studies.* Cambridge, Mass.: Harvard University Press, 2000.

———. "Why Has Critique Run out of Steam? From Matters of Fact to Matters of Concern." *Critical Inquiry* 31.2 (winter 2004): 225–48. JSTOR.

———. "Will Non-Humans Be Saved? An Argument in Ecotheology." *Journal of the Royal Anthropological Institute (N.S.)* 15 (2009): 459–75. Web.

Leal, Luis. "The Rewriting of American Literary History." *Criticism in the Borderlands: Studies in Chicano Literature, Culture, and Ideology.* Ed. Héctor Calderón and Jose David Saldívar. Durham, N.C.: Duke University Press, 1991. 21–27. Print.

Levine, Lawrence W. *The Opening of the American Mind: Canons, Culture, and History.* Boston: Beacon Press, 1997. Print.

Lionnet, Françoise. *Autobiographical Voices: Race, Gender, Self-Portraiture.* Ithaca, N.Y.: Cornell University Press, 1989. Print.

Little Bear, Leroy. "Foreword." *Native Science: Natural Laws of Interdependence.* Gregory Cajete. Santa Fe, N.M.: Clear Light Publishers, 2000. ix–xii. Print.

Lloyd, Genevieve. *The Man of Reason: "Male" and "Female" in Western Philosophy.* 1984. 2nd ed. Minneapolis: University of Minnesota Press, 1993. Print.

Loewen, James W. *Lies My Teacher Told Me: Everything Your American History Textbook Got Wrong.* 1995. Rev. ed. New York: New Press, 2008. Kindle file.

Lorde, Audre. *The Black Unicorn.* New York: Norton, 1978. Print.

———. *Chosen Poems: Old and New.* New York: Norton, 1982. Print.

———. "An Open Letter to Mary Daly." Moraga and Anzaldúa 94–97.

———. *Sister Outsider: Essays and Speeches.* Freedom, Calif.: Crossing Press, 1984. Print.

———. *Zami: A New Spelling of My Name.* Freedom, Calif.: Crossing Press, 1982.

Loy, David. *The Great Awakening: A Buddhist Social Theory.* Boston: Wisdom Publications, 2003.

Lyttle, David. "Emerson's Transcendental Individualism." *Concord Saunterer* 3 (1995): 80–103. Print.

MacPherson, C. B. *The Political Theory of Possessive Individualism: Hobbes to Locke.* Oxford and New York: Oxford University Press, 1962. Print.

Macy, Joanna. *Mutual Causality in Buddhism and General Systems Theory: The Dharma of Natural Systems.* Albany: State University of New York Press, 1991. Print.

———. *Understanding our interconnections.* 2007. Retrieved January 22, 2008. Web.

Maitino, John R., and David R. Peck. *Teaching American Ethnic Literatures: Nineteen Essays.* Albuquerque: University of New Mexico Press, 1996. Print.

Maparyan, Layli. "Feminism." *Rethinking Women's and Gender Studies.* Ed. Catherine M. Orr, Ann Braithwaite, and Diane Lichentstein. New York: Routledge, 2012. 17–33. Kindle file.

——. *The Womanist Idea.* New York: Routledge, 2011. Print.

Matthiessen, F. O. *American Renaissance: Art and Expression in the Age of Emerson and Whitman.* New York: Oxford University Press, 1968. Print.

May, Vivian. "Intersectionality." *Rethinking Women's and Gender Studies.* Ed. Catherine M. Orr, Ann Braithwaite, and Diane Lichentstein. New York: Routledge, 2012. 155–72s. Kindle file.

McCabe, Douglas. "'Higher Realities': New Age Spirituality in Ben Okri's *The Famished Road.*" *Research in African Literatures* 36.4 (2005): 1–21. Project Muse.

McGee, Micki. *Self-Help, Inc.: Makeover Culture in American Life.* New York: Oxford University Press, 2005. Print.

McGee, Patrick. *Telling the Other: The Question of Value in Modern and Postcolonial Writing.* Ithaca, N.Y.: Cornell University Press, 1992. Print.

McPhail, Mark Lawrence. "Complicity: The Theory of Negative Difference." *Howard Journal of Communications* 3.1&2 (1991): 1–13. Communication & Mass Media Complete.

——. "Passionate Intensity: Louis Farrakhan and the Fallacies of Racial Reasoning," *Quarterly Journal of Speech* 84 (November 1998): 416–29. Communication & Mass Media Complete.

——. *Zen in the Art of Rhetoric: An Inquiry into Coherence.* Albany: State University of New York Press, 1996. Print.

Meyer, Manulani Aluli. "Acultural Assumptions of Empiricism: A Native Hawaiian Critique." *Canadian Journal of Native Education* 25.2 (2001): 188–98. Web.

——. "Indigenous and Authentic: Hawaiian Epistemology and the Triangulation of Meaning." *Handbook of Critical and Indigenous Methodologies.* Ed. Norman K. Denzin, Yvonna S. Lincoln, and Linda Tuhiwai Smith. Thousand Oaks, Calif.: Sage Publications, 2008. 217–32. Print.

Mignolo, Walter. *Local Histories/Global Designs: Coloniality, Subaltern Knowledges, and Border Thinking.* Durham, N.C.: Duke University Press, 2000. Kindle file.

Miranda, Deborah A. "'What's Wrong with a Little Fantasy?' Storytelling from the (Still) Ivory Tower." Anzaldúa and Keating 192–202.

Momaday, M. Scott. *House Made of Dawn.* New York: Harper & Row, 1966. Print.

——. *The Way to Rainy Mountain.* 1969. Albuquerque: University of New Mexico Press, 1976. Print.

Moraga, Cherríe. *Last Generation: Prose and Poetry.* Boston: South End Press, 1999.

——. "Refugees of a World on Fire: Foreword to the Second edition." Moraga and Anzaldúa n.p.

——. "Salt that Heals: Remembering Gloria Anzaldúa." *A Xicana Code of Changing Consciousness.* Durham, N.C.: Duke University Press, 2011. 116–30. Print.

——, and Gloria Anzaldúa, ed. *This Bridge Called My Back: Writings by Radical Women of Color.* Watertown, Mass.: Persephone Press, 1981. New York: Kitchen Table: Women of Color Press, 1983. Print.

Morales, Rosario. "We're All in the Same Boat." Moraga and Anzaldúa 91–93.

Morejón, Nancy. *Nación y mestizaje en Nicolás Guillén.* Havana: Unión de Escritores y Artistas de Cuba, 1982. Print.

Mori, Toshio. *Yokohama, California.* 1949. Seattle: University of Washington Press, 1993. Print.

Morris, Meaghan. *The Pirate's Fiancée: Feminism, Reading, Postmodernism.* London: Verso, 1988. Print.

Morrison, Toni. *Sula.* New York: Penguin, 1973. Print.

——, and Robert Stepto. "'Intimate Things in Place': A Conversation with Toni Morrison. *Massachusetts Review* 18.3 (1977): 473–89.

Moschkovitch, Judit. "'—But I Know You, American Woman.'" Moraga and Anzaldúa 79–84.

Mosha, R. Sambuli. "The Inseparable Link between Intellectual and Spiritual Formation in Indigenous Knowledge and Education: A Case Study in Tanzania." *What Is Indigenous Knowledge? Voices from the Academy.* Ed. Ladislaus M. Semali and Joe L. Kincheloe. New York and London: Farmer, 1999. 209–25. Print.

Mouffe, Chantal. "Radical Democracy: Modern or Postmodern?" *Universal Abandon? The Politics of Postmodernism.* Ed. Andrew Ross. Minneapolis: University of Minnesota Press, 1988. 31–45. Print.

Moya, Paula M. L. "Cultural Particularity versus Universal Humanity: The Value of Being *Asimilao.*" *Hispanics/Latinos in the United States: Ethnicity, Race, and Rights.* Ed. Jorge J. E. Gracia and Pablo De Greiff. New York: Routledge, 2000. 77–97. Print.

Murray, David. *Forked Tongues: Speech, Writing, and Representation in North American Indian Texts.* Bloomington: Indiana University Press, 1991. Print.

Myers, Linda. "The Psychology of Knowledge: The Importance of Worldview." *New England Journal of Black Studies* 4 (1984): 1–12. Print.

——. *Understanding an Afrocentric World View: Introduction to an Optimal Psychology.* Dubuque, Iowa: Kendall/Hunt Publishing, 1993. Print.

——, et al. "Identity Development and Worldview: Toward an Optimal Conceptualization." *Journal of Counseling and Development* 70 (1991): 54–63. Print.

Nhất Hạnh, Thích. *Interbeing: Fourteen Guidelines for Engaged Buddhism.* 1987. 3rd ed. Berkeley, Calif.: Parallax Press, 1998. Print.

Nicolescu, Basarab. "Transdisciplinarity as Methodological Framework for Going Beyond the Science-Religion Debate." Metanexus Institute, 2007. Web.

Norton-Smith, Thomas. *The Dance of Person and Place: One Interpretation of American Indian Philosophy.* Albany: State University of New York Press, 2010. Kindle file.

Ohmer, Sarah. "Gloria E. Anzaldúa's Decolonizing Ritual de Conocimiento." *Confluencia* 26.1 (2010): 141–53. Academic Search Complete.

Oliver, Kelly. "The Look of Love." *Hypatia* 16 (2001): 56–78. Project Muse.

———. *Witnessing: Beyond Recognition.* Minneapolis: University of Minnesota Press, 2001. Print.

Ostriker, Alicia. *Stealing the Language: The Emergence of Women's Poetry in America.* Boston: Beacon, 1986. Print.

———. "Thieves of Language: Women Poets and Revisionist Mythmaking." *Signs: Journal of Women in Culture and Society* 8.1 (1982): 68–90. JSTOR.

Palumbo-Liu, David. "Introduction." *The Ethnic Canon: Histories, Institutions, and Interventions.* Ed. David Palumbo-Liu. Minneapolis: University of Minnesota Press, 1995. 1–27. Print.

Pariser, Eli. *The Filter Bubble: What the Internet Is Hiding from You.* New York: Penguin Press, 2011. Kindle file.

Parker, Joe, and Ranu Samantrai. "Interdisciplinarity and Social Justice: An Introduction." *Interdisciplinarity and Social Justice: Revisioning Academic Accountability.* Ed. Joe Parker, Ranu Samantrai, and Mary Romero. Albany: State University of New York, 2010. 1–33. Print.

Parmar, Pratibha. "Black Feminism: The Politics of Articulation." *Identity: Community, Culture, Difference.* London: Lawrence and Wishart, 1990. 101–27. Print.

Peat, F. David. *Blackfoot Physics.* 2002. York Beach, Maine: Red Wheel/Weiser, 2010.

Peavey, Fran. *Heart Politics Revisited.* Annandale, Australia: Pluto Press, 2000. Print.

Phillips, Layli. "Womanism: On Its Own." *The Womanist Reader.* Ed. Layli Phillips. New York: Routledge, 2007. Print.

powell, john a. "Disrupting Individualism and Distributive Remedies with Intersubjectivity and Empowerment: An Approach to Justice and Discourse." *University of Maryland Law Journal of Race, Religion, Gender and Class* 1 (2001): 1–23. LexisNexis.

———. "Does Living a Spiritually Engaged Life Mandate Us to Be Actively Engaged in Issues of Social Justice?" *University of St. Thomas Law Journal: Fides et Iustitia* 1 (2003): 30–38. LexisNexis.

Powell, Timothy B. "All Colors Flow into Rainbows and Nooses: The Struggle to Define Academic Multiculturalism." *Cultural Critique* 55 (2003): 152–81. Project Muse.

———. *Ruthless Democracy: A Multicultural Interpretation of the American Renaissance.* Princeton, N.J.: Princeton University Press, 2000. Print.

Puar, Jasbir. "'I would rather be a cyborg than a goddess': Intersectionality, Assemblage, and Affective Politics." Web.

Quintanales, Mirtha. "I Paid Very Hard for My Immigrant Ignorance." Moraga and Anzaldúa 150–56.

Rapping, Elayne. *The Culture of Recovery: Making Sense of the Self-Help Movement in Women's Lives.* Boston: Beacon Press, 1996. Print.

Rich, M., and A. C. Cargile. "Beyond the Breach: Transforming White Identities in the Classroom." *Race, Ethnicity, and Education* 7.4 (2004): 251–65. Academic Search Complete.

Richardson, Robert D., Jr. *Emerson: The Mind on Fire.* Berkeley: University of California Press, 1995.

Rindfleisch, Jennifer. "Consuming the Self: New Age Spirituality as 'Social Product' in Consumer Society." *Consumption, Markets and Culture* 8.4 (2005): 343–60. Business Source Complete.

Roberson, Loriann, and Carol T. Kulik. "Stereotype Threat at Work." *Academy of Management Perspectives* 21.2 (May 2007): 24–40. Business Source Complete.

Roberts, Jane. *The Nature of Personal Reality: A Seth Book.* New York: Bantam, 1984. Print.

Robinson, Reginald Leamon. "Human Agency, Negated Subjectivity, and White Structural Oppression: An Analysis of Critical Race Practice/Praxis." *American University Law Review* 53 (August 2004): 1361–420. LexisNexis.

——. "Race Consciousness: A Mere Means of Preventing Escapes from the Control of Her White Masters?" *Touro Law Review* 15.2 (1999): 401–38. LexisNexis.

Rudy, Kathy. "Radical Feminism, Lesbian Separatism, and Queer Theory." *Feminist Studies* 27.1 (spring 2001): 190–224.

Saldívar, Ramón. *Chicano Narrative: The Dialectics of Difference.* Madison: University of Wisconsin Press, 1990. Print.

Sanchez-Tranquilino, Marcos, and John Tagg. "The Pachuco's Flayed Hide: Mobility, Identity, and Buenas Garras." *Cultural Studies.* Ed. Lawrence Grossberg, Cary Nelson, and Paula Treichler. New York: Routledge, 1992. Print.

Sandoval, Chela. "Feminism and Racism: A Report on the 1981 National Women's Studies Association Conference." Anzaldúa 55–71.

——. "Foreword: AfterBridge: Technologies of Crossing." Anzaldúa and Keating 21–26.

——. *Methodology of the Oppressed.* Minneapolis: University of Minnesota Press, 2000. Kindle file.

——. "U.S. Third World Feminism: The Theory and Method of Oppositional Consciousness in the Postmodern World." *Genders* 10 (spring 1991): 1–25.

Schaefer, Carol. *Grandmothers Counsel the World: Women Elders Offer Their Vision for Our Planet.* Boston: Trumpeter Books, 2006. Print.

Schrager, Cynthia D. "Questioning the Promise of Self-Help: A Reading of *Women Who Love Too Much*." *Feminist Studies* 19 (1993): 177–92.

Schueller, Malini Johar. "Analogy and (White) Feminist Theory: Thinking Race and the Color of the Cyborg Body." *Signs: Journal of Women in Culture and Society* 31.1 (2005): 63–92. JSTOR.

Semali, Ladislaus M., and Joe L. Kincheloe. "Introduction: What Is Indigenous Knowledge and Why Should We Study It?" *What Is Indigenous Knowledge? Voices from the Academy.* Ed. Ladislaus M. Semali and Joe L. Kincheloe. New York and London: Farmer, 1999. 3–57. Print.

——, ed. *What Is Indigenous Knowledge? Voices from the Academy.* New York and London: Farmer, 1999. Print.

Shapiro, Svi. "Education and Moral Values: Seeking a New Bottom Line." *Tikkun* 20.2. (2002). Academic Search Complete.

Sheldrake, Rupert. *Morphic Resonance: The Nature of Formative Causation.* 1981. Rev. ed. Rochester, Vt.: Park Street Press, 2009. Kindle file.

——. *The Sense of Being Stared at and Other Aspects of the Extended Mind.* New York: Crown Publishers, 2003. Print.

Shumway, David. *Creating American Civilization: A Genealogy of American Literature as an Academic Discipline.* Minneapolis: University of Minneapolis Press, 1994. Print.

Silko, Leslie Marmon. *Ceremony.* New York: Penguin, 1977. Print.

——. "Yellow Woman and a Beauty of the Spirit: Essays on Native American Life Today." *Yellow Woman and a Beauty of the Spirit: Essays on Native American Life Today.* New York: Simon & Schuster, 1996. 60–72. Print.

Smith, Barbara. "Racism and Women's Studies." Anzaldúa 25–28.

Smith, Henry Nash. *Virgin Land: The American West as Symbol and Myth.* Cambridge, Mass.: Harvard University Press, 1950. Print.

Smith, Paul. *Discerning the Subject.* Minneapolis: University of Minnesota Press, 1988. Print.

Sojourner, Sabrina. "From the House of Yemanja: The Goddess Heritage of Black Women." *The Politics of Women's Spirituality: Essays on the Rise of Spiritual Power Within the Feminist Movement.* Ed. Charlene Spretnak. New York: Doubleday, 1982. 57–63. Print.

Spangler, David. *Apprenticed To Spirit: The Education of a Soul.* New York: Riverhead Books, 2011. Kindle file.

——. *The Laws of Manifestation: A Consciousness Classic.* 1995. San Francisco, Calif.: Red Wheel/Weiser, 2009. Kindle file.

Spivak, Gayatri Chakravorty. *In Other Worlds: Essays in Cultural Politics.* New York: Methuen Publishers, 1987. Print.

——. *Outside in the Teaching Machine.* New York: Routledge, 1993. Print.

Squint, Kirstin. "Choctawan Aesthetics, Spirituality, and Gender Relations: An Interview with LeAnne Howe." *MELUS* 35.3 (fall 2010): 211–24. Project Muse.

Steele, Claude. "Stereotype Threat and the Intellectual Performance of African Americans." *Journal of Personality and Social Psychology* 69.5 (1995): 797–811. PsycARTICLES.

Stuart, Andrea. "Feminism: Dead or Alive?" *Identity: Community, Culture, Difference.* Ed. Jonathan Rutherford. London: Lawrence & Wishart, 1990. 28–42. Print.

Sue, Derald Wing. "Whiteness and Ethnocentric Monoculturalism: Making the 'Invisible' Visible." *American Psychologist* (November 2004): 761–69. PsycARTICLES.

Suleri, Sara. "Woman Skin Deep: Feminism and the Postcolonial Condition." *Critical Inquiry* 18 (1992): 756–69. JSTOR.

Tate, Claudia. *Black Women Writers at Work.* New York: Continuum, 1983. Print.

Teish, Luisah. *Jambalaya: The Natural Woman's Book of Personal Charms and Practical Rituals.* San Francisco, Calif.: Harper & Row, 1985. Print.

Thoreau, Henry David. *Walden; Or, Life in the Woods.* 1854. N.p.: Dover Publications, 1995. Print.

Toohey, Michelle Campbell. "Paula Gunn Allen's Grandmothers of the Light: Falling through the Void." *Studies in American Indian Literatures: The Journal of the Association for the Study of American Indian Literatures* 12. 3 (2000): 35–51. Web.

Trinh, T. Minh-ha. *When the Moon Waxes Red: Representation, Gender and Cultural Politics.* New York: Routledge, 1991. Print.

——. *Woman Native Other: Writing Postcoloniality and Feminism.* Bloomington: Indiana University Press, 1989. Print.

Tsing, Anna Lowenhaupt. *Friction: An Ethnography of Global Connection.* Princeton: Princeton University Press, 2005. Kindle file.

Turner, Victor. *The Forest of Symbols: Aspects of Ndembu Ritual.* Ithaca, N.Y.: Cornell University Press, 1967. Print.

TuSmith, Bonnie. *All My Relatives: Community in Contemporary Ethnic American Literatures.* Ann Arbor: University of Michigan Press, 1994.

Valerio, Anita. "It's In My Blood, My Face—My Mother's Voice, The Way I Sweat." Moraga and Anzaldúa 41–45.

Valerio, Max Wolf. "'Now That You're a White Man': Changing Sex in a Postmodern World—Being, Becoming, and Borders." Anzaldúa and Keating 239–53.

Vanzant, Iyanla. 1998. *Tapping the Power Within: A Path to Self-Empowerment for Women.* Twentieth-Century Anniversary ed. Carlsbad, Calif.: Hays House, 2008. Kindle file.

Violet, Indigo. "Linkages: A Personal-Political Journey with Feminist of Color Politics." Anzaldúa and Keating 486–94.

Walker, Alice. *The Color Purple.* New York: Washington Square, 1982. Print.

——. *In Search of Our Mother's Garden.* New York: Harcourt Brace, 1984. Print.

——. *Now Is the Time to Open Your Heart.* New York: Random, 2004. Print.

——. *Possessing the Secret of Joy.* New York: Harcourt Brace Jovanovich, 1992. Print.

——. *The Temple of My Familiar.* New York: Harcourt Brace Jovanovich, 1989. Print.

Warren, Joyce. *The American Narcissus: Individualism and Women in Nineteenth-Century American Fiction.* New Brunswick, N.J.: Rutgers University Press, 1984. Print.

Watts, Duncan J. *Six Degrees: The Science of a Connected Age.* New York: Norton, 2003. Print.

Whitman, Walt. *Song of Myself.* 1855. N.p.: Dover Publications, 2001. Print.

wong, nellie. "When I Was Growing Up." Moraga and Anzaldúa 7–8.

Yamada, Mitsuye. "Invisibility is an Unnatural Disaster: Reflections of an Asian American Woman." Moraga and Anzaldúa 35–40.

Yamato, Gloria. "Something About the Subject Makes It Hard To Name." Anzaldúa 20–24.

Zaytoun, Kelli. "New Pathways towards Understanding Self-in-Relation: Anzaldúan (Re)Visions for Developmental Psychology." Keating 147–59.

——. "Theorizing at the Borders: Considering Social Location in Rethinking Self and Psychological Development." *NWSA Journal* 18.2 (2006) 52–72. Project Muse.

Zinn, Howard. *A People's History of the United States.* 1980. New York: HarperCollins, 1999. Print.

Zinn, Maxine Baca, Lynn Weber Cannon, Elizabeth Higginbotham, and Bonnie Thornton Dill. "The Costs of Exclusionary Practices in Women's Studies." Anzaldúa 29–41.

Index

Aanerud, Rebecca, 211n5

academy: boundaries, 27; conflicts, 2–3, 9; disciplines, 4, 5, 18, 19, 143–44; oppositional, 49, 54, 187. *See also* graduate school; nepantla; oppositionality

accountability, 49, 174, 176, 195. *See also* interconnectivity

activism, 25. *See also* oppositionality; revisionist mythmaking; womanist self-recovery

activist-scholar(s), 57–58, 89; limited by oppositional discourse, 7

aesthetics, 139–30; poet-shaman, 119–25, 223n17; western, 123. *See also* language

affinity, 107, 213n14; and identity, 110, 182, 231n19. *See also* commonalities; interconnectivity

affirmative, the, 10, 20, 31, 165, 229n24

agency, 35, 78, 87, 124, 130–31, 171; personal, 72, 150, 152, 162. *See also* language; self-reflection; womanist self-recovery

Alarcón, Norma, 31

Alexander, M. Jacqui, 4, 8, 48, 208n7, 230n8

Allen, Paula Gunn, 19, 22, 24–25, 66, 87–88, 96–98; biography of, 218n13; on creation stories, 156; reception of, 103, 149–50; self-definition, 82–83, 220n26; tactical (re)naming, 100–103, 106–7; as trickster, 102–3. See also *Grandmothers of the Light*; revisionist mythmaking; *Sacred Hoop, The*

alliances, 33–35, 93. *See also* affinity; commonalities

almas afines, 30. *See also* commonalities

American Dream, the, 77–78. *See also* individualism; meritocracy

American Renaissance, 62

anger, 50–51, 121

Anzaldúa, Gloria, 18, 22, 53–54, 67, 87–88, 96–98, 113, 154, 214n25; and academic training, 25, 210n24; biography of, 61–62; critique of social identity

AnaLouise Keating is a professor of women's studies at Texas Woman's University and the author of *Teaching Transformation: Transcultural Classroom Dialogues* and other books.

The University of Illinois Press
is a founding member of the
Association of American University Presses.

Composed in 10.75/14 Marat Pro
with Adrianna Extended display
by Jim Proefrock
at the University of Illinois Press
Manufactured by Sheridan Books, Inc.

University of Illinois Press
1325 South Oak Street
Champaign, IL 61820-6903
www.press.uillinois.edu